REDEFINING THE PAST

Essays in Diplomatic History
in Honor of William Appleman Williams

William Appleman Williams

REDEFINING THE PAST

Essays in Diplomatic History
in Honor of William Appleman Williams

Edited by Lloyd C. Gardner

Oregon State University Press
Corvallis, Oregon

The paper in this book meets the guidelines for permanence and durability of the Committee on Production Guidelines for Book Longevity of the Council on Library Resources.

Library of Congress Cataloging in Publication Data
Redefining the past.
  Bibliographies: p.
  Includes index.
  1. United States—Foreign relations—20th century.
  2. Williams, William Appleman. I. Williams, William Appleman. II. Gardner, Lloyd C., 1934-
E744.R42 1986   327.73   86-8427
ISBN 0-897071-348-5

Contents

Introduction

History as a way of learning has one additional value beyond establishing the nature of reality and posing the questions that arise from its complexities and contradictions. It can offer examples of how other men faced up to the difficulties and opportunities of their era.

William Appleman Williams
History as a Way of Learning

The essays in this collection do not cluster about a specific theme, nor do they present a single unified interpretative approach to issues in the history of American foreign policy. Above all, William Appleman Williams is a teacher. And good teachers are disappointed with conformity. No one would ever come away from reading Williams without a complete awareness of just how little regard he has had for accepted truths, even—when it came to that—his own.

With the publication of *American-Russian Relations, 1781-1947* (1952), a new voice—unwelcome to many at the height of the Cold War—challenged the standard "Containment" world view. More remarkable, perhaps, than anything Williams wrote about American-Russian relations as such was his dramatic recasting of the "Containment" thesis as a reflection of general assumptions Americans held about the world and revolution. Once that connection had been made, the history of foreign policy could no longer exist in a vacuum, sealed off against contact with contaminants brought in from outside sources.

Practitioners of the "old" diplomatic history had a rough time adjusting to Williams, in part because they were right: this was no longer their discipline. It had become, or was in the process of becoming, something quite different. Today, of course, Williams's influence has permeated the writing of American history, and not just the history of foreign policy.

What characterizes contemporary historical inquiry is a desire to move beyond accepted answers, and accepted questions, in an effort to arrive at new formulations of both. Williams put down a skilled draftsman's proposal for accomplishing those goals.

*　　*　　*

In the first section of this volume are essays which will introduce the reader to Williams and his work at much greater length. The second section offers a selection of writings by some of his co-workers, former students, and his own teacher at the University of Wisconsin.

Lloyd C. Gardner
Rutgers University
February 1986

Acknowledgments

Many people contributed to the realization of this project. Professor Darold Wax, Chairperson of the History Department at Oregon State University, initiated the whole idea—and has helped to guide it through to completion. His colleague, William Robbins, aside from contributing his own piece, was responsible for helping to "round up" the authors, and for coordinating my work with his own at the Corvallis end. Don E. McIlvenna compiled the bibliography, assisted by Jean Franklin at the computer. Jo Alexander of the Oregon State University Press managed to take twelve disparate essays and weave them into a unified whole. My thanks to all of them, and to the individual authors who put aside other research and writing to get this project out in timely fashion.

L.G.

About the Authors

Edward P. Crapol is Professor of History in the College of William and Mary. He received his Ph.D. at the University of Wisconsin in 1968. He is the author of *America for Americans: Economic Nationalism and Anglophobia in the Late Nineteenth Century* (1973), and several articles on 19th century foreign relations. He is currently working on studies of American women and foreign policy.

Ivan R. Dee took his B.J. and M.A. degrees at the University of Missouri. He is currently Director of Public Affairs at the Michael Reese Hospital and Medical Center in Chicago, Illinois. After founding his own press in Macon, Georgia, Dee moved on to Quadrangle Books in 1961, and was its Editor-in-Chief for eleven years, the period of its greatest expansion as an independent voice in the corporate world of publishing.

Lloyd C. Gardner received his Ph.D. from Wisconsin in 1960. Since 1963 he has been a member of the History Department at Rutgers University. His most recent publications are *A Covenant with Power: America and World Order from Wilson to Reagan* (1984) and *Safe for Democracy: The Anglo-American Response to Revolution, 1913-1923* (1984).

Fred Harvey Harrington's Ph.D. is from New York University in 1937. A long and distinguished career in the History Department at the University of Wisconsin devoted to both scholarship and institutional endeavors was capped by his being named president of that institution in 1962. He served in that post for eight years, and then as a program adviser in India, Sri Lanka, and Nepal for the Ford Foundation. Among his publications is *God, Mammon, and the Japanese: Dr. Horace N. Allen and Korean-American Relations* (1944).

Patrick Hearden is a member of the History Department at Purdue University, and received his Ph.D. at Wisconsin in 1971. His first book, *Independence and Empire* (1982), concerned the economic impact of the "New South" on American diplomacy. He has recently completed a manuscript on American policy toward Hitler's Germany.

Walter LaFeber is Noll Professor of History at Cornell University. He received his Ph.D. from Wisconsin in 1959. Author of the now classic *America, Russia, and the Cold War,* which has gone through several editions since it first appeared in 1966, LaFeber's most recent book is *Inevitable Revolutions: The United States in Central America* (1983).

Thomas McCormick received his Ph.D. from Wisconsin in 1961 and is now Professor of History at his alma mater. His book, *China Market: America's Quest for Informal Empire, 1893-1901* (1967) reinterpreted the "open door" policy. Author of several seminal articles, and collaborator with others in this collection in *The Creation of the American Empire* (1973), McCormick is completing a study of American policy in the Cold War.

Margaret Morley teaches at Northern Arizona University. She received her Ph.D. at Wisconsin in 1972. Her dissertation was on Henry Clay and American foreign policy, a topic which remains a major scholarly interest for her.

David W. Noble is Professor of American Studies and History at the University of Minnesota, where he has taught since 1952 after receiving his Ph.D. at Wisconsin in that year. Recent books have been in collaboration with Peter Carroll and David Horowitz, *The Free and the Unfree* (1977) and *Twentieth Century Limited* (1980). His latest book, a study of the historians who shaped our thinking about the recent past, *The End of American History,* appeared in 1985.

Carl Parrini took all his degrees at the University of Wisconsin. His Ph.D. came in 1963. He is currently Professor of History at Northern Illinois University, and is the author of *Heir to Empire: U. S. Economic Diplomacy 1916-1923* (1969) and several recent articles on investment theory and imperialism.

Bradford Perkins, a specialist on American foreign policy in the early national period and later 19th century, is Professor of History at Michigan. He received his Ph.D. from Harvard in 1952. Over the succeeding years he has published many books, including *Castlereagh and Adams: England and the United States, 1812-1823* (1964) and *The Great Rapprochement: England and the United States, 1895-1914* (1968).

William G. Robbins studied at several universities, taking his Ph.D. from the University of Oregon in 1969. Currently Professor of History at Oregon State University, Robbins is also editor of the *Environmental Review.* His books focus on western history. They include *American Forestry: A History of National, State and Private Relations* (1985) and *Lumberjacks and Legislators: Political Economy of the Lumber Industry, 1890-1941* (1982). A colleague of William Appleman Williams, he is a practicing marathoner.

Part One

The essays in Part One are concerned with evaluations of William Appleman Williams's impact on the teaching and writing of American history. William Robbins of Oregon State University offers an assessment of Williams's career at the University of Wisconsin and at Oregon State University, focusing not only on Williams's written works, but also on the ways he has influenced both students and colleagues. The second essay is by Ivan Dee, Vice President and Editor-in-Chief of Quadrangle Books in the 1960s. Williams's association with Quadrangle Books, as Dee points out in this fascinating portrayal of the relationship between academic scholarship and the publishing world, was, in part, coincidental, but it was nevertheless an important one at the outset of an exciting era of new interpretations.

Bradford Perkins of Michigan University reviews *The Tragedy of American Diplomacy* after twenty-five years, and gives readers a chart by which to measure the reverberations caused by this book that shook the academic world, while David Noble of the University of Minnesota offers an intellectual historian's evaluation of Williams's place in the evolution of American historiography.

William Appleman Williams: "Doing History is Best of All. No Regrets."

William G. Robbins

Although chance, occupation, or design sometimes take us far from our birthplace, the childhood memories and recollections of place have a strong attraction for most people. And so it is with William Appleman Williams who recalls affectionately the drifting snows of winter and the humid summer scent of hogs and maturing corn in western Iowa. His present home on the Oregon coast, brushed by winter squalls and the cool summer breezes of the Pacific, has an equally strong pull. For Williams, the home overlooking the majestic western sea is both haven for reflection and a way to "keep your ego in check." The ocean, he says, "tells you not to take yourself too seriously."[1]

It is, in part, that affinity for the sea, the harmony of rural Oregon, and the recollections of boyhood days in Iowa's farm country that have influenced Williams's perceptions of America. Those physical settings, notable for their isolation from the mainstreams of American culture, are conducive to the sense of place and community that has buoyed Williams as a writer of American history and helped to establish him as one of the preeminent historians of the modern era.

Strong and independent women—his mother, Mildrede Appleman, and grandmother, Maude Hammond (who provided home and affectionate instruction while the widowed mother was attending college)—informed his early life. Born Mildred Louise, his mother happily attached the "e" to distinguish herself from two other Mildreds in her first grade classroom. That peculiarity, according to her son, "caught the eye and mind" of administrators, ship pursers and airline attendants, "hustlers and sophisticates" on three continents, paymasters, students, and "ultimately the mortician and the coroner."[2] Mildrede's qualities of determination and will, as well as her maiden name, have also distinguished the son.

The father and grandfather were less conspicuous, though no less influential, in his upbringing. William Carleton Williams, raised on a farm in the Atlantic, Iowa, countryside, went off to the state college and then to the Army Air Corps in the fall of 1917 where he learned the art of being a "demonstration" pilot. That was prelude to his marriage to Mildrede Appleman in November 1918, a return to civilian life as a pilot "barnstormer," and finally to a succession of jobs in Iowa. When none of those proved satisfying (he was "probably a bit bored," the son reasons), "Billy" returned to active duty with the Army Air Corps in Oklahoma. He died in an airplane crash in war games exercises in March 1929.[3]

And therein enter Maude and Porter who, with Mildrede's assistance, provided the fatherless boy with "a good family life, a solid childhood, [and] a warm home." While Maude was stable and sensible, and kept the family together during the harsh years of the Depression, Porter was adventurous, witty, and "cared a bit too little for security for his family." But he also was devoted and caring for his wife, daughter, and grandson, and "not a bad grandfather to have around the house." Although he avoided yard work and other familial responsibilities of that order, Porter raised Mildrede as an equal and taught the grandson skills with hand tools that served him well in adult life.[4]

Athletic talents in basketball and high school academic achievements earned Williams a scholarship in 1939 to Kemper Military School in Boonville, Missouri, where he was inclined toward architecture. Two years later, as war raged over Europe and Asia, he was appointed to the United States Naval Academy. The "Academy," as he affectionately refers to the Annapolis school, provided "a first-rate liberal arts education" and a thorough grounding in the sciences, and broadened his awareness of power relationships, a perspective that would prove valuable to his future work as a historian.[5]

After graduating from the academy, Williams spent fifteen months in the Pacific as an officer on a landing ship. He was wounded during a naval engagement and transferred to Corpus Christi, Texas, for medical attention and recuperation, an experience that turned into a liberating one for the young naval officer. During his stay in the coastal city, he witnessed conspicuous examples of American power and racism and, with a fellow officer, joined with the Black community and the National Association for the Advancement of Colored People to address those conditions. The Texas experience taught him "a lot about American society, . . . that the reality" was far different than the popular mythology. Williams told a reporter in 1978 that the civil rights struggle in Corpus Christi, even more than the searing encounter with war, was the point "where I consciously became a radical." In the process, he also learned about the authority and influence of the business community.[6]

The civil rights affair was another factor that drew Williams to the study of history, because that discipline "seemed . . . to be the best place to go to make sense out of human activity." Thus, while he was still in the Navy, he wrote to the registrar at the University of Wisconsin and to the chairman of the history department, Paul Knaplund. According to Fred Harvey Harrington, who became Williams's major professor at Wisconsin, Knaplund was "impressed with Bill's motivation and steered him into his career." The fact that his mother was teaching third grade in Wisconsin and the strength of the university's history faculty were central to Williams's decision to leave the Navy and enroll as a graduate student in 1946.[7] He arrived in Madison at a time when Knaplund was building the history department into one of the most influential in the United States.

During his tenure as a graduate student at Wisconsin (1946-50), he shared company with several outstanding history doctoral candidates—Wayne Cole, Harvey Goldberg, John Higham, Jackson Turner Main, David Shannon, and Irv Wyllie. From that distinguished company, Harrington notes, "he would be the most influential," though he "came with little history under his belt, with a none-too-impressive GPA from an institution not known for turning out history types (A. T. Mahan excepted)." The department admitted him on probation with the stipulation that he take a semester of undergraduate work in history.[8]

In addition to Paul Knaplund, other faculty members recognized the exceptional qualities of the new graduate student. For his part, Fred Harrington was impressed when Williams indicated a desire to work in Russian-American relations. He liked the young doctoral candidate's "openmindedness," found him "inquiring, willing to change," and, he says, "tried not to curb him." From the graduate student's perspective, Harrington was one who "could dissect any decision, event, or movement into its constituent parts with a subtle, loving ruthlessness." Those qualities earned the Wisconsin professor such endearing nicknames as "Mr. Cold" and "The Fish Eye."[9] Williams impressed other Wisconsin faculty members in addition to Knaplund and Harrington, and he has subsequently repaid their kindnesses with affectionate references in his articles and books.

Of those, the person of William Best Hesseltine looms the largest. There were qualities about him, according to Harrington, that Williams liked; Hesseltine "was a scoffer, liked to say outrageous things and to have people combat him—WAW liked that, and liked H's ideas." Hesseltine's argumentative style, Williams later remarked, "did not so much teach you as he infuriated you to learn." Even, he remembers, when "Hesseltine came down on your first sentence like he was Darth Vader.'' Williams learned, too, from Paul Farmer and the sociologist Hans Gerth, scholars with impressively wide-ranging minds. While the likes of Hesseltine and others had Williams ''thinking, soaring,'' Harrington taught him the ''nuts and bolts of historical inquiry'' and attempted to ''hold him on the ground, at least during graduate school.''[10]

Long after he left Wisconsin, Williams remarked that he took to the institution ''[l]ike a fish to water. It was a terribly exciting experience.'' While Harrington, Hesseltine, Knaplund, Merrill Jensen, Merle Curti, and Howard K. Beale informed Williams about doing research, ''how to think straight,'' and how ''to make sense out of that material,'' his graduate peers were equally if not more influential. Williams recalls that his ex-GI friends were politically informed about their education and the way the university operated, and those in history wanted ''to figure out what the hell had been going on in the war.'' That particular group of graduate students, Harrington believes, was ''more influential'' than the faculty in shaping Williams's mind; some of them were ''activists and thinkers,'' and collectively they provided an exciting intellectual climate on the Wisconsin campus.[11]

Walter LaFeber, a Harrington student who also studied under Williams when the latter joined the Wisconsin faculty in 1957, points out that the graduate school situation was ideal for Williams. Harrington, for one, allowed his students great latitude in selecting dissertation topics, and ''both Harrington and Hesseltine also were open to different, off-center interpretations.'' Wisconsin and Williams were ''a perfect match,'' LaFeber notes; ''he needed room and encouragement for what he wanted to do, and Wisconsin was probably the only place in the United States that could provide both.'' It was also the one graduate program in the country where many of the Americanists ''were linked by ideological attachments to Progressive history, most notably the work of Turner and Beard.''[12]

For Wisconsin-trained historians economics were inextricably linked with politics and ideology and, therefore, important to historical understanding. For Williams and many of his contemporaries, Madison was an intellectual environment that encouraged fresh perspective and independent thought, the hallmarks of revisionism. According to Harrington, any historian worth serious consideration was a revisionist. Williams understood that to mean ''someone who sees basic facts in a different way.'' Harrington, Hesseltine, and Curti, LaFeber adds, urged the future historians not to rewrite but to ''rethink'' the past. Heady advice from a group that LaFeber likens to ''the historical equivalent to the 1927 Yankee Murderers' Row.''[13] By the mid-1960s, it could be argued that the Wisconsin institution was the most lively center for historical studies in the United States.

Another impressive and powerful intellectual force was Merrill Jensen who taught Williams and others about domestic revolution and about the contradictions in Thomas Jefferson. Jensen, who delighted in conversation, would occasionally become engrossed until the moment the bell rang for his next class. Then he would reach into the shelves above his desk and pull out a handful of 5 x 8 note cards and head for the classroom where he invariably delivered outstanding lectures.[14] Based on his observations of Jensen's note card technique and Harrington's habit of writing outlines five minutes before class, Williams developed his own method of drafting only short briefs for his lectures.

After Williams completed his master's degree in 1948, he spent five months in England attending a seminar on socialist economics at Leeds University. There, under the tutelage of economist A. J. Brown, he first considered the possibility of decentralized economic and political structures as an appropriate transition away from a failing capitalism. That approach, he said, appealed "to my whole value system and experience."[15] And it was a theme that became more prominent in his later articles and books, especially in *America Confronts a Revolutionary World* and *Empire as a Way of Life.*

When he returned to Wisconsin, Williams decided to do a doctoral thesis on the career of Raymond Robins, a social reformer and Progressive party leader. Robins, who was in Russia at the end of the First World War and witnessed the revolution of 1917, turned over most of his correspondence to Williams. The young doctoral candidate, who traveled to Florida for a visit, reported that the two "got along famously." Williams subsequently defended his completed dissertation in the summer of 1950.[16]

That manuscript, revised in book form, appeared as *American-Russian Relations* in 1952 and established Williams as a scholar to be reckoned with. He learned later that a Rinehart editor had forwarded the last chapter, an epilogue covering the years 1940 to 1947, to the American foreign policy establishment's publication, *Foreign Affairs.* Because he had challenged the validity of George F. Kennan's containment policy, the chapter was widely circulated and prompted considerable discussion among the foreign policy architects associated with the journal.[17] That experience sharpened and tempered Williams's perceptions about the publishing world and its relations with political power brokers.

*   *   *

Williams left the University of Wisconsin with impressive support, including that of his mentor, Fred Harvey Harrington, who was moving up the administrative ranks towards the presidency at Madison. The new chairman of the history department, Chester V. Easum, praised Williams as "one of the ablest individuals turned out by our graduate school in recent years." He applauded his "interest in students, and extraordinary ability to communicate his own enthusiasm to others." That praise, according to Harrington, was from a man "with zero sympathy for Bill's views on historical and current events." With those recommendations, Williams landed a one-year appointment at Washington and Jefferson College, followed by another temporary appointment at Ohio State University for the academic year 1951-52.[18]

During the Ohio State interlude, Williams met Paul Varg, a man he described as "a true gentleman"; Ray Dulles who was "kind and supportive"; Harvey Goldberg, a great intellect, radical, and teacher; and another institutional force at Ohio State, football coach Woody Hayes. When Williams gave Hayes's red-shirted halfback (who was to replace the redoubtable "Hopalong" Cassidy) an F in Western Civilization, the irate coach phoned "*Instructor* Williams" to inform him that he had erred in recording the grade. The ensuing conversation, Williams recalls, went as follows:

"Are you aware, *Instructor* Williams, of how much we have invested in this young man?"

"That is not a matter of record, Mr. Hayes."

"Well, I'm telling you that we've got one hell of a lot invested in this kid. And who the hell do you think pays your salary over there, *Instructor* Williams?"

"The taxpayers, Mr. Hayes."

"The hell they do: I pay your salary with my football team. Don't you think you ought to change that grade?"

"No, Mr. Hayes."

"Well, you better goddam well believe that I'll change your job, *Instructor* Williams."[19]

*   *   *

After the year at Ohio State, Williams moved on to the University of Oregon and his first tenure track appointment in the fall of 1952. A small but growing department that included Gordon Wright, Wendell Stephenson, Earl Pomeroy, Vall Lorwin, and Edwin R. Bingham, the Eugene environment seemed ideally suited for one seriously committed to historical scholarship. It was "a truly *fine* small liberal arts university," Williams remembers, with exciting people in several of the humanities disciplines and in the physics department. He also made friends with Bernard Malamud who was teaching at the "Aggie" school (Oregon State College) in Corvallis, forty miles north of Eugene. On one occasion, after a lengthy argument about *The Natural*—a discussion that included James Hall of the University of Oregon's English department—Malamud told Williams he was one of the first people to understand the novel as a metaphor about American history.[20]

Red-baiting and McCarthysim were also a fashionable part of the University of Oregon campus, and Williams remembers certain individuals who "tried to make life miserable for me and some other people." Eventually, Williams, Vernon Snow (Wisconsin), and Orde Pinckney (Berkeley), all left Eugene for other academic appointments. They feared a change for the worse when Stanford hired Gordon Wright away from Oregon. On one occasion as the faculty was leaving campus at the end of the day, a member of the history department fronted Williams at a hallway water cooler and asked bluntly: "Are you a communist?" Williams informed his inquisitor that the question was "an insult" and walked out the door.[21] That exchange boded ill for his security at Oregon.

Other facets of the Oregon experience, however, made a positive and lasting impression, especially the state's spectacular coast with its high rocky bluffs and long stretches of sandy beach. The ocean provided those intangible qualities, "the sound and drive of the surf," that moved one's psyche. Williams renewed his acquaintance with the rhythms of the sea during long weekend tours along the coast, capturing the best of those moments with photographic skills that he had developed over the years.[22]

During his stay at the University of Oregon, Williams compiled and edited the massive two-volume work, *The Shaping of American Diplomacy* (1956). Focusing heavily on selections that illustrated the relation between economic and foreign policy, he cautioned readers that it was important to "watch other men make foreign policy." Understanding the consequences of acting upon "various outlooks and beliefs," he argued, can help people change and formulate "their own" view of the world. Despite some disagreements, the documents indicated that there had been "a sense of continuity in outlook and action" in the conduct of United States foreign policy.[23]

The long hours of sifting through diplomatic records and correspondence also provided the groundwork for Williams's best-known book, *The Tragedy of American Diplomacy* (1959), and his most wide-ranging interpretive effort, *The Contours of American History* (1961). Although *Tragedy* was published after he returned to Wisconsin, most of the work on the original 200-page essay was done at the University of Oregon where he was one of the most productive members in the history department. But even then detractors belittled his performance, because he published articles in *Science and Society, Monthly Review,* and *The Nation.* His critics ignored the fact that established journals, like the *American Historical Review* and the *Mississippi Valley Historical Review,* refused to publish essays that raised unorthodox questions.[24]

Williams's experience with professional editors did not jibe with his graduate training. From Hesseltine and Harrington, students had come to expect "a high level of candor, honesty, and acceptance of new and different ideas"; neither of the two major professional journals, Williams contends, "demonstrated those qualities." His exchanges with Carey McWilliams (*The Nation*) and Paul Sweezy (*Monthly Review*), however, were of a different quality. They and their progressive journal associates offered "tough, useful editorial criticism." Paul Sweezy, he remembers, never quite forgave him "for saying that John Quincy Adams had something significant to say about American foreign policy and culture."[25] However, neither Sweezy nor Williams personalized the issue, and the two remain good friends.

While matters continued to simmer at Oregon, a series of personnel shifts at the University of Wisconsin opened the way for Williams to return to Madison. Fred Harrington was being pushed as the social science candidate for the presidency of the university, a move that would vacate the position in diplomatic history. Harrington phoned Williams about the situation, and the Wisconsin history department voted unanimously to extend an offer. But, there were problems—the position was untenured, the salary was not that attractive, and Williams did not want to leave Oregon, at least until he had finished *The Tragedy of American Diplomacy.*[26]

However, when Harrington called a week later and slightly sweetened the pie, Williams went to the department chairman at Oregon and asked the university to match the Wisconsin offer, a difference of $400. At some point, an Oregon administrator killed the match and thereby forced his decision. In the fall of 1957 Williams was off to Wisconsin where, he points out, "even some of the administrators" were exciting. As it turned out, the departure from Eugene involved more—a marriage of twelve years in which two people had "developed in different ways" also came to an end.[27]

*   *   *

Once at Wisconsin, Williams quickly established himself as a force in the profession and as a centerpiece of the Madison academic community. He trained more than thirty-five Ph.D.s during his eleven-year stay and wrote several books and articles that have become classics in American historical writing. Those were some of the most creative and productive years ever enjoyed by an American scholar. As Bradford Perkins states elsewhere in this volume, Williams raised fundamental questions about America and the world that have become conventional premises for examining United States foreign policy.[28]

Although he was known to the faculty at Wisconsin, Lloyd Gardner recalls that graduate students "knew practically nothing about WAW when he arrived." Only Walter LaFeber was familiar with *American-Russian Relations,* and he told Lloyd Gardner that Williams "was a much criticized author." But Gardner and LaFeber quickly learned more about the new historian when they were assigned to assist Williams in the foreign policy course. For one thing, the readings in *The Shaping of American Diplomacy* were different, Gardner points out, "and in combination with his lectures, it was an awesome year!"[29]

For LaFeber, working as Williams's teaching assistant was a memorable experience: "Sitting in that classroom and listening to him lecture I understood for the first time what a *teacher* . . . was supposed to do." His special genius, LaFeber remembers, was "his ability to stand outside and generalize and take fresh perspectives" to understand and explain American society. Although the "more orthodox" of the graduate students sometimes wandered out of William's lectures shaking their heads, LaFeber remarks, "their own thinking was never the same afterwards. . . . And that is the test of a great historian."[30] In short, Williams taught students *how* to think about history.

Lloyd Gardner points out that Williams "sometimes got lost in his spinning out of points . . . he would say there are four things to keep in mind about X. Then list only three." After those performances, students would rush to "the back of the room in a panic to ask us what the fourth was." Gardner and LaFeber, both ignorant of the vital "fourth point," confessed that they had no idea. "Why is this a good story?" Gardner asks. "Because we had never thought about foreign relations in the way that Bill did."[31] All *four* points, therefore, were new.

According to LaFeber, Williams forced students to think "about things differently, from a broader perspective and more critical in context." He was an "architect, not a post-hole-digger," and he did what most historians cannot do and that is "to put those post holes in a larger plan, a larger context and blueprint." That characteristic was Wisconsin's heritage, LaFeber believes. Williams learned those scholarly principles during his graduate years at the university, and that is what he taught his students when he returned as a member of the faculty.[32]

Even his office was different, Gardner recollects. Williams had the entire *Foreign Relations* series, the collected works of G. D. H. Cole and E. H. Carr, books on the sociology of knowledge, architecture, economics, and anthropology. "That is why," Gardner explains, "it is a little hard to take when I hear Bill charged with simplistic interpretations, or economic determinism."[33] The Wisconsin office, like his present one at Oregon State University, also sported an assortment of more esoteric and less scholarly items—model airplanes, imaginative posters, cards with the favored aphorisms of Mother Jones or Eugene Debs, and magnificent collages and mobiles given to him by students and friends.

Shortly after his return to Madison, several of Williams's students began publishing *Studies on the Left,* a journal that presented a radical critique of American institutions and policies. The University of Wisconsin also staged one of the first "teach-ins," opposing United States involvement in Southeast Asia.[34] As the war heated up, Williams's iconoclastic views gained increasing popularity among the throngs of young people who flocked to the antiwar movement in the latter part of the 1960s. "Mad Town" gained a reputation as a turbulent center of radical student activity and leftist politics.

Amidst the intellectual ferment and excitement of the Wisconsin years a second marriage began to disintegrate, and there were other distractions— the publication of often vicious reviews of his books, and the expensive and time-consuming fight against a subpoena from the House Committee on Un-American Activities (HUAC). The committee, evidently, was interested in the manuscript of *The Contours of American History* which had not yet appeared in print. Through a friend at the Wisconsin law school, Williams contacted Paul Porter, an impressive Washington, D.C., lawyer, who agreed to take the case.[35] As it turned out, the choice was fortuitous.

Williams visited with Porter, who took him "up and down and sideways and backward trying to figure out" what the committee wanted. Porter told his client that if he leveled with him, the manuscript would be surrendered only through a Supreme Court order. He had Williams review his career, and asked a lot of questions "about Texas . . . [and] the Black question," because the Communist Party had a long tradition of activism in southern civil rights issues.[36] The racist committee, of course, never lost an opportunity to connect civil rights activists with the party.

But HUAC was interested in other matters as well—because Williams had published in *Science and Society, Monthly Review,* and *The Nation,* because he served as an advisor to *Studies on the Left,* and because he had a small grant from the Rabinowitz Foundation. What the committee wanted most, however, was to stop the publication of *Contours.* To that end, they played Williams "like a yo-yo," telling him to report on a certain day to testify, and then canceling the appearance via telegram after he had boarded a train for Washington. "That way, you couldn't collect any money for it," Williams learned.[37] Thus, even though the committee often encountered legal obstacles in its arcane maneuvering, it still exacted a price from its victims.

Finally, when Porter had to argue an antitrust issue in front of some of the same representatives on another committee, he turned the Williams case over to Thurman Arnold, the former antitrust prosecutor in the Justice Department. Arnold convinced HUAC to back down and advised Williams that they should go before the committee "and pay our respects to them," pointing out that the alternative would be $50,000 in expenses and five years of legal battles. Recognizing that those resources were beyond his means, Williams, despite his reluctance to acknowledge the committee, went before HUAC for a ten-minute *tête-à-tête* after which the committee dropped the case. But, as Williams learned, HUAC *"will"* work its way." They sent his name to the Internal Revenue Service and that agency, he says, harrassed him "for the better part of twenty years."[38]

Meanwhile, establishment scholars took after the growing number of Williams's books. Foster Rhea Dulles attacked *The Tragedy of American Diplomacy* as the effort of "a brilliant but perverse historian" who was more interested in argument than doing history; John Braeman criticized *Contours* as the work, not of a historian, but of "a prophet leading the American people to salvation." It remained for Harvard's Oscar Handlin, however, to deliver the most impassioned tirade against *Contours* in the

Mississippi Valley Historical Review. Williams, he said, was wrongheaded, had created an "elaborate hoax," and, with the "literary striving of an unskilled freshman," had written a distorted and "farcical" book. In a new foreword to *Contours* published in 1966, Williams likened those attacks to "trench warfare," so wholly negative that they destroyed any possibility of dialogue.[39]

Much of the criticism directed at Williams and what was becoming known as the "Wisconsin school" was petulant and spiced with more than a little jealousy. The Wisconsin historians, after all, *knew* they were good. After lunch with Knaplund, Harrington, Hesseltine, Jensen, Beale, and later Harvey Goldberg, Williams points out, "what more could an intellectual ask for?" Each was a prominent figure in his field, and that made some of the elite schools "mindlessly jealous of Wisconsin," and the fact that a mid-western public institution was the center of progressive and revisionist scholarship. Lloyd Gardner observes that Williams has developed a variety of foils to counter Ivy League chauvinism, including an emphasis on "his midwestern twang as an act of defiance" when he visits the east coast.[40]

Williams is blunt about the issue: "After all, Wisconsin did write the best history for years . . . and produce the best students." But the "great thing" about the institution at that time "was that we just got on with the job and did not fret about Harvard, etc." Hesseltine, he argues, had the proper attitude: "Write your mind. Do not waste your mind arguing with your critics. Let them worry about the problems you raise." In Walter LaFeber's assessment, Williams "defined the field of American diplomatic history in such a way that everyone who works in it has to take his work into account." And, as for *The Tragedy of American Diplomacy,* Bradford Perkins notes that its influence "is beyond challenge."[41] Though his critics dominated the major professional publications with negative reviews of his books, Williams and the "Wisconsin school" were gaining national and international respectability.

Eugene Genovese, a rising force in southern and slave history in the 1960s, told an interviewer in 1970 that Williams was "the best historian the Left has produced in this country." According to the Brooklyn-born Marxist, he "created almost single-handedly a new school of American diplomatic history." Even bedrock conservatives like David Donald began to admit that Williams and the people he trained had so revolutionized the writing of American diplomatic history that they had become the establishment. In 1971, the *Wall Street Journal,* certainly no admirer of those who would overturn the established order, referred to Williams as the "dean of left-wing diplomatic historians."[42] The carping, of course, did not stop, but by the early 1970s Williams's most vocal critics were battling revisionist brushfires from every direction.

His professional associates have never questioned Williams's commitment to the study of history. Because it "is a vital part of creating, sustaining, and changing a culture," he argued recently, doing history "is serious and consequential labor." That philosophy has influenced nearly two generations of students, some of whom merely read his books and articles in faraway places. As a young faculty member at Wisconsin, Fred Harrington recalls, Williams was deadly serious about the importance of studying history. The former mentor "found it interesting that at parties, though he had fun, he always insisted on intellectual discussions as part of the fare."[43]

That sense of purpose and importance about doing history impressed Walter LaFeber, Lloyd Gardner, and Tom McCormick at a time when at least one of them was considering leaving graduate school. The scene was LaFeber's apartment where the three graduate students and their wives hosted a dinner for Williams shortly after he joined the Wisconsin staff. "A stunning evening," Gardner remembers, and one that lasted until 3 a.m.[44] Williams, who from long practice had developed the habit of writing until the early hours of morning, undoubtedly missed his nightly work on that occasion.

According to LaFeber, Williams convinced the three young graduate students "that history did not have to be viewed as traditional diplomatic historians were teaching it, that it could have real meaning for the present and could be a pioneering field." Because of that conversation, LaFeber says, he "decided to stick it out" and finish graduate school. He also points out that none of the three would "have looked at our work and careers in the same way had Bill not spent that evening and morning with us." Gardner is equally emphatic about the conversation: "It made the impact that lasted." From a self-professed "Wilson hater and FDR lover," he began to see both men "somewhat differently after that evening."[45]

*   *   *

As the antiwar movement heated up after 1965, students—especially the enlarged enrollment in Williams's Ph.D. seminar—made greater demands on his time. His responsibilities to the seminar were burdensome to the point that he no longer taught lower division classes, a task that he had always enjoyed. Finally, with the conceptual outline of another book in mind, Williams took a full research leave from Wisconsin in 1966-67 and settled in Newport on the Oregon coast to write *The Roots of the Modern American Empire*. Along the way he and his family (including three children via a second marriage) made stops in Nebraska and Wyoming and other repositories of agricultural journals and manuscripts.[46] But it was the coastal environment that counted; there he renewed his acquaintance with the sea and established contact with some of the faculty at Oregon State University, sixty miles to the east in Corvallis.

Because the university's library had a good collection of populist magazines and agricultural publications, he began to make regular trips into Corvallis. During those visits he became acquainted with George Carson, history department chairman and former editor of the American Historical Association's Service Center for Teachers series. He liked Carson, appreciated the force of his mind (and his integrity), and the chairman, in turn, invited Williams to speak to the department about his research. The Carson-Williams dialogue led to an inquiry and eventually the offer of a teaching position at Oregon State.[47]

One Oregon State historian recalls Carson, with a gleam in his eye, announcing at a staff meeting that Williams was interested in joining their department. But Carson had to do some maneuvering to get the administration's approval. For his own reasons, the institution's president, James H. Jensen, was skeptical about hiring a controversial, albeit nationally renowned, historian. Williams speculates that he may have been under pressure from individuals on and off campus. Because Jensen had known Harrington when the two of them were central figures in developing the Sea Grant university program, he phoned Harrington to ask if the Wisconsin maverick was "safe." After seventeen years at the Corvallis school, Williams laughs about Jensen's query: "Now, you ask me, what the hell can Harrington say but that I am safe. So that is that, and I get the job."[49] But the move to Corvallis in 1968, a major career shift, raised eyebrows in the academic community.

There would be no training of Ph.Ds at Oregon State University; in fact, the institution still does not offer even a master's degree in history. Why, then, the determination to leave one of the most lively centers of progressive learning in the United States? And to a university with, at best, a questionable commitment to the liberal arts? Although the reasons are complex, it was not a spur-of-the-moment act, and shabby treatment at Wisconsin did not figure in the equation. That institution, Williams makes clear, "treated me very well, and I am sure would have continued to do so."[49]

Williams believed the Ph.D. seminar had run its course. "I had trained students that were as good if not better than I was, and so why string it out?" He also wanted to teach undergraduates again, a near impossibility at Wisconsin because of the demands of the seminar. And there were less prosaic, nonprofessional reasons for the decision. He missed the sea; he did not like the idea of shoveling snow at the age of sixty-five; he wanted his children to associate with people of different classes. Equally important, because he did not want to retire in Madison, Williams wanted "to put down roots in a community" where he would spend the rest of his life.[50]

There was a sense of play involved as well. As he grew older, his professional career became "less and less . . . the essence of my life." And the Oregon coast provided an abundance for that play—a photographer's haven, excellent surf fishing, and most of all the quiet and leisured pace of rural living. The combination of teaching undergraduates and having a residence on the coast had other advantages. From the time he settled

15

permanently in Oregon, he points out, "I have been free to write the kind of essays that I thoroughly enjoy."[51] While he plied the tidal waters for rockfish, cultivated his talents in the poolroom, and indulged in the art of amateur photography, he also became an assertive figure in Oregon's academic and public communities.

There were less pleasant circumstances associated with the move to Oregon. A second marriage that had become problematic in Madison did not survive the new setting. There followed a stint as a single parent and then, in late 1973, the quiet but happy union with Wendy Margaret Tomlin, a British national living in Corvallis. That relationship has grown and matured and the Williamses are presently respected citizens of Waldport, a community of about 1,300 people.

There were battles and excitement during the first years at Oregon State University. Steeped in the Harrington tradition and always fond of informing his listeners that "Wisconsin was a university run as a true democracy," Williams enjoyed "raising hell" in college committees and the faculty senate, challenging them to create a true university. It was fun, he observed, "to tweak the nose of some of our colleagues with an awareness of what a university *should* be."[52]

But there also were disappointments with deans and other administrators at Oregon State. When a liberal arts dean attempted to impose a computerized teacher evaluation form on the college, Williams (and most of the faculty) strongly opposed the effort. Proud that his colleagues had resisted the imposition of what was euphemistically referred to as "the dean's instrument," he still thought the administrator's action disgraceful:

> Enough to have him cashiered out of the service in good seventeenth century style. The faculty in gowns around the mall and his hood ripped from his shoulders and his hat ground into the mud. All to the roll of drums. We ought to go back to such meaningful ceremonies in such cases.[53]

Despite the frustrations and what he perceived as institutional lethargy, Williams retained his sparkle of wit and a sense for the ironic. After a day of nagging committee work, a department meeting, and a miscellany of university errands, he suggested in exasperation that "Lewis Carroll would have written about Alice in Corvallis if he had known about it!" As he moved toward the presidency of the Organization of American Historians, he likened that group's conservative and inefficient stature to "a Cub Scout Troop without a Den Mother."[54]

Williams also developed the habit of referring to university president, Robert MacVicar, not by name, but with the acronym, *the sixth floor*. But his association with MacVicar—who served as president from 1970 to 1985—although more adversarial than his relation with Harrington, was candid and forthright. "MacVicar," he notes, "always played it straight with me." While Williams would publicly denounce the trade school mentality that prevailed at Oregon State, he also noted that the institution had the potential to "leapfrog" from assembly-line pedagogy and defining jobs in terms of the marketplace to create a university that emphasized "the process of becoming human beings . . . and citizens."[55] He has continued that dialogue through public lectures and newspaper columns, and in his contributions to humanities education at the university.

MacVicar is equally respectful of the historian. "People knew of Oregon State because of Williams"; he "was a stimulus to mature scholars on campus and a model for the younger ones." William Appleman Williams, the ex-president notes, "demonstrated in action the essence of the academic scholar." During his tenure at the university, MacVicar cited as "particularly noteworthy" Williams's efforts to advance the quality of the liberal arts and his contributions to the establishment of a humanities center.[56]

In the mid-1970s Williams joined a small group of scholars at Oregon State who applied to the National Endowment for the Humanities (NEH) for a grant to develop and improve interdisciplinary courses in the humanities. As part of that effort, he expanded his own curricular offerings to include courses in marine and maritime cultures. He recalls the "fun and excitement" of developing that program and the "truly *good* people" he met in the process. He also helped the university's Center for the Humanities gain institutional support to meet a successful challenge grant from NEH.[57]

*   *   *

Since the move to Oregon, the books and essays have continued to multiply. The more important of these—*America Confronts a Revolutionary World* (1976), *Americans in a Changing World* (1978), and *Empire as a Way of Life* (1980)—added to the author's reputation for raising unorthodox but thoughtful questions about the political culture of the United States. A marketing agent for Harper and Row who read the manuscript of the twentieth century text, *Americans in a Changing World,* cautioned his superiors that the book would not "sell in Peoria" because of its controversial tone. That rebuke did not move Williams to alter the manuscript. His motto: "When I get to my final draft, I've said what I've got to say, and if someone doesn't want to print it, that's fine."[59] Self-confident and assertive, with a reputation firmly established, Williams has lost none of his combativeness.

The criticisms of his work, some of them even more vitriolic in recent years, have also continued. Robert J. Maddox, a former Williams student, authored the most publicized attack in a 1973 book, *The New Left and the Origins of the Cold War.* Although it was rife with innuendo and short on solid argument, old line cold warriors welcomed the book. But that form of savagery, as Bradford Perkins suggests, continued to ignore the important questions that Williams raised.[59] Despite the play that the Maddox book received when it first appeared, Williams's increasing respectability in the scholarly establishment has obscured its significance.

Published at a time when recycled and simplistic social theories were becoming fashionable, *Empire as a Way of Life* was subjected to the same vicious criticism. *The New Republic,* in one of its reactionary moods, asked a shrill conservative, John Lukacs, to review the book. The result was an exercise in expletive and venom that virtually ignored the issues raised in *Empire.* Edward S. Shapiro followed with an equally bitter attack in *The Intercollegiate Review,* a reactionary academic journal. Shapiro cited the appearance of the book while Williams was serving as president of the Organization of American Historians as evidence that its membership was "overwhelmingly on the left."[60] Clearly, the intellectual vigilantism characteristic of the McCarthy era of the 1950s was alive and well in the early 1980s.

When he began writing weekly articles for the Salem *Statesman-Journal* in 1981, Williams opened himself to more public criticism in the letters-to-the-editor column of the newspaper, through his personal mail, and in anonymous and threatening phone calls. But there was little difference between those attacks and the irate rantings of some professional historians—they were personalized and failed to grapple with the issues.

John H. McMillan, publisher of the *Statesman-Journal,* valued the weekly columns because of Williams's broad-ranging interests. But he regrets that no one at Oregon State, "either publicly or privately," stepped forward to defend Williams or the newspaper from some of the irresponsible attacks. McMillan also faults the university for not celebrating Williams whom he describes as a world-class scholar. Indeed, he says, the university "seems almost embarrassed by him."[61]

In January 1985, Williams shifted to the larger circulation Portland *Oregonian,* where he agreed to do a less demanding biweekly column. His topics included traditional Williams material—George Orwell and *1984;* rethinking the Constitution; a comparison of Ronald Reagan and Herbert Hoover; John Winthrop and the City on the Hill; and frequent references to "sane conservatives" like John Quincy Adams.[62] Williams terminated his affiliation with that newspaper when an editor refused to publish one of his articles.

The newspaper columns reflect that same sense of wry humor and gently perverse teasing that his graduate students discovered nearly thirty years ago when Williams unabashedly rooted for the New York Yankees and Green Bay Packers; those who cheered for other teams, he said, were afraid of power. "He could say that," Lloyd Gardner remembers, "with the same seriousness as he discussed the roots of the Cold War." In one Sunday column he compared the intellectual power and achievements of Herbert Hoover and Ronald Reagan: "Reagan reads scripts written by other people. Hoover wrote books. . . . Hoover did his homework. Reagan takes naps and thinks it is clever to avoid tough questions."[63]

Both as a historian and as a public citizen William Appleman Williams continues to inform and challenge us. John Byrne, who became president of Oregon State University in November 1984, acknowledges that Williams is the kind of "'troublesome character' we need in institutions of higher education." Whether you agree or disagree with him, Byrne says, "he makes you think." For his part, Williams has never seriously entertained any other objective. "That is why," he told the 1973 meeting of the American Historical Association, "warts and all, I remain, faithfully yours, an intransigent revisionist." Twelve years later he could still say that it had been fun, that *"doing* History is the best of all. No regrets."[64]

"The Tragedy of American Diplomacy": Twenty-Five Years After

Bradford Perkins

The influence of William Appleman Williams's *The Tragedy of American Diplomacy,* published a quarter century ago, is beyond challenge. An iconoclastic attack upon conventional wisdom, it is equally important because it framed arguments about its subject. In both ways it is very much like the study of the Constitution by Charles A. Beard, a scholar whom Williams reveres. And when historians finally escaped the conceptual fetters imposed by Beard and Williams they found that they could not—indeed, did not want to—ignore much that these figures suggested.

In 1959, *Tragedy* made a rather modest splash. The *New York Times* did review it, and the *Christian Science Monitor* denounced it as a Stalinist tract. But the *American Historical Review,* which then used smaller type and fewer words for reviews of minor publications, placed Williams's book in that category. Most reviewers praised the author's originality, then savaged his emphasis on economic factors. A political scientist, who suggested that the book was a mistake unlikely to be committed in his profession, believed it would be ignored: "The approach taken by Williams is no longer in the mainstream of international relations study."[1] But within only a few years *Tragedy* was definitely in the mainstream.

Reviewers concentrated on Williams's most persistent theme, that almost all Americans held "the firm conviction, even dogmatic belief, that . . . domestic well-being depends upon . . . sustained, ever-increasing overseas

This paper was first published in *Reviews in American History,* volume 12, number 1, March 1984. Reprinted by permission of the publisher and author.

economic expansion.''[2] Despite the decision to annex the Philippines, the preferred strategy of economic expansion was pursuit of the open door, the globalization of John Hay's China-oriented declarations of 1899 and 1900. As Williams phrased it, "When combined with the ideology of an industrial Manifest Destiny the history of the Open Door Notes became the history of American foreign relations . . .''[3] Most policies, from McKinley onward, were determined by a desire to keep doors open, by open door imperialism designed to create informal empire.

Americans saw no contradiction between promoting their trade and improving the world by stimulating economic activity or, as Williams says, in putting "their self-interest to work to produce the well-being and the harmony of the world.''[4] But although Americans professed to believe—even believed that they believed—that every nation had a right to determine its own path, in fact they felt, and came to insist, that the American way was the only one. They failed to see that the kind of economic activity they encouraged, in Third World countries at least, was exploitative, that it institutionalized dependency and discouraged socioeconomic progress.[5] This blindness led the United States, with increasing activism, to pursue counter-revolutionary policies. Today's policies, in this view, represent "the final stage in the transformation of the open door from a utopian ideal into an ideology, from an intellectual outlook for changing the world into one concerned with preserving it in the traditional mold.''[6] This argument meshes with and perhaps reinforces the economic one, and both emphasize expansionism, but the motivational priorities are strikingly different.

Second only to open door imperialism, the persistence of expansionism is the theme most often identified with *Tragedy*. Yet, although Williams included a brief, strained interpretation of James Madison's *Federalist #10* to suggest that America had been expansionist from the beginning, he really began his account toward the end of the nineteenth century.[7] *Tragedy* is an explanation for the overseas commercial expansion and ideological offensive of an industrialized America faced with the specter of surplus production. Williams and others later pushed the expansionist theme backward, but there is little reason to identify the original version of *Tragedy* with this theme.[8]

In any case, the expansionist thesis expressed a near truism. At least until our time, American leaders have been committed to growth, economically and sometimes territorially. Early economic policy, limited in effect by limited power, sought to create an open door empire for agriculturists and shipowners. Still, although Williams would later object to the "question-begging" argument of those who insisted that he ought to define empire and expansion,[9] there surely is imprecision in commingling territorial expansion to control new areas of production with efforts to dispose of a surplus through expanded trade, to say nothing of a quest for ideological dominion.

In 1962 and again in 1972, Williams extensively revised *The Tragedy of American Diplomacy*. He increased its length by half, adding detail and extending the chronology. He also made scores of changes which hardened the arguments. In 1959 *Tragedy* described Hay's Open Door Notes as a "policy . . . for America's overseas expansion," a comment with which few would disagree; the third edition described it additionally as a policy "through which America's preponderant strength would enter and dominate all underdeveloped areas of the world."[10] The original edition stated that most of Wilson's opponents in the fight over the Treaty of Versailles "emphasized the need to continue economic expansion with greater vigor," while Williams later added that they also wished "to oppose . . . revolutions with more determination . . ." than Wilson.[11] Revised editions stressed, far more than the original, that the concept of an Axis menace in the 1930s predated any military threat. "It occurred instead," Williams wrote, "as those nations began to compete vigorously with American entrepreneurs in Latin America and Asia," and he also argued that "the strategy of the open door"—here used in the economic sense—"did lead to war."[12]

The changes reflected Williams's growing alienation. In 1959 he "seemed to imply that America could achieve a more humane and successful foreign policy by recognizing its former errors and only mildly reforming itself."[13] Then came America's violent reaction to the Castro revolution, and after that Vietnam. A new introduction began, "The tragedy of American diplomacy is aptly summarized, and defined for analysis and reflection, by the relations between the United States and Cuba"—intervention, exploitation, and counterrevolution, a paradigm of policies the world over. The new conclusion repeated an eloquent appeal for the tolerance of revolution but added that, for this to come about, "existing American society had to be changed."[14]

In 1959 *Tragedy* was a passionate essay. Later, in Jerald A. Combs's words, "colleagues and students applied [Williams's] theory in particular episodes in a harvest of monographs."[15] These were cycled back into revised versions of *Tragedy* as sources for new passages or footnotes to support sections which had inspired them in the first place. While revised editions are still thinly documented, the *ex post facto* apparatus of scholarship gives them a more traditional air.[16] Still, it is as a manifesto, not a monograph, that the book should be judged.

Writing on the "Open Door Interpretation" years later, Williams disclaimed sole responsibility for it. A group at the University of Wisconsin, he wrote, interacted to produce a mode of analysis of which *Tragedy* was the most general statement. Williams paid special tribute to "the particular genius of [Fred Harvey] Harrington."[17] Indeed, impressive works by the "Wisconsin school" were at least begun as dissertations under Harrington. But Harrington's views were less monothematic than Williams's. Two of his students, David F. Healy and Robert Freeman Smith, produced studies of relations with Cuba which were highly critical of American policy but did not insist that commerical considerations reduced others to insignificance.[18] Still, whether the product of Williams's conceptualizing or a synthesis of group ideas, *Tragedy* challenged traditional views and laid out alternatives.

One discussion of "William Appleman Williams and the 'American Empire'" sensibly distinguishes, as many fail to do, between those who share Williams's revisionism only in the general sense, as is the case with many Cold War critics, and a true "school," those who essentially expand upon passages in *Tragedy,* which in practice usually means application of the concept of open door imperialism.[19] Most renowned of the latter is Walter LaFeber's *The New Empire* (1963), which, although begun under Harrington, closely fits *Tragedy*'s mold. Unlike the latter, it concentrated only on the expansionist thrust prior to 1898, but the persistent theme was the search for markets to absorb an industrial surplus that seemed to threaten the economy. Tariff reciprocity, policy toward a Brazilian revolution, the quarrel with England over the boundary between British Guiana and Venezuela, and the coming of the Spanish-American War were all examined in light of their support of this theme. LaFeber's arguments were sometimes questionable or overdrawn, and he acknowledged that he had passed by episodes that did not fit his pattern. Still, *The New Empire,* an early elaboration of the market thesis, both showed the influence of *Tragedy* and seemed to support its claims.[20]

Subsequently, students of Williams, following his shift of emphasis into the period before 1898, produced a cluster of works which buttressed both *Tragedy* and *The Roots of the Modern American Empire* (1969), the product of his new concern. Howard Schonberger maintained that farmers, merchants, and railroad-builders sought to improve access to overseas markets during the building spree after the Civil War, an argument more convincing if emphasized as a complement to rather than a substitute for interest in creation of a national market. Tom E. Terrill dismissed arguments over the tariff as essentially quibbles over tactics, since everyone was a commercial expansionist, thus blurring passionate disagreements and downplaying the success of protectionists. Edward P. Crapol emphasized the search for national economic independence and overseas markets. He argued, with only mild qualification, that Republicans won the election of 1896 because they convinced voters they knew "how best to foster overseas commercial expansion . . . ."[21]

Other works applied the market theme to the thirties and forties. Lloyd C. Gardner's *Economic Aspects of New Deal Diplomacy* (1964) ferreted out evidence that material considerations, not sentimental pan-Americanism or security-based or even ideological opposition to the Axis, lay at the heart of policy. In the introduction to a paperback edition in 1971 Gardner half-apologized for the lack of balance, but his ideas have found a modest place in later works on Rooseveltian diplomacy. More polemically, Dick Steward and David Green examined policy toward Latin America under Roosevelt and Truman, emphasizing the selfishness of tariff reciprocity. Frederick C. Adams made much the same point with reference to the Export-Import Bank.[22] All these books showed the danger, implicit in *Tragedy* itself, of pressing a single theme beyond its capacity to explain, of becoming uncritical pupils in a "school."

The open door argument proved more impressive when not made to deny the importance of other factors. Thus Thomas J. McCormick's *China Market: America's Quest for Informal Empire, 1893-1901,* which dismissed ideological arguments as something "dipped into" to camouflage economic greed, was less satisfactory than Marilyn Blatt Young's *The Rhetoric of Empire, 1895-1901,* a study informed by Williams's concept but adding political and cultural factors. Similarly, Carl P. Parrini's *Heir to Empire: United States Economic Diplomacy, 1916-1923* suffered by comparison with Michael J. Hogan's *Informal Entente: The Private Structure of Cooperation in Anglo-American Economic Diplomacy, 1918-1928* because Parrini, too, was reluctant to go outside Williams's boundaries.[23]

These examples, even when supplemented by Cold War literature, to which we will return, do not exhaust the possible list of works influenced by *Tragedy.* Still, large areas of study remain almost untouched by Williams's schema. No one has really applied his insights to policy in the early republic (the Monroe Doctrine would seem an inviting target) or expanded on Norman A. Graebner's argument, predating *Tragedy,* that a yearning for Far Eastern markets helps to explain the expansionism of the 1840s. Of course, historians continue to explore territorial expansion, especially the Louisiana Purchase and the acquisitions under Polk. Williams's distaste for expansionism may perhaps be detected in Alexander DeConde's *This Affair of Louisiana* (1976) and David M. Pletcher's *The Diplomacy of Annexation* (1973), but neither of these now standard works more specifically embraces his views.[24]

In 1975 Howard Schonberger proclaimed "the increasing domination of the historiography of American foreign policy by New Left scholars."[25] In fact, New Left history, to say nothing of Williams's particular brand, had not then approached domination. Nor did the open door interpretation continue to crest after 1975, by which date most of the monographs discussed above had been published. Critical studies have been and are numerous, but by no means all bear the New Left mark, and narrow ones in the style of Crapol and Terrill are rare. Furthermore, most historians, both before and after 1959 or 1975, simply continued to work in traditional ways.

Tragedy of course stimulated—that is to say, influenced—critics as well as followers. One, in fact, provoked Schonberger's arrogant claim: William H. Becker published articles which powerfully challenged one of Williams's (and LaFeber's) basic assumptions, demonstrating that fears of a "glut" were not widespread in the years before World War I. Later he carried his attention down to 1921, examining government-business cooperation and concluding that "the expansion of the export of manu-factured American goods between 1893 and 1921 is remarkable more for lack of close government cooperation [with business] than for closer ties with business and government in the making of these sales." Equally critical, though not directed solely at Williams, was Alfred A. Eckes's 1975 article, "Open Door Expansionism Reconsidered: The World War II Experience." Eckes showed that, contrary to revisionist assertions, America's leaders did not believe that only expanded exports could prevent a postwar depression and also showed that the economic order they created was not designed with that consideration in mind. Eckes later published a history of this structure which stressed its political purposes and rebuked "economic determinists [who,] in their quest for synthesis, magnify economic factors at the expense of other policy objectives and thus wrench history out of perspective."[26]

Most impressive of several critiques of Williams's overall approach was Robert W. Tucker's *The Radical Left and American Policy* (1971). Although this book did not deal exclusively with Williams and was written with Cold War revisionism as its prime target, it provided an extensive, thoughtful analysis of *Tragedy*'s conceptual base. Tucker saw an essential ambiguity in *Tragedy*'s central argument. As he phrased it, "the reader is never quite clear—because Williams is never quite clear—whether America's institutions necessitated expansion or whether America has been expansion-ist out of the mistaken conviction that the well-being . . . of these institu-tions required constant expansion." This was a valid point; Williams's position was opaque. A careful reading, however, shows that he was unwilling to embrace determinism to the extent of making his argument absolutely dependent on it. And wisely so. A determinist argument would have col-lided with obvious facts: exports were, until recently, a small fraction of national output, and nations subject to open door imperialism absorbed only a small part of that fraction. In the end, Tucker rightly concluded that, despite ambiguity, Williams saw policy "as largely responsive to a deeply rooted, although apparently mistaken, conviction about the requirements of the nation's institutions."[27]

But, Tucker continued, if this was Williams's view, his argument did not differ fundamentally from those of other critics, notably so-called realists, who also argued that American policies were based on mistaken calculations. "If," wrote Tucker, "the radical critique is understood to mean that we have been expansionist out of mistaken conviction, . . . and that in expanding we have sought to universalize American values . . . , then even if it is granted that capitalism is the foremost of those values it is still not easy to see wherein the critique is sharply distinguished from a more conventional criticism."[28]

America did want an American-style world. But, wrote Tucker, *Tragedy* mistakenly defined this world, and American policy, in economic terms: "America's interventionist and counterrevolutionary policy is the expected response of an imperial power with a vital interest in maintaining an order that, apart from the material benefits this order confers, has become synonymous with the nation's vision of its role in history."[29] This statement, accepting Williams's postulate of an expansionist America, was accompanied by important qualifications. It referred to the Cold War years; Tucker challenged Williams by pointing out how little, not how much, the United States had usually done before 1939 in response to threats to its kind of world. He also argued that "the method of indirect and informal empire," which Williams considered uniquely American and especially nefarious, "is not an American invention. It is not even a Capitalist invention."[30]

On balance, Tucker was highly critical of *Tragedy*. Nevertheless, he repeatedly praised Williams, and other radicals, for challenging the view, held even by nonradical critics who attacked policies without questioning motivation, that the country's basic outlook had been unselfish. "If nothing else," he concluded, "the radical critique has forced us to acknowledge the extent to which an obsessive self-interest has been central in American foreign policy."[31]

Another critic, J. A. Thompson, shared many of Tucker's conclusions and added others of his own. (He did not, however, credit Williams with useful demythologizing.) He objected that loose use of words such as "expansion" and "empire" allowed Williams to create a false impression of continuity. He argued that open door imperialism was so imprecisely defined that it comprehended "any political action [however weak] designed to promote foreign trade." Even more, he said, for those who accepted *Tragedy*'s argument, "'imperial expansion' seems to be synonymous with successful economic competition . . . ," even if the government did not act at all.[32] Thompson's essay, published in 1973, in effect summed up the arguments against *Tragedy*. That so much labor had gone into this reaction is itself proof of *Tragedy*'s influence.

Tragedy, then, had clearly made its mark. Williams had asserted the pervasiveness of national self-interest, reversing the realists' complaint and the patrioteers' boast that it had often been neglected. He had shown that national interest comprehended economic concerns as well as security interests. He had suggested a symbiosis between officials and businessmen. If predecessors had touched upon aspects of these things, Williams was first to synthesize them.

On the other hand, zeal carried him too far. In the 1972 edition of *Tragedy,* Williams deplored the attitude which "defines history as a stockpile of facts to be requisitioned on the basis of what is needed to prove a conclusion decided upon in advance."[33] But he himself had done exactly that, selecting and organizing the data not only to prove a conclusion but also to isolate it from competing ideas. Furthermore, he had postulated consistency, even effectiveness, where a less committed observer would have found hesitation, contradiction, and variety.

These failings, when added to the shortcomings pointed out by such people as Becker and Tucker, led many to reject Williams's interpretations out of hand, often dismissing them as simplistic Marxism. But Williams is neither Marxist nor simple.[34] Those who read him carefully, who refused to serve as *post hoc* footnoters or members of a scholarly Inquisition, moved his influence to a new level.

Critical was the incorporation of economic motivation into any account of American policy, not as an afterthought but as an integrated part of the whole. Critical, too, was an awareness of the relationship between business and government, although these historians pointed out that the relationship was by no means without friction. They gave ideology a major role, including a commitment to capitalism which was deep, not hypocritical. And they added other factors, notably bureaucratic politics, that Williams had ignored.

Hankerers after paradigms and models objected to the new eclecticism. Recently, Thomas J. McCormick, whose *China Market* was an early product of the Wisconsin school, objected that so-called postrevisionist students of the Cold War, and by extension all those who viewed history as complex and uncertain, worked on "The operative premise . . . that multiplicity, rather than articulation, is equivalent to sophistication. Systematicism is not their strong suit."[35] He and others have suggested a "corporatist" structure which would transcend the narrowness of Williams and the anarchy of postrevisionists and those who think like them. The corporatist approach may be loosely defined as a recognition of causal multiplicity, always including ideological factors, with, however, a heavy emphasis on economic factors. However employed, the approach is heavily in debt to Williams.

Much work in this vein, often undertaken before the label was invented, has dealt with World War I and its aftermath. The authors agree that an activist nation sought world power, largely through the use of economic weapons. Often they are very critical of Williams and his followers, who, Melvyn Leffler complained, fail "to weigh and to balance the relative importance of commercial considerations *vis-à-vis* other economic, fiscal, strategic, and political factors . . . ." Some time later, Leffler produced an impressive study which sought to restore the balance without denying importance to "commercial considerations." In *Informal Empire,* Michael Hogan gave prominent place to ambitions for trade and stressed collaboration between government and private interests, but he argued, too, that leaders sought a stable world through as much as for economic growth. Singly and together, such authors have raised Williams's approach to a more complex level, but his influence is clear.[36] Whether this approach will work as well for periods of intense political crisis and military confrontation remains to be seen.

N. Gordon Levin sensitively employed *Tragedy* in a different fashion in his study of Woodrow Wilson. Although Levin especially thanked Louis

Hartz, a conservative, and Hartz's concept of American exceptionalism informed the book, the preface to *Woodrow Wilson and World Politics* (1968) paid homage to Williams and other radicals. Levin defined Wilson's goal as "the attainment of a liberal capitalist world order . . . , safe both from traditional imperialism and revolutionary socialism, within whose stable liberal confines a missionary America could find moral and economic pre-eminence."[37] Like Williams, he showed that Wilson vigorously sought trade expansion, particularly through the strategy of the open door. And Levin believed, like Williams, that Wilson's United States was an expansionist nation seeking to establish and lead a world system based in large part on capitalist values.

But Levin joined these themes, drawn from *Tragedy*, with Hartzian ones to create a sophisticated whole. He stressed Wilson's conviction that American political and social values were the finest in the world and that their acceptance by all nations would assure peace and progress. He took great pains to make clear that Wilson not only did not see but could not conceive that his two purposes—expanded trade and an Americanized world—might conflict with one another. The intellectual impressiveness of *Woodrow Wilson and World Politics* is further confirmation of the wisdom of viewing *Tragedy* as what it is, a stimulus and not a blueprint.

No other book is more closely identified with Cold War revisionism than *The Tragedy of American Diplomacy*. Although only about one-fourth of the 1959 edition dealt with the period after World War II, earlier pages had prepared the ground for its treatment of the recent period, not only by staking out arguments but, more broadly, by establishing the critical thrust that is the heart of revisionism. Still, for various reasons, the nature and extent of *Tragedy*'s influence is difficult to establish.

In the first place, Cold War revisionism was very diverse, in marked contrast to the conceptual unity of the literature on open door imperialism in earlier periods. Revisionists agreed with Williams, of course, that the United States bore chief responsibility for the tense confrontation with the Soviet Union. Beyond that they varied greatly, often disputatiously.[38] Obviously, all critics of Cold War policies, even those who acknowledge their debt to Williams's spirit, cannot be identified as disciples, although careless writers have been tempted to do so.[39]

It is tempting, particularly since Gabriel Kolko came to share the leadership of revisionism, to identify him as a follower of Williams. There are of course similarities, particularly of spirit. But there are also differences, for example, in analyzing Soviet policy or motives for the Marshall Plan, which reflect dissimilar assumptions. Kolko brought to his study of the Cold War approaches developed in earlier, critical treatments of Progressive reform. He was far more rigorous in analysis than Williams, more Marxist, and the acknowledgment in *The Politics of War* of obligations to Arno Mayer and Barrington Moore reflected this. Kolko joined the revisionist crusade initiated by *Tragedy,* and he forced his way to its front rank, but he cannot be considered Williams's disciple except in the most general sense.[40]

That the nature of *Tragedy*'s arguments changed when it examined the Cold War also complicates matters. Here, Williams's treatment was unusual in that, for almost the only time, he evaluated the policies of another nation. *Tragedy*'s logic did not require such an excursus, and the sympathetic discussion of Russian motives and actions sounded like special pleading. In 1959, reminding Americans that the Soviet Union had emerged from World War II in a weakened state and that many Soviet policies were defensive was fresh and important. It was questionable to describe the Soviet Union as an essentially pluralistic society—a pluralistic oligarchy, if you will—and to view Stalin's actions as solely a response to American aggressiveness. Most revisionists embraced the first set of arguments but rejected or ignored the second.[41]

Such arguments weakened *Tragedy* as a whole, allowing critics to charge that it was a pro-Soviet tract. In the first chapter of an attack on the New Left treatment of Cold War origins, Robert J. Maddox savaged Williams, at one time his teacher, as he did all the authors with whom he dealt. He pointed to real and, more often, dubious examples of their misuse of sources, endeavoring to show a pro-Soviet bias. Maddox's vituperative tone and narrow concentration on policy toward Eastern Europe in 1945 and 1946 severely limited his effectiveness. Even historians critical of Williams objected that Maddox presented "a surfeit of innuendo and a paucity of hard evidence." They also objected, quite rightly, that "in his zeal to expose Williams's imprecision, Maddox loses sight of Williams's scope." Although Maddox's spleen was unique, Williams's gratuitous comments on Soviet behavior diverted others, as well, from the scheme and philosophy that was *Tragedy*'s chief claim to attention.[42]

The last section of *Tragedy* also differed from earlier portions in that the economic theme was muted. Williams continued to present evidence that American leaders sought foreign markets, and he saw this as a major factor in policy toward the Third World. He argued that, especially at Potsdam, the United States fought for Eastern European and Far Eastern markets. Still, in these pages economic expansionism played a small part, at least by comparison with the emphasis given it in earlier parts of the book.

Instead, Williams stressed "the ideology of the open door . . . ." Open door expansionism became in essence an aggressive crusade to propagate American values across the world: "As far as American leaders were concerned," he wrote, "the philosophy and practice of open door expansionism had become, in both its missionary and economic aspects, *the* view of the world." Williams refused to "assign priorities to the various facets of the *Weltanschauung,*" economic or other, only asserting rather lamely that "the open-door outlook was based on an economic definition of the world . . . ." Still, in his view, the employment of American power "in keeping with the traditional policy of the open door crystallized the Cold War."[43]

Thus the open door concept was extended to accommodate almost any interpretation stressing American aggressiveness. As Mark Stoler has written, "While Williams's Open Door approach theoretically provided a general framework of analysis, the framework proved to be so broad that its numerous adherents could apply either a rigid economic determinism or virtually ignore economics and economic issues and concentrate instead on vaguely related political beliefs and actions."[44] Whereas the first three-quarters of *Tragedy* provided a clear guide for those who wished to follow it, the treatment of the Cold War was a more diffuse *cri de coeur*.

Perhaps predictably, since *Tragedy* abandoned the single focus on markets, few who can be identified as Williams's followers applied that theme to the Cold War years, certainly not to the extent of obscuring others. Books by two men who had been at Wisconsin with Williams and had written market-centered monographs illustrate this point. While Lloyd C. Gardner's *Architects of Illusion* (1970), a study of policy makers who led America toward a false goal, stressed economic considerations, Gardner did not minimize ideological ones, as he had in *New Deal Diplomacy*. Walter LaFeber's *America, Russia, and the Cold War* (1967) differed even more from his earlier book. LaFeber's study is sometimes described, usually with the qualification that it is temperate, as economic determinist. In fact, although economic factors were examined, others received more stress, particularly the desire for an open door world in the broadest sense. (A theologian, Reinhold Niebuhr, rather than a businessman, was most often cited as spokesman of the American consensus.) LaFeber deplored the effort to Americanize the world, but he avoided Williams's extravagances. When it was first published, LaFeber's work seemed very revisionist; today it is widely perceived as the best survey of its subject, an indication of how much of revisionism (and *Tragedy*'s spirit) has been absorbed.

Yet it was also possible to reach conclusions broadly similar to LaFeber's without sharing his orientation. In a study of the early Cold War, Thomas G. Paterson also described the pursuit of an American-style, American-dominated world—in *Tragedy*'s jargon, an open door world. America's "often haughty, expansionist, and uncompromising" policies, Paterson wrote, drove a hesitant (but not innocent) Soviet Union to forceful reactions of its own. But he denied that economic goals were important and even that a capitalist outlook dominated America's world view. Economic power was the frequently misused weapon of political diplomacy, not its goal, Paterson argued. Thus he distanced himself from Williams's followers, although *Soviet-American Confrontation* levied the same basic charges against Washington policy makers.[45]

It was equally possible simultaneously to embrace and to reject key parts of Williams's argument. Bruce Kuklick, author of *American Policy and the Division of Germany* (1972), described himself as "parasitic" on Williams but devoted pages to an attack on him. Kuklick agreed that the United States, by its aggressive policies, produced the division of Germany.

31

But he denied that the open door had dominated policy since at least the 1890s. To so argue, he insisted, was "deeply ahistoric"; it suggested a nonexistent consistency in American aims, whereas postwar policy toward Germany was determined by time-bound conditions. Although he used different terms, when Kuklick described the goals of policy they differed little from those suggested by *Tragedy*—liberal democracy, American influence, and world trade expansion. Provocative though he thought these goals, Kuklick insisted they were more than self-serving. American leaders expected benefits for their country, but also for the world. Like N. Gordon Levin, Kuklick maintained that the American vision "simultaneously embraces moral commitment and politico-economic interest."[46] This endorsed rather than challenged much of what Williams had written, though not what both critics and simplifiers read into *Tragedy*.

These examples suggest that the influence of *Tragedy*, "the first important scholarly revision of recent American diplomacy . . . ," has been inspirational rather than specific. It is ridiculous to argue that other revisionist studies are "little more than extended footnotes on interpretations Williams first put forward."[47] Few have applied the open door concept in quite the same way, even granted that, dealing with the Cold War, Williams shifted his definition. Few have viewed the Soviet system as sympathetically as Williams did in 1959, and few have drawn the conclusion, added in revision, that "developments after 1952 [Stalin's death in 1953?] in Russia, and . . . the events of 1956 in Poland and Hungary . . ." indicated a softening of that system.[48]

For about a decade after 1965, historians did battle over the Cold War. Not only books and articles but historiographical essays abounded.[49] Then the battle moderated. Differences remained, but few revisionists any longer denounced their opponents as mere apologists for the State Department, nor were they denounced in reply as perpetrators of academic fraud moved by communist sympathies. Moreover, the site of battle, so to speak, shifted. Almost no historian any longer wrote on the Cold War with the purpose of holding Joseph Stalin guilty before the bar of history. The last major effort in this style was the work of two British authors, Sir John Wheeler-Bennett and Anthony Nicholls, published in 1972. A useful barometer of change is provided by new editions of John W. Spanier's survey, which, without abandoning the hard line of the original, have progressively incorporated revisionist ideas.[50]

Some, particularly those who identify themselves as postrevisionists, suggest that a Hegelian dialectic has taken place: orthodox thesis challenged by revisionist antithesis has produced the higher truth of postrevisionist synthesis. Yet it can be argued that postrevisionists, although they concede American failings, really aim to destroy revisionism. It can also be argued, by those who hanker after philosophical clarity, that they merely present a potpourri, not a synthesis. As Warren Kimball complains, "leaving no reason unturned is not the same as developing a new thesis." Moreover, just as the revisionist label blurs the variety within that camp, so postrevisionists differ greatly in tone and conclusion. There is a world of difference between John Lewis Gaddis's pioneering postrevisionist study, *The United States and the Origins of the Cold War,* often critical of American policy but harsher on the Soviets, and Daniel Yergin's dramatic book on the same subject, so negative toward the Americans that Jerald Combs, for example, can describe it as a "moderate revisionist account."[51]

Whether or not labeled postrevisionists, a large majority of those now writing on the Cold War owe substantial debts to Williams and other revisionists. They recognize economic factors, largely ignored by orthodox historians of the past, and they agree with Williams in placing policies aimed at trade expansion within a broader context. While they do not endorse *Tragedy*'s view of Stalin's Russia, they almost unanimously argue that Soviet leaders, though grasping and brutal, had no blueprint for world revolution. And they agree, most of all, that it is misleading to view American policies as purely defensive rather than at least in part as efforts to extend American interests and influence. Many find useful the concept of empire, though often blanching at the term itself, and at least since the tragedy of Vietnam began to unfold a chorus of voices has criticized the overextension of that empire.[52]

Of course, some of these conclusions seem obvious, and some had been argued before Williams wrote. At least since George F. Kennan's famous lectures in 1950, realists had condemned the overextension of American interest and the overcommitment of power, although they did not consider these to be inevitable products of the *Weltanschauung* and usually exempted policy toward Western Europe (but not the Truman Doctrine's hyperbole) from their criticism. This view was developed in surveys of the Cold War by Norman A. Graebner in 1962, before revisionism took hold, and by Ronald Steel, then outside the revisionist camp, in 1967.[53] Still, granting the point, it remains true that what seemed obvious to realists had not really been absorbed until argued—perhaps overargued—by revisionists, for whom William A. Williams was the bellwether.

A dozen years have passed since Robert W. Tucker pondered on the extent of "the influence exerted by the radical critique. That it has exerted an influence is clear," he concluded. "What is not clear is the extent of this influence . . ."; indeed, any effort to gauge it was, in Tucker's view, unlikely to succeed.[54] In a precise sense, this is true, not least because influence is so difficult to define. Need only the spirit or must the specifics of Williams's account be adopted if influence is to be claimed? How much of either? Moreover, regarding *Tragedy,* the effort to establish influence is particularly difficult because, as has been argued, the book makes two different, though reconcilable, arguments. Later writers can reject or ignore one or the other of them, perhaps apply one to a period in which for Williams it was a lesser theme, yet draw inspiration from *Tragedy*.

Assessing *Tragedy*'s influence on histories of the Cold War is especially difficult. The mere passage of time, the realist critique of moralism and extravagance, Gabriel Kolko's strident determinism, and the brutal education provided by Vietnam all contributed to the tide of criticism. *Tragedy,* nevertheless, was the first fundamental assault on the merits of American objectives. If few works in its direct descent have won the acceptance extended to LaFeber's history of the Cold War (and LaFeber is much readier to see the world in all its complexities), most revisionists are deeply beholden to *Tragedy* in a more general but fundamental sense.

It is clearer that the heyday of the open door imperialist argument—the theme, concentrating on trade expansion, for which Williams is best known— has passed. Few now see *Tragedy* as the best, certainly not the only, guide to pre-World War II diplomacy. Those books most narrowly applying its theme, whether to the late nineteenth century or a later time, are sometimes credited with adding a minor dimension to understanding, no more, and the stream of new studies is nearly dry.

What survives is the influence of *The Tragedy of American Diplomacy* on those who receive it intelligently and selectively. When Tucker wrote, the debate was a battle, not a dialogue. Most disputants, although not Tucker, argued either that *Tragedy* was a sacred writing, true and all-explaining, or a mere tissue of lies and distortions. As the combatants became exhausted, progress began. Historians recognized that too little attention had been paid to factors emphasized by Williams. Although they varied greatly in the extent to which they allowed this recognition to influence them and often rejected important parts of his arguments, they produced better history. Studies of the 1920s and works on the Cold War lumped together under the postrevisionist label are but two examples of this process.

Whether a new schema, a structure as complete as Williams's, will result is questionable. Postrevisionism can be a mish-mash of contending judgments, and the corporatist thesis is both vague and insufficiently tested. Historians today—and not merely historians of American diplomacy—often rather self-consciously seek for some system into which all eras and events may be fitted. These searches may fail, as Williams's did. But no comprehensive scheme, no broad generalizations, and few but the narrowest studies of episodes in American foreign relations will be written, if they are to shine, without an awareness of and an accommodation to William Appleman Williams's *The Tragedy of American Diplomacy.*

Revisionism Revisited

Ivan R. Dee

Among the many curiosities of the 1960s in America, one of the least curious events (for many) was the rise and decline of Quadrangle Books, a medium-sized Chicago publishing house which made much of its reputation by publishing what at the time was called "revisionist history." In fact, this was only part of what Quadrangle published, but most of its books were indeed serious, left of center, and concerned with history, politics, sociology, and "current affairs." While the Left found easy access to large publishing houses in the sixties (Doubleday probably published more radical titles than anyone else in the business in those years, but they were lost in Doubleday's immense list), smaller houses also did their share, Quadrangle more than most.

Almost no one in book publishing thought Quadrangle would succeed with its uncommercial mix. We were, after all, almost an anomaly in our time. The sort of book we liked best was one we could first publish in hardcover for modest sales through bookstores, then put into paperback for use in college courses. This scheme made sense for a publisher without powerhouse advertising or sophisticated distribution channels. Basic Books and the Free Press were notable and similar—though better-established— enterprises: serious specialized publishers who nonetheless attempted to sell through trade bookstores.

By the end of the sixties Quadrangle had carved a niche for itself with this approach to publishing; by the early seventies it had disappeared, lost in the corporate structure of the *New York Times*. Along the way, Quadrangle made a good many friends among historians. One of them was William Appleman Williams.

In our struggle to build a successful publishing house, Bill Williams and his work played an essential role. I cannot claim that our coming together resulted in a major chapter in the history of American book publishing, or in the publishing of American history; but the synergism produced by this unusual relationship made a difference to Bill, to his students, and ultimately, I think, to the profession.

*   *   *

When I came to Quadrangle in 1961, I had just spent a year publishing books on my own in Macon, Georgia, an unlikely locale for entering the business. I had been sent there for my last year of active duty in the Navy and had stayed another year to start a publishing house with a good friend. At the time it seemed to me the best way to get into a business which I had discovered was looking only for college travelers. So most of what I knew about publishing was self-taught in a tiny office over Kaplan's credit furniture in Macon.

Quadrangle at the time was a little more than a year old. It had been started by a Hyde Park car dealer named Michael Braude. He had put up the initial capital at the urging of Alex Morin who had come from the University of Chicago Press to run it. Quadrangle had published fifteen or twenty books in its first year, almost all imported from England and the Scandinavian countries, and all decidedly scholarly—in the social and behavioral sciences, economics, and business. It was also the American distributor for Edinburgh University Press. (When, shortly after my arrival, I received a cable from Edinburgh inquiring about TRAPPIST TENDENCY, I searched high and low for some record of the book but could find nothing. Several months later I discovered this was Scottish humor: their way of asking why Quadrangle hadn't been in touch with them.)

I came to Quadrangle with an enthusiasm born of my belief that by publishing good books I could make a "social contribution." I also had considerable interest in history. I had done graduate work in American and Russian history after taking a journalism degree at the University of Missouri. When it came to serious scholarship, history was one field I knew reasonably well as an intelligent layman, and I pursued it.

Melvin Brisk, a former newspaper reporter, came with me to Quadrangle. He dealt with business and sales details while I handled the editorial side, but we both did a bit of everything. We replaced Alex Morin who had had a falling out with Braude, the angel. Our office, on the second floor of an old loft building next to the elevated tracks on West Lake Street in Chicago, had been home to the Free Press before it became a success story—bought by Macmillan and moved to New York. (We were always confronting the hallowed ghost of Jeremiah Kaplan of the Free Press, especially when we looked at our profit-and-loss statements.) In these dilapidated, rather gloomy offices, reached by a wooden staircase of at least thirty steps, we had our first contact with the University of Wisconsin History Department.

It was late 1962 or early 1963 when I first corresponded with William B. Hesseltine. He was working on a book having to do with a bizarre episode of the Southern Confederacy in Egypt. Hesseltine was probably introduced to us by Larry Burnette of the Wisconsin State Historical Society, who advised us on a series of facsimile reprints in American history—our meager entry into the field. Bill Hesseltine came to see us in Chicago one day, survived the climb up that heart-wrenching staircase, and signed a contract for the book.

Not long after, Hesseltine put me in touch with Bill Williams. I had heard of a long essay that Williams was composing, and persuaded him to let me see it. In December 1963 I wrote to him:

> Dear Prof. Williams:
> I have read the fifty-three pages of manuscript, and I think the work is incisive and provocative. [It was ultimately to be published as *The Great Evasion*.] It is always difficult to predict how a book like this will be received. If the rest of the manuscript is as tight and cogent as the part I read, it could possibly become a 'primer' of sorts for your side of the argument.
> I would like to see the remainder, partly because most of our staff [my lone colleague] is in New York this week for a sales meeting, and I am anxious to get other reaction here in the house. But I am most definitely encouraged and favorably inclined to go ahead.

This was the beginning of a mutually admiring correspondence and friendship which lasts to the present day, though the letters are far less frequent than they used to be.

I soon went to Madison to meet Bill. At his office in Bascom Hall, I found him squatting on his desk chair, smoking a cigar and reading a manuscript. He was relaxed and accessible. I was still a learner, still pretty deferential to professors who had been teaching me things only a few years before. I suspect Bill liked this quality in me. For my part, I liked his openness, his willingness to involve me in his arguments. He would always make me feel important to him both as an intellectual sounding board and as an editor and publisher of his work.

It turned out to be not all that much work. *The Great Evasion* (subtitled "An Essay on the Contemporary Relevance of Karl Marx and on the Wisdom of Admitting the Heretic into the Dialogue About America's Future") was the only original manuscript Bill Williams ever published with Quadrangle. The book was only a long essay to begin with, but during the editorial process it was expanded by half. In March 1964 Bill wrote to me: "Done. A total of 89—I just counted them—89 pages of typed revision in an original ms. of 187. I think you got your money's worth, old friend."

Money was an aggravation to most Quadrangle authors at one time or another. In its early years, the house didn't have much of it. We had decided in 1963, after two years of doing nothing but imported books, that we wanted to publish original American scholarship. We were still in the first year of trying to do that, and we were miserly with advance money for authors. We offered Bill no advance at all when we sent him a contract for *The Great Evasion,* but he asked for $500 and we caved in. One of his letters to me in the spring of 1964 testifies to the tenderness of this subject. He wrote:

> I am not really put out, and in no sense angry, about what I take to be your policy on advances. But I do think that you ought to reconsider it if you want to attract the bright young people in this business . . . I was thinking tonight: here we are, an established if controversial writer of serious historical analysis presents a basically clean manuscript that is attractive. The publisher asks for reasonable and intelligent and perceptive revisions (no joking, I mean it, the suggestions are first-rate). The author undertakes to do them promptly and without any guff. This is work. So the book comes out in approximately six months. The author receives a fundamentally minor advance for work done promptly on a manuscript that ties up the publisher's capital a relatively short time and which must be expected to return—at a minimum—the equivalent of at least three times the advance.
>
> I could not help thinking tonight that this is the smallest advance I have ever had for what in some important respects is the best and most exciting manuscript I have done. My real point is not an indirect request for more money born of being tired at midnight, but rather the suggestion that you really ought to be a bit more candid in laying out your advance policy *ahead* of time and ahead of any dickering about it . . .
>
> Enough. I'm tired and the entire basement is filled with cigar smoke.

My response to Bill when such complaints arose was not to tell him that Quadrangle was always one step behind its creditors but rather to point out how overworked our accounting department was (the "department" consisted of a billing clerk and a part-time bookkeeper) or how good our intentions were, or to ask where he could possibly get our kind of personal attention elsewhere. These were the same rejoinders I used over the years as authors complained about the size of their advance or the tardiness of their royalty checks. In publishing with Quadrangle, authors indeed made commitments.

*   *   *

The Great Evasion was published in the fall of 1964 to a quiet reception. Journals of opinion and a few newspapers reviewed the book. In the *New York Review of Books,* Robert Heilbroner called it "vulgar, self-serving, imprecise, and shallow," a judgment so nasty as to provoke suspicion and cause a young editor to question himself. "The Heilbroner thing really disgusts and discourages me," Bill wrote to me. "I should have stayed in the Navy." But most reviews were admiring. More important to us, the book established Quadrangle as a publisher sympathetic to revisionist history, an identification that was to last for many years. I doubt that we could have realized this role with the publication of any other single author. Bill Williams was different. Regarded by many as the father of revisionist history, he was more revered by those students he had sent into the profession, as well as by others who had read his work, than almost any other historian, revisionist or otherwise.

It soon became clear to me that Bill's stature in a part—admittedly a controversial part—of the profession, and his ability to attract authors to Quadrangle, might be more helpful to us than his own books. As it happened, over the years the only other Williams book we were able to add to the Quadrangle list was a paperback edition of *The Contours of American History,* whose rights we bought from World Publishing. (I still regard *Contours,* by the way, as Williams's brightest and most thoughtful book.) But we got our money's worth in other ways.

Not so long after we met, Bill was already sending suggestions, and they continued for years: "I've written Walt LaFeber, Lloyd Gardner, and Thomas McCormick to get in touch with you. . . ." "This kid Sklar, who is doing the tremendous study of Wilson and the Far East, is getting on now, and you should write him immediately . . ." "When I write some of my closer friends, I need 50 each of your back list, your current catalogue. . . ." "If you want to write G. Kolko in re his ms. on railroads, here is his address . . ." "What about Shapiro at Notre Dame on Latin American Dictators? . . ." "This looks interesting enough to be worth your consideration . . ." "The book on Hoover could be superb and just might have some real influence . . ."

Bill sent me suggestions and opinions all the time I was at Quadrangle, until 1972. No editor could have claimed a more interested and helpful author. I would habitually bounce ideas off him, and he would respond not only with a historian's knowledge but with an amateur publisher's savvy. When he liked an idea, he usually knew who might execute it. We were eventually to publish Walt LaFeber, Lloyd Gardner, and Tom McCormick as well as others who were devotees of Williams or who admired him while disagreeing with many of his ideas.

"Revisionism" was not an intellectual or political position I had sought when we decided to build a strong list in American history. But twenty years later I believe that, with all its faults, the best of revisionist history was the most interesting history written in the 1960s. This is not so much because it happened to coincide with the temper of those times, for the best of what Williams and others wrote was intellectual light-years beyond the ideas presented as scholarship by the New Left in the sixties. Unlike many left-leaning faculty in those years, the best revisionists did not end up aping their students. I can remember Bill complaining on many occasions that his radical students weren't tough-minded. He once told me how a student had tried at length to persuade him to endorse the latest radical escapades in Madison. Bill refused to go along. "What are you going to do next," he asked the student, "swallow goldfish?" I admired his unwillingness to be fashionable. This quality was not often appreciated by those who put revisionist historians in the same critical bag with New Left "thinkers."

No, revisionist history was interesting not because of the political climate but because it challenged its own profession. It asked questions that had not been asked in a great many years, perhaps since Beard, and poked holes in traditional interpretation. Quadrangle didn't subscribe to every piece of revisionist thinking it published. Publishers aren't in a position to take sides on issues, only to let authors do so. But the most interesting people and the most interesting books that came to Quadrangle in those years were clearly those from revisionist historians.

*   *   *

Publishing revisionist history in the 1960s was, in some ways, not as easy as it might have seemed. It did not sell remarkably well. Sometimes it was difficult to find quality (as opposed to trendy) manuscripts. On the other hand, early on we turned down good manuscripts simply because we weren't expert enough to get the right kinds of readings of them, and because revisionists were, in some quarters, *persona non grata.* I recall returning to Eugene Genovese the manuscript of *The Political Economy of Slavery,* later to be published by Pantheon and to receive a front-page review on the *New York Times Book Review,* the first of several that Genovese's books were to enjoy. When we received the manuscript I had sent it to a Southern historian, warning him that this interpretation of slavery had a decidedly Marxist perspective. Several days later he phoned me back. "Marx, hell," he thundered in his broad Southern accent. "This ain't Marx, this is Bay-*ping!*"

There were other mistakes too, but I quickly adopted the stance I had heard attributed to Alfred Knopf: I didn't have time to worry about the books we didn't publish, I was too busy worrying about the ones we did. There was some bravado and a sense of real "business" in this aphorism, and it carried me past more than a few embarrassing moments.

In 1968, after seven years of fairly grueling work at Quadrangle, the firm at last began to show a small profit. This was not an extraordinarily long incubation as undercapitalized book publishing goes, but it was neither revisionist history nor bestsellers that finally brought us into the light. I cannot recall a single book that sold more than ten thousand copies in its first year of publication. But over this time we had been quietly (sometimes too quietly) building a backlist, and most of it was selling steadily. We had made a commitment (even though we hadn't sufficient capitalization) to publish fifty books a year because we thought we needed that many in order to be a significant house. In other words, we damn near *willed* it. By 1967-68 we were publishing fifty books a year, twenty-five each season, and doing this with an astonishingly small staff.

Moreover, while we did not ignore profitability, we were continuing to publish books that we strongly believed in, regardless of their potential return. And our principal, Mike Braude, was backing us up in this endeavor. At "review" meetings over take-out Chinese food in Braude's Hyde Park home, he would rail and storm about Quadrangle's financial woes; but if we proposed a book that we considered important yet not likely to make much money, Braude's inevitable response was the moral equivalent of Jerry Rubin: "Do it."

*   *   *

In the course of events, then, circumstances brought us together with the *New York Times*.

I had proposed to the *Times* a series of paperback readers for college courses, to be drawn from the pages of the *Times Magazine* and the newspaper proper over the years, and edited with introductions by leading historians, sociologists, or whatever. They liked the idea. It had a twist different from a series of books the *Times* had tried unsuccessfully with Encyclopaedia Britannica. Our series, as it turned out, succeeded almost at once.

At the same time we began Quadrangle's first regular if modest advertising program. Our ads ran once a month on the Wednesday book page of the *New York Times*. There weren't all that many of them, but they had been brilliantly conceived by Earle Ludgin of the famous Chicago agency that bore his name. I suspect he wrote at least the headlines himself. "If you move your lips when you read," the first one proclaimed, "you probably won't be interested in these Quadrangle Books." Subsequent ads used the same kind of snob appeal. I have always been convinced that these ads did as much as anything else to make us attractive to the *Times* as a potential property.

The *Times* was going through a period when it had plenty of surplus capital, when the newspaper itself wasn't making much money (this was before the union settlement which permitted the paper to automate), and when the name of the corporate game was "diversification." During a lunch with Allen Ullman, the *Times*'s book publishing maven (he was a refugee from the sales department at Random House), in New York in mid-1968, he obliquely asked me if we were available. "Are you saying you're interested in buying us?" I asked. "Yes," he replied.

Mike Braude had been entertaining offers for Quadrangle for a few months, tired of keeping up with the capital demands the firm now generated. He already had a substantial offer from Harper & Row, in the neighborhood of $750,000, and was in New York to talk with them. I phoned him immediately and told him to wait. Within a period of weeks the *Times* had offered to buy Quadrangle for about Harper & Row's figure, including the absorption of accounts payable.

At Quadrangle we all were pleased. Had we been purchased by Harper, which certainly didn't need our name, we would have disappeared. But the *New York Times* (the *New York Times*!) had no book publishing business of its own; it would have to build us. For the first time we would have enough capital to do the things we wanted. Or so we thought. As it turned out, we were naive. Bill Williams later told me that he had mixed feelings when he heard about the sale to the *Times;* he was more familiar than I was with corporate tidiness.

At the time, however, success reigned, along with hope and I-told-you-sos. Early in 1969 an intrepid little band from Quadrangle, including Mel Brisk, Mike Braude, myself, and our attorney, went to New York to sign the final papers for the sale. Afterwards we took the elevator up to Punch Sulzberger's office where all the vice presidents dropped by for cocktails late in the afternoon. It was a splendid gathering, but I should have known then that we were in trouble. Looking around the room, I could see that the most interesting man there was Braude, the car dealer.

The *Times* soon moved to shore up the business aspects of our operation. Money became plentiful. For years we had shipped our books out of an old warehouse in Brooklyn that did its work by hand. Its only advantages were speed and reasonable cost. Now the *Times* moved our entire inventory to a computerized warehouse in Lawrence, Massachusetts. This modern enterprise so badly fouled us up that we had to move all our books again within a year. Over the next three years we were to move our warehouse twice more—a staggering headache.

After a year, the *Times* also arranged with Random House to distribute and sell our books. We had always used commission salesmen, who were inexpensive and quite satisfactory for the serious books we published, books that didn't demand heavy promotion in stores or the widest distribution. In that first year with Random House we lost $300,000, our largest loss ever. Later the *Times* moved our distribution package to World Publishing, then in its own death throes, with equally irritating results.

As for our editorial approach, there had been some carping at the *Times* but no pressures toward change. Then, around 1970, we published a book by Michael Walzer, the left-thinking political scientist then at Harvard, called *Political Action*. After the book was published, Allen Ullman called me from New York to say that he had read it (in itself a small victory for us) and found it most interesting. But, he asked, wouldn't it be a better idea to publish a book which presented both sides of this issue rather than just one side? Wouldn't you get a bigger market that way?

I explained that it would indeed be possible, but that it would be a different kind of publishing. It was not a great leap from Ullman's questions to the gradual establishment of a separate Quadrangle publishing operation at the *New York Times* offices, where another Quadrangle list began to appear simultaneously with the one we did (in exile) in Chicago. The New York list included *101 Ways with Hamburger* and other such titles, many of them drawn from *Times* writers or articles. When Allen Ullman retired, this operation was run by a fellow named Herb Nagourney, whose character was probably better suited to the appliance business.

By 1972, when the *New York Times* exercised an option to move Quadrangle to New York, the character of the house had begun to change so substantially that I no longer saw much point in going along. I stayed in Chicago, my home, fully aware that I might never publish books again. I haven't to this day, though I can't say that I have given up the idea.

Soon after reassembling in New York, Quadrangle became Times Books. It sold off most of its college paperbacks, concentrated heavily on *Times* authors, laid out big advance money for blockbusters, changed presidents every few years or so, and limped along, accumulating losses as part of the *New York Times*'s "Information and Education Group." It never fulfilled the expectations of *Times* management who had spent surplus dollars for it in quest of another Random House; nor the hopes of those who built Quadrangle at considerable personal expense. An unobtrusive note at the bottom of a column in the *Times*'s 1984 annual report testified, "The sale of Times Books [to Random House] in November 1984 completed the Company's departure from the book, education, and library services business."

*   *   *

I now subscribe to the *Journal of American History* every other year. I give the issues a cursory glance and then pile them up. When the renewal form arrives, I decide it's a waste of money. After a year passes, I start feeling guilty that I may be missing something. So I subscribe, and the process begins again.

My point is that most American historical writing is now lame—or so it seems to me. The writing of history inevitably reflects the mood of its own time. Through most of the seventies and into the eighties, American historians appear to have been satisfied with a rather narrow monographic interest that is bland and antiseptic. This kind of history proves points but rarely makes larger arguments. It is not interpretive in ways which reflect upon the whole of American experience, or the events of this century, or the issues of our time. In a phrase, it lacks a social conscience.

Young historians, who ought to be doing most of the writing as well as asking most of the questions, are like many young people in the rest of our society at the moment. They are careful, safe, selfish, career-minded, and dull. If we have yuppie accountants, yuppie lawyers, and yuppie stockbrokers, it's not difficult to believe that we also have yuppie historians. Bodies improve, commerce flourishes, but the society suffers.

I'm not complaining that history should be wholly ideological, or that only such history is worth reading. But I do believe that good history demands a point of view. Bill Williams used an epigram from Napoleon at the beginning of *The Contours of American History:* "You commit yourself, and then—you see." This sort of commitment is what I find lacking in most of the American history written today. Whether it is a commitment of left or right, of consensus or conflict, or liberalism or conservatism matters less than its being there at all. No history need be swallowed whole, but it ought to have enough fiber to chew on.

I expect a "new" American history before long, though I don't expect it to be a "revisionist" history in the old sense. There will be new concerns and new perspectives. My hope is not that the new history will be *correct,* but that it will be as fresh, as energized, and as challenging as some of the work that Quadrangle was fortunate enough to publish.

William Appleman Williams
and the Crisis of Public History

David W. Noble

In an essay published in 1984, Thomas Bender called attention to the fact that Charles and Mary Beard's *The Rise of American Civilization* was "the last successful synthesis of our history." A major reason for that success, according to Bender, was that for the Beards, writing in the 1920s and 1930s, "the justification of history was public and present. History was a part of the living present, and it was to be used to grasp and grapple with the world." Their history was, for Bender, "an interpretive, explanatory synthesis informed by moral judgment." Pointing to current laments by professional historians that there seems to be a diminishing lay audience for their writing, Bender shares their dismay; and he calls for efforts by historians in the future to regain the Beards' ability to construct successful public histories. But the combination of interpretation, explanation, and moral judgment necessary for communication between the historian and the public comes, according to Bender, only from a powerful cultural mythology. And he is not able to offer suggestions for an alternative mythology to that shared by the Beards and their readers. "The historian's faith available to Charles and Mary Beard in framing and establishing a point of view for their book is simply not available to us. Our uncertainty makes it difficult to establish a strong narrative line," he declared, and "probably we must turn to the rhetorical mode of irony in our quest for a synthesis of these, our troubled times."[1]

Gene Wise, in his 1973 book, *American Historical Explanations,* identified the 1940s as the decade when a Progressive paradigm, expressed most fully in the writings of Frederick Jackson Turner, Vernon Louis Parrington, and Charles Beard, lost the dominant position it had held within the history profession for a half century and was challenged by an emerging counter-Progressive paradigm. Narratives of unqualified progress no longer seemed credible to many young historians, such as Arthur Schlesinger, Jr. or Richard Hofstadter, whose careers were beginning in the 1940s, and they were attracted to the use of irony as a way of qualifying the story of American history as progress. Wise called these younger historians counter-Progressives because their major concern was not that of replacing the moral judgments used by the Progressive historians to define a conflict between the forces of progress and those of reaction with another set of moral judgments. Rather than offering an alternative paradigm, or what Bender calls an alternative mythology, they used irony to criticize what were now for them the unrealizable expectations of the Progressive paradigm.[2]

Perhaps it is because Bender in 1984 is still committed to the counter-Progressives' use of irony as the basis for historical narrative that he does not mention William Appleman Williams who, more than any other professional historian since the 1940s, has striven to be a public historian. Williams has always agreed with the Beards that "the justification of history was public and present. History was a part of the living present, and it was to be used to grasp and grapple with the world." Bender writes that the Beards were "self-conscious successors to George Bancroft, whose last volumes were published as the Beards prepared for college." Williams in his turn has seen himself as a successor to Charles Beard, whose last book appeared in 1948 when Williams was in graduate school. Charles Beard's first book. *The Industrial Revolution* (1901) was, according to Bender, "intended to give workers a sense of their industrial past so that they might more effectively shape and control their future." Williams's first book, *American-Russian Relations* (1952), also was intended to give American citizens a sense of their diplomatic past "so that they might more effectively shape and control their future." Like Beard's first book, that of Williams marked the beginning of a lifelong commitment to public history.[3]

Williams's absence from Professor Bender's essay might be explained simply by the fact that, while Williams has always tried to write for a public rather than a professional audience, he has not been as successful as Beard in reaching the general reader. Unlike Beard, his writing has not "entered into the culture of the educated classes of its time as a central, explanatory myth." It thus could be argued, in Bender's terms, that because Williams has not reached an audience comparable in size to that which read Beard, Williams has not "devised a serious but popular synthesis of the vast scholarship produced in our time."

But certainly Williams has "devised a serious synthesis" over the last four decades as he has attempted to move beyond the legacy of irony bequeathed by the counter-Progressives of the 1940s to the current generation of historians. He has tried to replace the failed moral judgment of Beard and the other Progressive historians with an alternative set of moral standards. And he has constructed a mythic understanding of American history which is dramatically different from that of Beard. Perhaps it is because this myth is so drastically different from the one which held the imagination of American historians from 1776 to 1941 that it has been so difficult for other historians and the reading public to give up their nostalgia, even qualified as it is by irony, for the "innocent" mythology of American exceptionalism last expressed in the 1930s by the Beards.

The immense distance which separated Williams by the 1980s from the position of Charles Beard in the 1940s is illuminated by Williams's essay, "Radicals and Regionalism," published in 1981. Human existence, Williams wrote there, "is defined by four variables: place, time, space, and scale." Modern historians, according to Williams, have believed that place must be defined as the "nation state" and that time was "the present defined as the future."[4] Central to the Progressive paradigm to which Williams was introduced in the 1940s was the assumption that American history was that of the nation state making progress toward greater democracy as it moved into the future. In 1981, however, Williams denied that the development of the nation state had brought or could bring democracy. Participation by citizens in the creation of a virtuous community was, for Williams, the basis of any real democratic experience. He claimed, however, that such experience was possible only in a space much smaller than that of the nation state. Such a democracy needed decentralization while the history of the nation state was inexorably that of centralization. By the 1960s, after groping for an alternative to the Progressive paradigm in the 1940s and 1950s, Williams had achieved "an interpretive, explanatory synthesis" of American history, "informed by moral judgment." The view of American history which led him to advocate the dismantling of the American nation state in favor of a number of regional political entities was linked to his rejection of the belief that political democracy was possible only when the nation state was able to create the conditions for economic growth. This belief that economic expansion would automatically bring about more political democracy had produced tragedy from the moment that the first English invaders had begun to dispossess the American Indians from their homelands until the contemporary era when an aggressive American foreign policy using military power to control economic resources beyond our national boundaries threatened to destroy the world in a nuclear holocaust.

The path that Williams followed from his doctoral dissertation written in the late 1940s to his present belief that there is no usable past connected with the history of the American nation state began with his participation in the dramatic revision of the Progressive paradigm achieved by the counter-Progressives during the 1940s. In *The Rise of American Civilization,* the Beards had identified the American nation state with democracy and claimed that the United States, therefore, was unique. No other nation state had its origins in the agricultural resources which awaited English settlers in the seventeenth century and which provided the necessary economic base for a political life which was democratic. When those agricultural resources ceased to provide the basis for economic plentitude at the end of the nineteenth century, industrialism, according to the Beards, had provided such a foundation. And industrialism, unlike the agricultural frontier, was not based on finite physical resources but rather on the infinite resource of the human mind which provided an unending flow of technological progress.

For the Beards, however, no other industrializing nation could achieve democracy because all other nations had undemocratic traditions. In the United States, industrialism had fused with the democratic tradition rooted in the colonial period. In the other nations, however, industrialism fused with their undemocratic traditions. Although the Beards saw the American nation state as inherently democratic, they did see it constantly threatened by the undemocratic, European tradition of capitalism. The Beards distinguished between productive private property which sustained a sense of democratic political virtue and the parasitical private property of capitalists which, because of its patterns of self-interest and economic dependency, corrupted political life. In making this distinction, they were implicitly drawing on the English tradition of Republican Virtue which underlay much of the Anglo-American political imagination during the Revolutionary crisis.

There were, according to the Beards, capitalists in America but since the American national tradition was democratic, these undemocratic individuals were un-American. The great political struggle of the 1930s was between the American national tradition of democracy which, recognizing American exceptionalism, tried to segregate the United States from a world of perpetual political corruption and the international exponents of capitalism who struggled to undermine the uniqueness of American virtue by forcing it into the world community. This struggle had been going on since Alexander Hamilton conspired to import the undemocratic elements of English capitalism.

In the Beards' story, when the plenitude of the agricultural frontier had waned, so had its productive ethic, including a national sense of public virtue. Then, for the Beards, capitalism had become politically dominant until the growth of an industrial frontier made possible the politics of Progressivism. Symbolized best, in the Beards' narrative, by Theodore Roosevelt and Franklin D. Roosevelt, Progressivism in 1901 and again in 1933 proposed a nationalist policy of democratic collectivism. The Beards rejoiced in a strong presidency which could voice the public interest against the antisocial individualism of the capitalists. They rejoiced in the rapid development of a large national bureaucracy which could replace capitalist anarchy with a planned economy. In their optimism about the inevitable triumph in the twentieth century of a Progressive democracy combining the plenitude of an inexhaustible industrial frontier with the organic tradition of a national democracy rooted in the colonial experience, the Beards focused attention on the tragedy of World War I. American participation in that international conflict had restored the vitality of the capitalists who lived in the United States. Unable to compete with the fusion of industrial productivity and the national democratic tradition, un-American capitalists had been in retreat from 1901 to 1917. American intervention in the international conflict in 1917 had made it possible for capitalists to successfully engage in parasitical economic activity and regain political control in the United States during the 1920s. But the Great Crash of 1929 had destroyed both their economic and political power; and the election of Franklin D. Roosevelt in 1932 marked the final triumph of Progressivism as Roosevelt moved to institute national planning and national collectivism on a large scale and commit the United States to a perpetual policy of political and military separation from a chaotic and corrupt outer world.

But after 1935 Charles Beard's articles and books on American foreign policy were filled with angry warnings that Roosevelt was betraying his historical mission. His actions as president were leading the United States into the European war which Beard, by 1935, was certain would explode in the immediate future. If Roosevelt succeeded, he would revitalize the undemocratic and parasitical capitalist presence in the country and would seriously endanger the survival of the national tradition of a virtuous, productive democracy. Beard was deeply worried that this national tradition which had managed to survive American participation in World War I could not, however, survive if the country participated in World War II.[5]

On one level, of course, Beard was correct. The Progressive paradigm which provided the basis for his analysis of American history as a conflict between reactionary European capitalism and progressive American democracy died during World War II. Beard could believe in 1940 that his position of nonintervention expressed national tradition and, therefore, was the only patriotic one. The greatest intellectual revolution associated with American participation in World War II was that, after 1945, this position was defined as unpatriotic; it had become un-American. The new mythology was that the colonial heritage of the United States was capitalist as well as democratic. This capitalist heritage was understood to be productive, not parasitical. And the new paradigm held that it was the economic foundation of capitalism which made the political world of democracy possible. Most fully articulated by the Protestant theologian, Reinhold Niebuhr, who as a young man in 1915 had shared the Progressive paradigm, counter-Progressivism also specifically refuted Beard's understanding of American entry into World War II.

Since the essential history of the American nation, for Beard, was the separation of its democratic exceptionalism from the undemocratic society of Europe, any diplomatic activity which involved the New World with the Old World was the work of Old World capitalists within America. By definition, for Beard in 1940, there was no American diplomatic history; diplomatic history was always un-American. The United States, therefore, could have entered World War II only because of a successful conspiracy by aggressive capitalists who wanted to end the separation of the democratic and virtuous New World from the undemocratic and corrupt Old World.

But, for Niebuhr, writing in the 1940s, it was a capitalist and democratic America which had been forced by German and Japanese aggressiveness to reluctantly abandon its mistaken belief in two worlds and to accept its responsibility in a single world community to help restrain those demonic nations which were attempting to overcome the natural pluralism of the world of nations and to impose an unnatural uniformity. Built on a European inheritance of capitalism and representative government, the American society which emerged during the colonial period was one, according to Niebuhr, which appreciated both pluralism and power. Americans, symbolized by the Founding Fathers, understood the necessity of using power but also of avoiding excessive power through a system of social, economic, and constitutional checks and balances. While realistic and pragmatic in their domestic history, Americans, for Niebuhr, had not applied these principles to the international community. There they had been unrealistic and rigidly ideological, insisting that the United States existed in isolation from the rest of the world. Because they were beguiled by this fantasy of two separate worlds, they refused to see that they must also use power responsibly in the world of nations while encouraging a pluralism that would restrain any nation from attempting to dominate its neighbors. But Niebuhr rejoiced in 1945 that Americans had finally learned this lesson because of their experience with the need to use responsible power against the irresponsible use of power by Nazi Germany and Imperial Japan. They were no longer misled by the false promises of men such as Charles Beard who had insisted that Americans were innocent of the events beyond their national boundaries.[6]

When one analyzes the paradigmatic assumptions on which Williams built the narrative structure of his first book, *American-Russian Relations,* and his second, *The Tragedy of American Diplomacy* (1959), the extent to which his historical imagination was influenced by the rapid development of counter-Progressivism becomes apparent. He accepted the idea that the American national tradition was a successful synthesis of capitalism and democracy. He also accepted the idea that American foreign policy should express the values of the national tradition which, according to men like Niebuhr, was committed to pluralism and the exercise of power within a system of checks and balances. Since, for this counter-Progressive paradigm, the United States had participated in World War II to defend these principles against the dictatorial ambitions of Germany and Japan, the continued defense of these principles was the foundation after 1945 for American entry into a Cold War against the Soviet Union. That country was now the chief threat to the natural pluralism of the world order as it conspired to impose its vision of an unnatural universal on the particulars of the many national cultures.[7]

When Williams, however, used these counter-Progressive paradigmatic assumptions as the basis for his narrative of the diplomatic relationships between the United States and the Soviet Union before the onset of the Cold War, he found strong contradictory evidence. It was true, he wrote, that the makers of American foreign policy had been pragmatic "realists" during the nineteenth century. "From 1781 to the present," he wrote, Russia and the United States "have adjusted policy with regard to the conflict between each country's territorial and economic expansion and the actual or potential value of each nation to the other in terms of a world balance of power. Prior to the Bolshevik Revolution of November 1917, ideological considerations were clearly secondary."[8]

Rejecting Beard's assumption that capitalists, although present in America, did not participate in American history, Williams was shocked to learn that Niebuhr's assumption about the pragmatic realism of American capitalists did not apply to their foreign policy toward the Soviet Union between 1917 and 1945. Nothing but rigid ideological intolerance of any revolutionary activity which was not identical in purpose and method to the American Revolution could explain the blind rage expressed by American foreign policy leaders in the 1920s and 1930s toward the Soviet Union. The new Marxist Russia was economically and militarily weak in 1917 and continued to be so throughout the 1920s and 1930s. And yet Wilson had joined his wartime allies in sending troops into Russia in a vain attempt to suppress the revolution. During the 1930s, the Soviet Union did not share with Japan or Germany the energy or the will to drastically alter the world order. But an absolute hatred of the Soviet Union kept American leaders from cooperating with Russian leaders to contain Japanese and German aggressiveness. Only such an ideology could explain "the failure of the United States to collaborate with the Soviet Union against Japanese expansion from 1920 to 1922, during Tokyo's invasion of Manchuria in 1931, and later, when Japan began to wage hostilities against China in 1937."

Agreeing with Niebuhr that balance of power was the right policy for the United States to pursue, Williams now related the declension from the pursuit of that policy in the nineteenth century to the decision by American leaders in the 1890s that the United States needed an overseas frontier because "the financial and industrial powers of the United States soon came to dominate their domestic market and looked abroad for new opportunities." Assuming that the world's future would be one of corporate capitalism, they were prepared to repress revolutions which did not conform to that ideal and threatened to create alternative futures. This was their policy toward the Mexican Revolution which began in 1910 and it was, of course, the policy toward the Russian Revolution in 1917. Their continued hostility toward the Russian Revolution in the 1920s and 1930s stemmed from the fact that the existence of the Soviet Union compelled American leaders to be aware of their inability to totally define and control the development of an international marketplace. And the success of the Bolshevik revolution offered a model to other nations that did not want to define their futures in American capitalist terms. Williams, therefore, had nothing but contempt for those who interpreted American policy after 1919 as isolationist. "The policy of the United States toward the Soviets," he argued, "exemplified the victory of those domestic forces that, though generally labeled isolationist, in fact desired the further and unrestricted overseas expansion of American economic and political power." "Far from isolation," he concluded, "the American policy of these interwar years was one characterized by decisions and actions taken with sole reference to unilaterally determined goals— decisions and actions for the consequences of which Washington disclaimed all responsibility."[9]

Reinhold Niebuhr, in his 1952 book *The Irony of American History,* had explained the development of the Cold War as the reluctant response of a pragmatic United States after 1945 to the aggressiveness of an ideological Soviet Union. And he had warned his readers not to become as obsessed with ideology as their Russian enemies. If that happened, Americans, mobilizing to achieve total victory, would destroy their own pluralist democracy. But when Williams looked at the writings of George F. Kennan, a leading American theoretician of the Cold War in the late 1940s, he saw an establishment figure calling for such a total victory. Williams, therefore, did not argue, as Niebuhr had, that current American political leaders were working within a tradition of pragmatism, flexibility, and compromise. From 1917 to 1947, American policy toward the Soviet Union had been ideological, inflexible, and uncompromising. Williams's prophecy in 1952 was that the continuation of this policy would indeed destroy whatever aspects of democracy still existed within the United States. "Freedom," he declared, "is not nurtured by states preparing for war. Rather does it find more opportunity to flower in the atmosphere of mutual accommodation achieved and sustained through negotiated settlements."[10]

Much of what Williams had to say in *American-Russian Relations* about the beginning of a revolution in American foreign policy at the end of the nineteenth century was implicit rather than explicit. But in an article published in 1955, "The Frontier Thesis and American Foreign Policy," he expressed his awareness that he was offering a new perspective on the 1890s as a watershed decade in American history. From the perspective of Beard's Progressive paradigm in 1940, the American people never had any desire to go outside their continental homeland. It was the temporary influence of un-American capitalists, motivated by the ideology of English imperialism, therefore, which had caused the United States to acquire an overseas empire during the Spanish-American War. For counter-Progressives such as Richard Hofstadter, it was the irrational reaction of fringe groups such as farmers or descendants of the colonial aristocracy to the inevitability of historical change which had caused them to express their frustrations in a foreign adventure.

Williams confronted these assumptions that American imperialism in the Spanish-American War was an aberration. "One of the central themes of American historiography is that there is no American Empire," but, he asserted, "[t]he United States has been a consciously and steadily expanding nation since 1890. A set of ideas, first promulgated in the 1890s, became the world view of subsequent generations of Americans and is an important clue to understanding America's imperial expansion in the twentieth century." And he turned to the writings of Frederick Jackson Turner to provide a way of understanding why the 1890s marked the beginning of systematic overseas expansion by American economic and political leaders. "Turner's frontier thesis," Williams argued, "made democracy a function of an expanding frontier." The response of American decision makers in the 1890s to Turner's announcement that there was no longer an internal frontier followed Turner's logic—the political health of the nation depended upon the development of an overseas frontier. "Turner," Williams declared, "gave Americans a national world view that eased their doubts, settled their confusions, and justified their aggressiveness." Like the Spanish-American war, World War I and World War II were not aberrations from an established anti-imperialist isolation; they were, for Williams, the inevitable price that the shapers of foreign policy were willing to pay for their commitment to the necessity of an overseas marketplace.[11]

Niebuhr and other counter-Progressives such as Hofstadter celebrated Franklin D. Roosevelt as the epitome of the intrinsic pragmatism of the American tradition of capitalism and democracy. But when Williams looked back in 1955 at the foreign policy of the New Deal, he saw none of that anti-ideological flexibility. By the late 1930s, he wrote, those New Dealers who were shaping foreign policy had begun to "openly apply Turner's thesis to the new economic situation. An expanding economy became the dogma of an industrial economy." And that expansion demanded overseas markets and overseas sources of raw materials. Niebuhr had described Roosevelt's "realistic" attitude toward World War II as an acceptance of a policy of compromise within the framework of a world where power was to be balanced and kept from being concentrated. And Niebuhr, who in 1945 understood Stalin as holding the same "realistic" goals, had then decided that the Soviet leaders had turned back to the ideology of world revolution, forcing the United States into the Cold War. But, for Williams, the president "seemed, from the spring of 1942 to the fall of 1944, to base his plans for the postwar era on the idea of a concert of power. Then, in October 1944, he in effect reaffirmed the Open Door policy.'' Contrary to Niebuhr, American ideology had preceded Russian ideology.[12]

The Tragedy of American Diplomacy, published in 1959, provided Williams with the opportunity to present a more complex context for the self-destructive impasse of this American foreign policy which called for victory in the Cold War. Niebuhr, in *The Irony of American History,* had written that ''the tragic element in a human situation is constituted of conscious choices of evil for the sake of good.'' Williams also found the United States to be in the tragic situation of consciously choosing an evil, war, for the sake of what it judged to be good. Niebuhr had seen tragedy growing out of an ironic situation which ''is differentiated from tragedy by the fact that the responsibility is related to an unconscious weakness rather than to a conscious resolution.'' Now Williams in *The Tragedy of American Diplomacy* was describing the United States of the 1890s in such ironic terms. But Niebuhr also had insisted that ''an ironic situation must dissolve if men or nations are made aware of their complicity in it. Such awareness involves some realization of the hidden vanity or pretension. This realization either must lead to an abatement of the pretension, which means contrition, or it leads to a desperate accentuation of the vanities to the point where irony turns into pure evil.'' Williams would claim that the irony of the pretentious foreign policy that had begun in the 1890s would become tragedy in the 1930s when war was chosen as a necessary tool for its fulfillment. But Williams still hoped that it was not too late to replace the movement from irony to tragedy with a movement from irony to contrition.[13]

In starting his narrative with an America in 1890 which was both democratic and capitalist, Williams did not try to describe the late nineteenth century in any detail, but rather moved immediately to establish the ironic vanity leading toward tragedy. ''The tragedy of American diplomacy is aptly symbolized, and defined for analysis and reflection,'' he wrote, ''by the relations between the United States and Cuba from April 21, 1898'' to the present. Americans had gone to war ''to free Cuba from Spanish tyranny, to establish and underwrite the independence of the island, and to initiate and sustain its development toward political democracy and economic welfare.'' But Americans did not realize that the only economic tools which were available to express these generous impulses were those of corporate capitalism, which soon ''dominated the economic life of the island by controlling, directly or indirectly, the sugar industry, and by overtly and covertly preventing any dynamic modification of the island's one-crop economy.'' The elites in the United States government who were making foreign policy moved swiftly to sustain this corporate domination; they were willing to intervene ''with economic and diplomatic pressure and with force of arms, when Cubans threatened to transgress the economic and political restrictions set by American leaders." And the American public, smug in their national pride that their model of democracy and capitalism could liberate all the peoples of the world, refused to criticize this foreign policy which would not tolerate alternative forms of modernization. The unintended consequence of this rigid and narrow definition of how progress must be made was to drive subsequent Cuban revolutionists such as Fidel Castro, and similar revolutionists throughout the world who wanted more democracy and prosperity for their nations, to look toward the Soviet Union for support. The Cold War paranoia of those who, like Niebuhr, saw a huge conspiracy to overcome the particulars of history with a universal order, was a self-fulfilling prophecy.[14]

Niebuhr intended that *The Irony of American History* provide Americans with a new way of understanding their history. They must become self-conscious of their heritage of a pluralist democracy if they were to avoid the temptation of the Cold War to become the mirror image of the Soviet Union. Williams also intended that *The Tragedy of American Diplomacy* provide Americans with a new way of understanding their history. Becoming self-conscious of the necessity of pluralism, they must see how their foreign policy for half a century had denied that pluralism. If the Soviet Union was striving after a world order built on its national model, it was the mirror image of a United States foreign policy already firmly established in 1917 when the Bolshevik revolution took place.

Appealing to history as "a way of learning" and "getting closer to the truth," Williams affirmed that, "It is only by abandoning the clichés that we can even define the tragedy. When we have done that," he concluded, "we will no longer be merely acquiescing in the deadly inertia of the past." Since 1945, he declared, we have been trapped within the myth that the United States was an isolationist nation until 1941. But look at the 1890s, look, he wrote, and see the "broad support for expansion, and particularly overseas economic expansion," see how that "rested upon an agreement among conservatives and liberals (even many radicals joined for a few years) and Democrats and Republicans from all sections and groups of the country." See how the planning for an overseas frontier "was the most impressive intellectual achievement in the area of public policy since the generation of the Founding Fathers."[15]

"In a truly perceptive and even noble sense," Williams declared, "the makers of the Open Door policy understood that war represented the failure of policy." But the policy also "derived from the proposition that America's overwhelming economic power would cast the economics and the politics of the poorer, weaker, underdeveloped countries in a pro-American mold." Designed to end the continual warfare caused by the imperial ambitions of the great powers, the Open Door policy, ironically, increased world tensions because American corporations in their search for markets and raw materials aborted the prosperous development of the poorer nations and then enlisted the United States government to coerce those nations when they rebelled against this pattern of exploitation.[16]

The basic contradiction in the Open Door policy, according to Williams, did not become clear until World War I. "Given entry into the war on the grounds that 'the world must be made safe for democracy,'" he stated, "the crucial questions became those about the definition of democracy and the means to insure its security." Wilson, however, represented the consensus of American leaders that democracy must include a synthesis of the nineteenth century marketplace of natural harmonies with the large corporation.[17]

Herbert Hoover was the figure that Williams used to dramatize this moment in American history when the irony was revealed and American leaders faced a tragic choice. They could choose the continued and escalating use of force to achieve an Open Door empire or, acknowledging the arrogance of their insistence that the world conform to the American model, they could become contrite and surrender their effort to shape history in their own image. Shocked by the failure to reshape the entire world through the use of war, or even to suppress the Bolshevik revolution by sending troops into Russia, Hoover committed himself to the original intention of the Open Door policy—to achieve American influence abroad only through the power of the economy. It was this form of internationalism that Franklin Roosevelt denounced as isolationist in 1941 when he embraced war as a necessary tool for American overseas expansion. Hoover, however, in Williams's analysis, did not have the strength to surrender the Open Door policy even though he was certain that if the United States repeated the experience of World War I the nation would become permanently militarized. For Williams, President Roosevelt's foreign policy, therefore, was a perversion of the Open Door policy. "Men who began by defining the United States and the world in economic terms, and explaining its operation by the principles of capitalism and a frontier of historical development," Williams wrote, "came finally to define the United States in military terms as an embattled outpost in a hostile world. When a majority of the leaders of America's corporate society reached that conclusion, the nation went to war."[18]

With Roosevelt's death in 1945, the new president, Harry Truman, and his advisors continued to look on war as a successful tool for the Open Door policy. The United States had destroyed Japan and Germany as rivals for world leadership. This left only the Soviet Union as a possible competitor. And they decided on an immediate showdown with Stalin which would force him to acknowledge that the international future was to be defined in Open Door terms. "This decision," Williams declared, "represented the final stage in the transformation of the Open Door from a utopian idea into an ideology, from an intellectual outlook for changing the world into one concerned with preserving it in the traditional mold."[19]

Williams's next book, *The Contours of American History,* demonstrated that he had no hope that there were cultural resources in the United States which might reverse the tragedy of this entrenched foreign policy. This book, an overview of the entire American past, fulfilled the logic of the counter-Progressive paradigm by beginning American history in Europe. Most counter-Progressives, however, found that a European heritage of capitalism, representative government, and Protestantism provided the foundation for a society which retained its democratic pluralism as it expanded from the Atlantic to the Pacific. But, for Williams, the most significant aspect of the European heritage for Anglo-American colonial society was mercantilism, while its commitment to pluralism and social responsibility did not survive the western expansion of the nineteenth century. The internal contradiction in mercantilism which, in Williams's analysis, ultimately destroyed it, was that it tried to sustain a sense of community while engaging in an imperialistic foreign policy. Because the colonists, retaining this contradictory European inheritance, believed it was necessary for the economic health of their society to engage in constant territorial aggrandizement, they were finally forced to give up their inherited faith in "a political system and philosophy involving an interlocking network of freedoms, duties and obligations between individuals inhabiting specified areas of land" and in a "small state" as "the only feasible unit of self-government." This surrender of the ideal of a pluralistic community was expressed, according to Williams, in the political philosophy of the Founding Fathers who cut all ties between the individual and place, as well as the ties between the individual and community, when they insisted that there was no relationship between the size of a nation and the experience of self-government. Looking hungrily at the vast expanse of the continent which stretched westward from the boundaries of their new nation, men like Jefferson, Williams wrote, were certain that a spatial expansion which would last for a thousand years made traditional political concerns for the relationship of the individual to the community irrelevant.[20]

As Williams went into the 1960s, he no longer believed, therefore, that the development of the Open Door Empire in the 1890s was a declension from a more responsible nineteenth century democracy. Continental expansion from 1790 to 1890 was characterized by the war of white settlers against the pluralism of the many American Indian nations. Always the advancing Anglo-Americans had tried to impose their cultural patterns, which they claimed were universal, on the particulars of a variety of cultures. Williams could no longer write, as he had in *The Tragedy of American Diplomacy,* that American policy had been pragmatic and non-ideological before the 1890s. In the 1950s, he had hoped that the Cold War represented an aberration, a declension from a usable past when the moral judgment of Americans had respected pluralism and the particulars of human history. But by the 1960s he found these counter-Progressive assumptions about the American political tradition to be completely in error. The dominant American political culture had no respect for limits. It had substituted spatial expansion for traditional concerns of social justice within the boundaries of a community. But Williams, unable to agree with the counter-Progressives, could not turn back to the Progressivism of Turner and Beard. They too had celebrated the imperialism of the continental conquest, and they also shared with the Founding Fathers the belief that the expanding nation state rather than the local community was the best environment for the cultivation of self-government. Neither Progressives nor counter-Progressives, therefore, offered a concept of social justice which could be achieved within political boundaries and which could serve as a positive alternative to the current policy of Open Door imperialism, the ideological roots of which stretched all the way back to the earliest ambitions of the European nations to establish colonial empires in the Western Hemisphere.

Searching for an ideal of a nonimperialistic community outside the traditions of American national history, Williams gained a reputation as a radical with the publication of his next book, *The Great Evasion.* Here he asked Americans to use the writings of Karl Marx as the foundation for a moral judgment which could give a positive meaning to a search for social justice within the boundaries of a particular society. Williams hoped to change the mind of those Americans who, calling themselves liberals or progressives in the 1960s, believed that their country had such a unique past that the writings of Marx had no relevance to the American experience. Could these American liberals and progressives explain, Williams asked, the failure of the prophecies of men like John Dewey and Charles Beard who had insisted that there was enough strength in a national democratic tradition to make Marx irrelevant as a critic of the American present or a prophet for the American future? They had failed because they had not recognized that American history was a national variation of the capitalist history which had begun in early modern Europe. As long as American intellectuals insisted on American uniqueness, they would never adequately explain why their dream of a democratic society was not fulfilled nor be able to create a successful alternative to Open Door imperialism. American academic and religious progressives, Williams insisted, had refused to confront "Marx's central theses about the assumptions, the costs and the nature of capitalist society. We have never confronted his central insight that capitalism is predicated upon an overemphasis and exaltation of the individualistic, egoistic half of man functioning in a marketplace system that overrides and crushes the social, humanitarian half of man."[21]

Specifically, Williams continued, Marx had predicted that a capitalist society would have an imperialist foreign policy. And, as Williams had demonstrated in his first three books, the record of American diplomatic history proved Marx right. But Williams wanted now to broaden the discussion of imperialism to include the westward expansion of Anglo-American culture. Turner and Beard had used the metaphor of exodus from an Old World of oppression to a New World of liberty to define European migration to America. But when Williams rejected that metaphor of two worlds and described the migration as the transfer of capitalist culture from Europe to America, he also, in dramatic contrast to Turner and Beard, defined European settlement as a process of conquest. The constant succession of wars between the Euro-Americans and the nations of the American Indians from 1600 to 1880 had, for him, become part of American diplomatic history; and so had the colonial slave trade and the enslaved Afro-Americans within Anglo-American culture.

Marx also had predicted increasing economic misery under capitalism and American liberals in 1960 insisted that current national prosperity proved Marx wrong. Williams already had pointed to the role of deficit spending by the national government in providing the illusion of economic vitality. But he urged the liberal yea-sayers to reconsider how much poverty did exist within the United States and to also consider the dependence of the qualified national prosperity on the exploitation of an external proletariat, the citizens of the underdeveloped world whose resources and labor were siphoned off as profits for the developed world.

Finally, Marx had predicted increasing alienation within the capitalist nations. The two major examples for this trend which Williams chose to stress were the confusion, anger, and resentment being expressed by the present generation of adolescents and the decline of voter participation in elections throughout the twentieth century. Marx had argued that capitalism must betray its utopian promise to make every individual a productive participant in the economy. The history of corporate capitalism in the United States had fulfilled that prediction with "the loss of any participatory role in the principal decisions of the capitalist marketplace," by a growing and dependent wage-earning force which had lost "control over any private property which played a part in the productive activities in the system." It was inevitable, Williams concluded, that the loss of meaningful participation in the productive economic system would lead these wage-earners to feel alienated from the political system. The average citizen "is becoming a mere consumer of politics as well as a mere consumer of goods." But these workers could not imagine an alternative system in which they would be vital participants in the economy and in politics because they were ensnared in a culture where "the sharing of profits is mistaken for the sharing of direction and control of the enterprise itself, just as the sharing of the leader's charisma is mistaken for the sharing of power."[22]

Using Marx's teachings, liberals could learn, Williams insisted, "that a free society is that in which the individual defines himself, and acts, as a citizen of a community rather than as a competing ego. In a very real sense, therefore, the frontier for Marx is the space and resources made available for human development by loving thy neighbor as thyself." In envisioning the end of American history as capitalist expansion, Williams advocated drastic decentralization of the nation as a political unit because a "true community is more easily obtainable, and more extensively developed, in small rather than large units." A new America, beginning a new history, "will be beautiful instead of ugly" and "will facilitate human relationships instead of driving men into separate functional elements."[23]

By the late 1960s, however, Williams no longer believed that the writings of Marx pointed toward decentralization. Williams had argued that modern American culture was rooted in early modern Europe and that the cultural weaknesses of the United States were also those of modern European civilization. Marx, of course, had criticized European capitalism. And Williams had insisted that Marx's criticism applied to American capitalism. But it began to occur to Williams that Marx was offering a variation of the modern outlook rather than an alternative. Williams, for example, in *The Great Evasion* had accepted Marx's position that industrial capitalism was a necessary stage in history as progress. It was industrial capitalism which created the engines of productivity that made affluence possible for all the people of the world rather than for a privileged few. But Williams had criticized the growth of an American empire, first on the North American continent and then overseas, which promised increasing wealth. He saw that the civilian and military bureaucracies necessary for that expansion and that accumulation of wealth destroyed the possibility of true community. Did Marx's advocacy of unlimited wealth then also lead to huge civilian and military bureaucracies in socialist and communist countries? Were Marxists also frontiersmen unable to stop and define spiritual community as they pursued a future of more and more material goods? In *The Great Evasion,* Williams had explicitly separated Marx's teachings from the political practice of the Soviet Union. But in his next book, he came to believe that he had been mistaken. The Soviet Union, with its vast bureaucratic state and military machine, had become the mirror image of the United States because Marx in the manner of capitalist philosophers believed that democracy was possible only in an environment of increasing wealth.

In *Some Presidents from Wilson to Nixon* (1972), Williams, therefore, was engaged in working out his own vision of the future, one he hoped was free from the ironic weakness in Marx which had led to the tragic culture of the Soviet Union. He related what seemed to be the permanent crisis of the presidency to the crisis of an overextended political system linked to an overextended economic system. Increasing wealth depended upon forcing the particulars of history to conform to the logic of industrial rationality and efficiency. If industrial production were to continue to grow, political power must be extended to force individuals as well as physical nature to imitate the universals implied in the logic of rationality and efficiency. But, for Williams, there were inevitable limits on the ability of political power to dominate the human and natural diversity which was characteristic of the earth. "There are only two ways to govern a continent," he declared, "one is to assert the will of a minority as a well-organized plurality. The other is to divide the continent into natural regional communities and allow each people to decide its own fate—including its relationships with other social communities." He urged Americans to understand the tragic failures of their presidents from Wilson to Nixon as evidence of the failure of a political system which tried through the triumph of the will to force unnatural uniformity on natural diversity; political diversity as a system was more in harmony with human and physical experience.[24]

In his 1976 book, *America Confronts a Revolutionary World,* Williams extended the moral of presidential failure to impose uniformity within a geographic area as diverse as the United States to the failure of the presidents since Wilson to force all the revolutions that had occurred in the twentieth century to imitate the American revolution. Refusing to acknowledge that history was composed of particulars and not universals, they had pursued foreign policy goals that always ended in frustration and defeat.[25] And in his 1978 textbook, *Americans in a Changing World,* Williams tried to teach Americans how the pursuit of uniformity not only led to the frustration of their domestic politics and foreign policy but also to the frustration of their personal lives when they permitted themselves to be uprooted from their families, neighborhoods, and geographic localities in order to fit the uniform standards of the marketplace. He called on the history of the Native Americans for a usable past to provide a prophecy for a less destructive future. "Not only were [the first Americans] good farmers (who cleared enough land to let half lie fallow)," he declared, but "they demonstrated a sophisticated understanding of how to create and sustain a symbiotic relationship with the land." These "first Americans," he wrote, "had painfully evolved a sense (and the rituals) of time, place, and space that could have helped the majority of twentieth-century Americans sustain their own traditions of community and common humanity during the process of urbanization and industrialization."[26]

But asking Americans in 1980 to define their present situation as a declension from the Native-American world of decentralized communities was an almost impossible task. In *Empire as a Way of Life* (1980), Williams lamented that, "Once people begin to acquire and take for granted and waste surplus resources and space as a routine part of their lives, and to view them as a sign of God's favor," it is difficult for them to give up the philosophy that more is better. But, he affirmed, we must nevertheless try to "create a culture on the basis of agreeing upon limits." Williams had made clear how far he had moved from 1964 when he had joined Marx in promising a cooperative community with great affluence. Now he declared that the promise of a decentralized America meant tremendous economic sacrifices by everyone. But what was the choice? The pursuit of rising standards of living had led to empire and to an arms race with Soviet Russia. "Empire as a way of life," he insisted, "will lead to nuclear death." The alternative to this internal and external chaos caused by our national and international centralization was decentralized community; and such "community will lead for a time to less than is necessary. Some of us will die. But how one dies is terribly important. It speaks to the truth of how we have lived."[27]

As a public historian in the 1980s, Williams continued his efforts to create an audience which shared his vision of a decentralized America. In the essay of 1981, "Radicals and Regionalism," he emphasized that Americans who wanted to break with empire as a way of life must embrace ideas which they always had identified with conservatism—localism, rootedness, and a self-conscious religious identity. "Twentieth-century American radicals," Williams complained, had become "so blinkered by Marx's acceptance of the productivity of the capitalist political economy that they had ignored or dismissed ostensibly conservative truth." But if corporate capitalism was pushing for both national and international centralization, "surely a vigorous radicalism," Williams affirmed, "is defined by decentralization and the diffusion of power." American radicals, he continued, "must confront centralized nationalism and internationalism and begin to shake it apart, break it down, and imagine a human and socially responsible alternative."[28]

Radicals, therefore, should consider a constitutional convention where the centralized nation state with its international ambitions would be broken down "into a confederation of regional governments based upon proportional representation and the parliamentary system within each region and in the confederation itself." The foreign policy of the confederation parliament would be completely defensive, enabling "each culture to proceed with its self-determined development within its legitimate boundaries."[29]

Williams, the public historian, had always insisted that people could and should use their understanding of history to shape their historical destiny. The choice now lay with the public and with professional historians. They must choose whether they would understand their past and create their future through the paradigms of Progressivism, counter-Progressivism, Marxism, or Radical Regionalism.

Part Two

This section consists of monographic and interpretative essays on a variety of problems in American history. Carl Parrini of Northern Illinois University discusses interpretations of imperialism. Studies of American imperial theorists usually begin and end with Alfred Thayer Mahan and Senator Albert Beveridge. Parrini examines the role of lesser known—but perhaps more important—"practicing" thinkers such as Charles Conant, a key figure in developing overproduction suppositions at the end of the nineteenth century. Parrini's ability to locate American thought in a broader framework makes his essay an especially useful contribution to an understanding of imperial theory— and its applications.

Edward Crapol of the College of William and Mary takes up the question of an abolitionist foreign policy. Increasingly, as a result of recent scholarship in the intellectual roots of foreign policy, scholars have become concerned with examining extraofficial or alternate programs for conducting a nation's foreign affairs. The results have suggested there really is no division between domestic and foreign policy questions, but that the two must be looked upon as symbiotic in nature.

The problem of theory and practice is examined from another perspective by Fred Harvey Harrington, Emeritus Professor of History and President of the University of Wisconsin. Although the Orient has had a great attraction for American policy makers, the vision of the Great China Market always remained a vision. Relations with Europe, on the other hand, were always the immediate concern of the men who made policy.

Harrington suggests why this was so, and with what fateful consequences. Latin America, likewise, has taken second place to Europe in the minds of policy makers. But as Walter LaFeber of Cornell University demonstrates, recent invocations of the Monroe Doctrine are intriguing examples of the creation of a "useful past" by contemporary policy makers in an effort to justify expanded definitions of "national security."

Not all policy makers have accepted the role of the United States as international policeman. As Patrick Hearden of Purdue University argues, some, like Herbert Hoover, believed there were definite limits to what could be accomplished in foreign policy to alter the basic conditions of American society—or to reshape the world. Hoover's conservative critique of an "imperial America" posited, however, an illusory freedom of action not really possible in the modern world. Liberal-left critics like Freda Kirchwey of the *Nation* believed, on the other hand, that there was a basis for cooperation in the postwar world, even when superpower rivalry with the Soviet Union was taken into account. Margaret Morley of Northern Arizona University reviews Kirchwey's efforts to persuade her readers and influence policy makers in this direction.

At the outset of the postwar era the atomic bomb seemed to give the United States an instrument to deal with world problems. Throughout the nation's history Americans had had great faith in the marvels to be wrought by technology, and had been amply rewarded for their devotion; but applying the technological fix to political dilemmas in the Cold War proved much more difficult. Lloyd Gardner of Rutgers University attempts an explanation of the reasons why. At the heart of any dialogue about the nature and design of the "American Century" is the issue of consciousness and purpose. Thomas McCormick of the University of Wisconsin concludes the book with a highly sophisticated analysis of the determinants of foreign policy as a combination of responsibilities for national welfare and the functioning of the modern world system. The founders of the modern American empire, far from being absent-minded, were well aware of the obligations imposed on them in the aftermath of two world wars and the Great Depression. The very limitations of "dollar diplomacy"and of "atomic diplomacy" required an effort of imagination that would incorporate all the leverage available to policy makers to achieve "total diplomacy." It is the world they created yesterday that we as historians and citizens must deal with today.

Theories of Imperialism

Carl Parrini

It is the purpose of this essay to examine the principal similarities and differences among socialist and nonsocialist interpretations of modern imperialism. It will be important to keep in mind that there are differences among the members of each group as well as between the two.

It will also be necessary to restore to our memory the fact that socialist and nonsocialist interpretations of imperialism shared common fundamental premises for many years around the turn of the twentieth century; they did not diverge on basics until some time later. It was not until the 1930s that socialist and nonsocialist theorists came to disagree definitively over whether modern imperialism was economically motivated and essentially caused by the dynamics of modern capitalism. In general, socialist theorists continued to maintain that imperialism, though affected by many factors, was essentially economic in nature, while nonsocialist theorists began to argue that imperialism was to be explained by psycho-cultural motives (including drives to power) essentially unrelated to and often inconsistent with economic rationality or motivation.[1] But the definitions of modern imperialism prevalent from 1900 to World War I and for some years thereafter reveal no such divergence; indeed, a near unanimous consensus existed between socialists and nonsocialists.[2]

This consensus held that imperialism was essentially an economic phenomenon. Differences arose over whether imperialism was the result of the conscious choices of statesmen in the industrial capitalist countries, or the inevitable result of the industrial capitalist political economy and social structure. Differences also arose over whether imperialism benefited the

For their comments and criticisms I would like to thank Jo Alexander, Lloyd Gardner, Margaret George, Marvin Rosen, and Martin J. Sklar.

imperial nation at the expense of the subject society, and whether imperialism characterized not only the relations between industrial and nonindustrial societies but also those among the industrial nations themselves. Corollary issues developed around such questions as whether imperialist nations sought outlets for surplus capital as against simply goods, and whether they sought cheap and exclusive sources of raw materials as strategically necessary to their industrial well-being and military security.[3]

Since World War II, other issues have arisen. Scholars have questioned the reality of "surplus capital." Exponents of the modern neoclassical synthesis among historians have tended to deny its reality, resurrecting Say's law of markets as though the whole historical criticism of Say's law among economists had never taken place. Keynesians and neo-Keynesians, for their part, have responded with increasingly more complex treatments of the question. Scholars, diplomats, and politicians have also differed since World War II about the degree to which the costs of imperialism outweigh any benefits to be derived from it. They have also differed as to the ways in which the growth of multinational corporations has fashioned a degree of economic interdependence among nations which has made the practice of exclusive empire impractical and unworkable.[5]

Part I of this essay attempts to demonstrate the nonsocialist origins of the surplus-capital theory of modern imperialism, indicating in particular the central relevance of Charles A. Conant's thinking to American policy making before World War I. Part II deals with other of the leading issues that have divided theorists: *1)* whether imperialism was an unavoidable structural characteristic of industrial capitalism; *2)* whether imperialism shaped relations among industrial countries as well as between them and nonindustrial countries; *3)* whether modern imperialism was "parasitic"; and *4)* whether surplus capital has persisted since the "Keynesian Revolution."

I

In general those authorities critical of the economic interpretation of imperialism have labeled it the "Hobson-Lenin" thesis. One of the first such critiques was William L. Langer's essay, "A Critique of Imperialism." Langer did not search for the origins of the surplus-capital theory of imperialism, nor attempt to determine the degree to which it was generally accepted. He simply noted that "since the outbreak of the World War the theoretical writing on imperialism has been very largely dominated by the Neo-Marxists," "who following in the footsteps of the Master [Karl Marx] have carried on his historical analysis."[6] In this way, Langer was able to confine his analysis of the surplus-capital theory to the Marxists, and thus avoid the question of the degree to which statesmen generally, and American statesmen in particular, had accepted the theory and acted upon it. Langer claims to trace the theory to Lenin via Hobson who "in turn took over the idea from the very bourgeois American financial expert, Charles A. Conant.''

Langer's essay set the pattern for subsequent critiques of the surplus-capital theory of imperialism: *1)* discuss the historiography; *2)* avoid re-searching statesmen who say that they accept an analysis that posits the existence of surplus capital; and *3)* discredit such statesmen as devotees of Hobson or Lenin.

It was also Langer who established the pattern of lumping Hobson, Lenin, Rosa Luxemburg and Rudolph Hilferding together in a kind of neo-Marxist synthesis which obscured the differences between them.[7] This practice was also conceptually distorting in a variety of ways. For example the linking of Lenin with Hobson without very careful qualification blurs major differences. Hobson believed that the destabilizing phenomenon of surplus capital could be eliminated by international free trade, income redistribution through government social spending, and strengthening of the bargaining power of labor by means of successful trade union organiza-tion.[8] In contrary fashion, Lenin argued that tariff elimination, even were it possible, would have no effect on the capital surplus. He further argued that capitalism as a system could never redistribute income to labor nor allow enough social spending to consume the surplus. Real power in all industrial capitalist societies, according to Lenin, was in the hands of those who controlled finance capital, despite the degree of apparent democracy.

On the issue of tariffs Charles A. Conant is closer to Lenin than to Hobson. He argued that imperialism—as a phenomenon caused by surplus capital—affected all the industrial capitalist nations irrespective of tariff systems. Conant also agreed with Lenin that income redistribution suffi-cient to solve the problem was unlikely under the existing political structure of industrial capitalism.[9]

Similarly, the linking of Luxemburg and Lenin is analytically unjusti-fied in many respects. For instance, Luxemburg argued that the Third World is necessary to industrial capitalist "realization" of profits. Lenin, on the other hand, asserted that realization was possible without the Third World, that indeed the "great imperialist war" (1914-18) was about central and southeast Europe. Lenin saw the Third World as "reserve areas" of capitalism, to be developed as capital investment outlets in the future. It is only when its identification with the "neo-Marxists" has been refuted that the surplus-capital theory of imperialism can be adequately tested.[10]

The notion of "surplus capital" (defined as capital for which there are no outlets sufficiently profitable, in relation to risk, to induce capitalists to invest) has complex origins, but there is no substantial evidence that they are any more socialist than nonsocialist. For instance, in the First Annual Report of the United States Commissioner of Labor, in 1886, Carroll D. Wright took the position that each of the United States, Great Britain, France, Belgium, and Germany "has overstocked itself with machinery and manufacturing plant far in excess of the wants of production.'' Wright went on to observe that

> what is strictly necessary has been done oftentimes to superfluity. This full supply of economic tools to meet the wants of nearly all branches of commerce and industry is the most important factor in the present industrial depression. It is true that the discovery of new processes of manufacture will undoubtedly continue and this will act as an ameliorating influence, but it will not leave room for a marked extension such as has been witnessed during the last fifty years or afford a remunerative employment of the vast amount of capital which has been created during that period. The market price of products will continue low, no matter what the cost of production may be. The day of large profits is probably past. There may be room for further intensive, but not extensive, development of industry in the present era of civilization.

Wright did point to potential investment opportunities, ''outside of the area of a state of industrial civilization, in China, Japan, India, Australia, Persia, and South Africa,'' in which ''there is a vast deal to be done.'' But that development he thought would take place very slowly. Wright also anticipated that investment of capital in banking insurance and other credit service fields ''will give to each of the great nations of Europe and America something to do, but,'' he observed rather pessimistically, ''the part of each in this work will be small and far from enough to insure more than temporary activity.''[11]

At the heart of the surplus-capital theory is a successful critique of (John Stuart Mill's restatement of) Jean Baptiste Say's law of markets. Existing scholarship has generally credited John Maynard Keynes with successfully making the first such critique. However, Charles Arthur Conant, in his essay, ''The Economic Basis of Imperialism,'' published in the fall of 1898 in the *North American Review,* attacked (Mill's restatement of) Say's law of markets, and its general inapplicability to modern industrial capitalist society.

In this essay, Conant dealt with the problems of *1)* historical time; *2)* unforeseen changes in consumer preferences; *3)* the development of capital saving techniques; *4)* public investment programs involving socialization of the surplus; *5)* the role of innovation; *6)* the creation of investment empires in the Third World; *7)* the supposed equilibrating role of the rate of interest in *(a)* the creation of more or less savings and *(b)* the allocation of investment; and *8)* relationship of effective demand to growth and stability. These were, of course, matters which John Maynard Keynes later took up. But Conant was the first to consider them in the English language literature in terms of their implications for the economic and social stability of industrial capitalism as a system. The stimulus for Conant to consider these questions came from two sources: the growing investment crisis which he actually noted taking place in the United States and other industrial capitalist states, and a book by the French economist and capitalist Paul Leroy-Beaulieu published in 1879 entitled *Essai sur la repartition des richesses et sur la tendance à une moindre inegalité conditions.* Leroy-Beaulieu had claimed that if European "laborers and capitalists continued to pile up saving in later years as they had done up to that time, the supply of loanable capital would become so great that its earning power would be materially reduced."[12]

Conant began his critique by asserting that about 1893 there had been clear undeniable evidence that the industrial capitalist nation state system created investment funds for which there were no investment outlets at prospective rates of return commensurate with the inherent risks. The evidence which he cited was of several types. He noted that consols, *rentes,* and German Government Bonds were being refunded at much lower rates of interest than their original issue price, indicating that the cost of low-risk capital to the governments of Britain, France, and Germany had been greatly reduced. That investors would accept these lower interest rates indicated there was a shortage of low-risk, even minimally profitable, investment outlets. Conant also cited evidence of plant duplication in railroads and industry as factors depressing investment returns outside government obligations. But because the educated reading public of his day by and large agreed with this assessment, Conant did not think it necessary to set forth more evidence of the existence of the capital surplus. Instead he proceeded to attack the theoretical issues involved.

Conant's attack on Say's law took several interrelated forms. First, he pointed out that even John Stuart Mill had acknowledged, in his defense of Say, that in order for production and consumption to be in equilibrium two initial assumptions had to be granted: *1)* "that production shall always take the right channels, producing only that for which there is a demand at prices at least equal to the costs of production;" and *2)* that "there shall be a perfect mobility of capital and labor to meet the changes in demand." Conant posited that "these conditions are difficult of realization under the modern system of production," requiring the almost unvarying ability to accurately project past trends into future events. Errors of information about future prices might lead to errors of calculation as to demand and supply which could in turn result in large numbers of price changes which would magnify the inaccuracy of estimates of future demand. This, Conant explained (quoting J. B. Clark), could "cause goods to be created for which in time there is no effectual demand" at prices sufficiently high to allow the entrepreneur to recover his long-run full costs of production. Such an entrepreneur would likely go bankrupt. Those investors who had bought his bonds would lose their capital (or a good part of it), which might make them reluctant to invest because of negative expectations, not simply about future profit potentials, but about the very security of the principal of their investment. In his 1898 essay Conant noted that economic crises "have been due in an increasing degree in recent years to the vain seeking for safe investments which could not be found."

Conant also attacked the assumption which orthodox economists made of the equilibrating role of the rate of interest, and dealt with all aspects of the problem later touched by Keynes. He pointed out that "the instinct of saving is to a considerable degree independent of the earning of dividends . . . the expectation of dividends from investment is a modern phenomenon, which is only one phase of the passion for saving, instilled by the evolution of civilized society." In other words it is not an increase in the rate of interest which calls savings into existence, nor does a decrease in the rate of return lead to dis-saving or consumption."It is doubtful," he explained, "if the first of these supposed effects of low interest—the dimunition of saving—will be felt to any serious extent in modern society." While he admitted that "saving might be somewhat impaired by diminished returns, there is a counter influence in the necessity for larger savings than before to obtain a given return.'" As a further counter to any tendency to diminish savings, Conant explained, "there is a constant addition to the number of those making savings under the tendency of growing social wealth to swell the numbers of the well-to-do classes."

But if supply and demand do not entirely, or even mainly, determine the rate of investment, what are the factors affecting the rate of investment? Conant implied that investor estimates of future risk were now the major factor. To Conant this explained why capital was being invested in the duplication of plant and equipment, which earned low and indeed, sometimes, no return. The higher rate of return promised in a Third World investment did not sufficiently outweigh the exchange and other political risks involved.

Conant also dealt with the problem of effective demand for "capital goods" as against "consumer goods" in the development of economic crises. "The steady fall in the earning power of capital," Conant explained, "points to excess of saved capital beyond effective demand." "There was a time," Conant explained, gone since modern corporate reorganization, "when every dollar of saved capital was required for productive enterprises in Europe and the United States." But this was no longer the case because "labor-saving machinery in farming and manufacturing had promoted saving in almost geometrical ratio from year to year." This in turn resulted in severe investment disproportionalities; it allowed "too much of the product of labor" to be "devoted to the creation of new [production] equipment of doubtful or at least postponed utility." In Conant's analysis that meant that not enough of the product of human labor (or "gross national product" as we would call it) was being applied to the "purchase of the products of the existing equipment." Like John Maynard Keynes later, Conant was pointing to the fact that the investment system was threatened with a relatively chronic condition of perverse operation—too

70

much investment in capital goods production, insufficient investment in the production of consumption goods.

Conant also noted that there were "monetary" as distinguished from "real" causes for the probable break between production and sale. Conant cited Wihelm Roscher to note that "by the intervention of money the seller was placed in a position to purchase only after a time, that is to postpone the other half of the exchange transaction as he wishes. Hence it follows that the supply does not necessarily produce a corresponding demand." In this connection Conant worried about underconsumption.

Nonetheless Conant did not see socialization of the surplus as a viable solution, not because it would not work economically, but because, unlike J. A. Hobson, Conant took the existing political decision-making process in the advanced industrial countries as given and largely unchangeable. Anything in the way of income redistribution "short of complete state socialism" would not, in his view, consume the capital surplus, and he did not believe that the majority of the voting population underpinning the existing American political system wanted such wrenching social change. He also rejected Hobson's assertion that international free trade would solve the problem of surplus capital, pointing out that it existed in both free trade and protectionist nations. In similar fashion he rejected the idea, later highlighted by Joseph Schumpeter, that innovation, both technical and organizational, could somehow consume the capital surplus. He did acknowledge that the organization of large corporations and of international trade mechanisms in the Third World could consume some of the capital, but did not believe that this would consume the whole capital surplus.

Conant, then, posited the existence of surplus capital, in the sense that it could not at certain times and under certain circumstances yield a rate of return high enough to compensate for the risks attached to its investment, in the view of those having fiduciary responsibility for its safe placement. Since he also considered and rejected, for various reasons, all the means for its consumption suggested later by John Maynard Keynes, this left open, in Conant's view, the option of external world market techniques of utilizing the surplus. Explicitly in his 1898 "Economic Basis of Imperialism," and implicitly in other of his published works, Conant argued that there was "a necessity that the United States shall enter upon a broad national policy," in order to find "new markets and new opportunities for investment . . . if surplus capital is to be profitably employed." At this date he had not come to a conclusion as to how the United States might obtain those markets and investment opportunities abroad, "and for asserting their rights for the free commerce of the East." But he did think that it was possible that the United States might "actually acquire territorial possessions," or "protecting sovereignties nominally independent," or even "content themselves with naval stations and diplomatic representations," to protect its access to markets and investment outlets. Economic imperialism, the building of an investment empire, seemed to Conant absolutely necessary. Otherwise American investors would "continue the needless duplication of existing means of production and communication, with the glut of unconsumed products, the convulsions followed by trade stagnation, and the steadily declining return upon investments which this policy will invoke."[13]

Conant's definition of surplus capital was accepted and acted upon by those at the center of the policy-making nexus. For instance Elihu Root, both as an official of the United States Government and as a decision maker in the private banking community, accepted the existence of surplus capital, and the need for both government and banking to act. Root argued that "since the first election of President McKinley [in 1896] the people of the United States have accumulated for the first time a surplus of capital beyond the requirements of internal development." Because, in Root's assessment, the United States had "paid our debts to Europe," we were "beginning to look beyond our own borders, throughout the world to find opportunity for the profitable use of our surplus capital, foreign markets for our manufactures, foreign mines to be developed, foreign bridges, railroads and public works to be built, foreign rivers to be turned into electric power and light."[14] The Bureau of Insular Affairs (BIA) (the United States "colonial office") came under Root's jurisdiction as Secretary of War in the Roosevelt administration. In private life, Root was the senior partner in the law firm Root and Cravath, which acted as the legal arm of the Morton Trust Company of New York, one of the city's four largest trust companies. Much of the capital surplus seeking safe and profitable investment was contained in the trust accounts of these banks. As Secretary of War and as general counsel to Morton Trust, Root bridged the policy-making gap between government and the banks in their joint effort to stabilize the economic situation. Indeed Root consciously fashioned the functions of the Bureau of Insular Affairs in such a way that it operated to stabilize Third World areas for investment. In the course of implementing this effort, Root worked closely with Conant, and probably arranged the appointment of Conant to the Board of Directors of the Morton Trust Company, as its treasurer, in 1902.[15]

One of the first experiments which the War Department and its BIA conducted in the preparation of a Third World area for economic development was in the political, administrative, and monetary restructuring of the Philippine Islands. American leaders concluded that at least a part of the cause of the reluctance of American capital to invest in the Philippines and hasten their modernization was a chaotic currency situation which seemed to investors to threaten not just potential returns from investment but the principal itself. Conant suggested that a financial expert be sent to the islands to examine their currency and try to construct proposals for their stabilization and in the summer of 1900, he was himself appointed to undertake this mission.

Conant, working in cooperation with William Howard Taft, who had become chairman of the Philippine Commission, developed a plan which called for the establishment of a gold exchange standard, one which would remove currency exchange risks. Taft and Conant were close personal friends and worked intimately together in the Philippine modernization campaign. Taft agreed with Conant's surplus capital analysis. Indeed, when he was being questioned by the United States Senate Committee on the Philippines, in January of 1902, on the issue of what benefits the United States might come to expect from its work in the Philippines, Taft explained to the senators that such US control of the islands provided to American investors "the opportunity of investing surplus capital under the protection and security of our own government." To those senators who, in his view, imperfectly understood the matter, Taft recommended that they consult "the book of Mr. Conant on *The United States in the Orient,"* because Taft "did not know of any place where it is better shown." The chairman of the committee, Henry Cabot Lodge of Massachusetts, explained as early as November 22, 1900, that

> it has been my firm belief that the Philippine Islands would not only become an important market to us for our finished goods, but what is still more important would furnish a large opportunity for the investment of surplus capital, and thus reduce the competition of accumulated capital at home, which is tending to lower very much the rates of interest, and to create in many places, needless competition by the establishment of plants which cannot hope to earn any decent return.

What Root, Taft, Conant, Lodge, and President Theodore Roosevelt attempted to do to stabilize the Philippines as a relatively low-risk area into which American surplus capital might be invested at profitable rates provided an experimental laboratory for the development of routinized policies designed to prepare Third World areas for the receipt of investment and hence "modernization." Although Philippine modernization and the investment of American capital there proceeded slowly, American leaders were well enough pleased with the general pattern which they had worked out to attempt to extend the system to China, and to advocate its extension to the colonies of other powers in Asia. This process was begun with the construction of a United States Commission on International Exchange (CIE) on March 3, 1903, upon recommendation of President Theodore Roosevelt, Secretary of State John Hay, and Secretary of War Root, with legislative enactment by both houses of Congress. The CIE was to try to reform China's currency as a way to prepare it for the investment of the surplus capital of all the industrial powers, based on an investment open door for all in Asia.[16]

The belief in the existence of surplus capital, as a constantly recurring phenomenon, provided a framework for American policy in China from 1900 to 1914, and beyond.

II
Justification for Application of the Term "Imperialism" to Varieties of Social Phenomena

One of the basic issues among intellectuals who accepted the economic analysis of imperialism was the question of whether or not imperialism was structural to capitalism, an inevitable development without essential choice—a state rather than a consciously adopted policy. Paul Leroy-Beaulieu argued, for example, that it was a choice which statesmen were free to adopt or not. But he warned that failure to build an international investment could lead to periodic declines in profit rates which could make socialism more attractive to segments of French society. In similar fashion Conant argued that the building of an investment empire was very desirable, but that it was in every sense a conscious choice over a number of undesirable alternatives. Elihu Root, Henry Cabot Lodge, Henry C. Morris, Paul Reinsch, and implicitly Theodore Roosevelt also argued for choice over inevitability. J. A. Hobson, an anticipator of the modern welfare state—and in many respects a proto-Keynesian—argued that imperialism was a choice, but an undesirable one. Karl Kautsky, Engels's literary heir and the chief intellectual of the second socialist international, also argued that it was a choice not an inevitable sociological stage. In this Kautsky made a sharp break with the existing socialist consensus based on a structuralist reading of Rudolph Hilferding's pioneering work, *Das Finanzkapital.*

Lenin asserted that imperialism was inherent in capitalism, because it was the final stage of the system. But, contrary to a widely held view, he did not assert that no investment outlets existed within the advanced, industrial capitalist states, but merely that the monopolistic organization of industry would not permit the long-term investment of capital at constantly reduced rates of return, but would force those who made the investment decisions for large corporations to seek short-run profit maximization. This he believed would lead to foreign investment, but to relatively modernized nations rather than to Third World areas, since he was fully aware that capital tended to go to nations which were relatively stable and possessed infrastructures and relatively modernized labor forces. In general Lenin regarded Third World areas as "reserve areas" in which future capital surpluses might be invested, once modernization was well underway.[18]

But in somewhat contradictory fashion Lenin took over from J. A. Hobson the concept that imperialism was largely parasitic and nondevelopmental, because of its unwillingness to undertake long-term modernized industrial development in Third World areas. This seemed to contradict his assumptions that capitalism developed at an uneven pace, and that, other things being equal, higher rates of return would attract capital investment; so that, were it profitable, long-run all-round development in the Third World was not inconsistent with the economic interests of the holders of surplus capital.

Lenin's thesis also seemed to imply that investment empire builders sought monopolistic investment outlets. Although he acknowledged that Kautsky was at least partly right when he claimed that there was a tendency toward ultra- or interimperial cooperation in the joint development of the resources of the Third World, Lenin did so in a polemical way. He argued that there was a countertendency toward monopolization and hence imperialist war over efforts to monopolize resource markets and investment outlets and, further, that this tendency was historically more significant as it was leading to more wars among the capital-surplus powers, as structural imperatives. These wars, according to Lenin, would result in periodic national and social revolutions which would destroy capitalism before any sort of real ultraimperial cooperation brought any stability to the system.[19]

Lenin deliberately confused the intellectual question of whether or not imperialist statesmen might learn to cooperate for the greater good of the capitalist system with the more immediate issue of which current policies would be more desirable for the socialist movement. In doing so, he put Kautsky on the defensive, particularly because Kautsky had published his thesis on "Ultra-imperialism" in *Neue Zeit* in September of 1914, just as World War I was breaking out. But of course Kautsky was not claiming historical determinacy in any immediate sense for his theory. His position was that imperialism was not necessarily a last stage of capitalism, but the result of conscious choice by statesmen over other possible choices and that some future statesmen could choose ultraimperial cooperation. Kautsky saw considerable evidence of this in some of the cartel structures (and, he might well have added, in the consortia approaches to the apportionment of investment outlets in China). He thought this to be a trend which would be strengthened by the growth in national liberation movements in the Third World which threatened a potential "collective" denial of investment outlets to all the capital surplus powers. This, he believed, would probably stimulate the developed industrial capitalist states to cooperate to police the Third World, which would lead to further cooperation in joint development of raw material sources and investment outlets.[20]

Kautsky's argument stressed the significance of the political response of the collective international industrial capitalist system to the necessity for it to subordinate its respective national profit interests to the stability of the system as a whole. Kautsky was implicitly arguing that industrial capitalism now possessed a sufficiently flexible system of administration to make it capable of rejecting the short-term profit drives of the property-owning classes—to eschew competition—and cooperate to bring stability to the system as a whole. Without saying so directly Kautsky was arguing that the politics of capitalist industrialism were not merely reflections of their economic base. He was thus rejecting the view that capitalist society could be separated into an economic base and an epiphenomenal superstructure made up of all else including culture and politics. This contrasted sharply with Lenin's implicit assertion that the tendency to competition was rooted in the base and would thus disrupt and shatter any political tendencies toward cooperation between industrial nations. Lenin and Kautsky differed deeply about the significance of the political aspects of imperialism; Lenin treated them as of secondary and derived significance, while Kautsky considered them as part of an integrated political economy, in which the politics and the economics interacted in qualitatively complex ways. The probable root of this difference was over the issue of whether or not monopoly capitalism was a final stage of capitalism as defined by Marx when he argued that capitalism would continue to exist so long as it had not exhausted its possibilities for the further "expansion of the productive forces." Lenin assumed that these possibilities had been exhausted, and thus that the capitalist system had arrived at its final stage. Kautsky assumed that the system still possessed that ability to expand the forces of production. Such differences involved contradictory selection of contemporary data by Lenin and Kautsky, and projection of those data into the future. The imperialist war seemed to Lenin the aspect of that present which would most characterize the future, whereas movements toward cooperation between imperialist nations seemed to Kautsky to predict the forseeable future of capitalism.[21]

These positions in turn implied differences over whether or not the industrial capitalist states had the capacity to undertake the modernization and industrialization of the less developed areas of Europe and the so-called "backward" nations. Lenin implied that such possibilities were exhausted. Kautsky implied that once the World War was over the cooperative trend in the development of less developed areas would be resumed. One test of the strength of their models would be the degree to which one or the other predicted the future. Neither was entirely satisfactory. Adherents of Lenin's model could argue that anticapitalist revolutions in the First World continued to characterize international politics, up through the defeat of the German revolution in 1923; supporters of Kautsky's thesis could plausibly argue that all the while, but especially after the Dawes Plan and German stabilization, industrial capitalism continued to modify its structure in such a way as to move toward ultraimperial or interimperial institutions and practices. If both models were further projected into the future, the trend leading toward World War II would tend to support Lenin, but developments since World War II—the enormous increase in productive forces in the industrial as well as industrializing world and the creation of interimperial institutions such as the International Monetary Fund and the International Bank for Reconstruction and Development, which allowed market and investment outlets to be apportioned without war—tend to validate Kautsky's model to a much greater degree.[22]

Although neither Lenin nor Kautsky openly discussed the ability of bourgeois institutions to apportion investment outlets, raw material sources, and export markets peacefully, the issue was at the heart of their differences. For instance Lenin accused Kautsky of holding that "monopolies in economics are compatible with non-monopolistic, non-violent, non-annexationist methods in politics . . . Kautsky's theory means refraining from mentioning existing contradictions, forgetting the most important of them." Lenin cites Kautsky's assertion that "from the purely economic point of view it is not impossible that capitalism will go through a phase . . . the phase of ultra imperialism . . . when wars shall cease under capitalism, a phase of the joint exploitation of the world by internationally combined finance capital."

Lenin did not consider whether the rules of industrial capitalist nation market apportionment, as exemplified in neoclassical theory and in practice, made such developments likely. He merely explained that Kautsky's theorizing about ultraimperialism simply "served an exclusively reactionary aim: that of diverting attention from the depth of *existing* antagonisms" [Lenin's emphasis]. But if one does examine classical and neoclassical economic theory it is quite clear that from a purely economic point of view cooperation among competing capitalisms to rapidly develop markets, investment outlets, and raw material supplies was perfectly consistent with bourgeois economic theory. And, at least in some respects, bourgeois economic practice—as exemplified not just by the international cartels which Kautsky cited, but also by the trend toward policies followed by the large banking combinations in Germany, the United States, and, to a lesser extent, other capitalist societies, which stressed their community of interest—tended also to sustain Kautsky's predictions.[23]

Another area of dispute between socialist theoreticians arose over the question of the degree to which the industrial capitalist nations utilized modes of capital surplus empire building to shape their relations with other developed industrial countries. Relative positions on this matter were complex. Both Luxemburg and Kautsky argued that the existence of Third World "agrarian zones" was essential to the ability of surplus capital investors to realize their profits. In a contrary way, arguing on the basis of Hilferding's model, Lenin assumed that what he called the "uneven development" of capitalism meant that relatively less developed, although modernized, nations would be an investment outlet, at least in theory, to a more developed industrial nation. But in his historically deterministic way Lenin insisted that such outlets were monopolized by free trade as well as high tariff nations, and that such monopolies made war inevitable, but not simply over the Third World but over the industrial areas themselves as they were described in Lenin's model.[24]

The issue of whether or not imperialism is parasitic rather than developmental is complex. There were and are differences in the socialist and nonsocialist literature. Marx himself was rather of two minds. He was critically cynical about the "civilizing" mission of the British in India during the nineteenth century. He pointed to the immediate misery for the people of India involved in the dissolution of traditional structures. Yet Marx was himself a believer in progress. He implied some parasitism within the context of overall development. He expected industrial capitalism to conquer the world; and he regarded this conquest as progressive although brutal.[25]

The late Bill Warren argued that industrial capitalist imperialism was developmental rather than parasitic. This is not because imperialist countries are innately progressive, but because there is conflict between the investors and the Third World governments. "The conclusion emerges," Warren argued in 1973, "that, over foreign manufacturing investment in the Third World, conflicts occur within a long-term framework of eventual accommodation mutually acceptable and mutually advantageous to both sides." Thus the underdeveloped countries increasingly and inexorably are able to exert relatively greater leverage in the conflict and bargaining process.

Warren denies the thesis developed by, for example, the American Marxist economist, Harry Magdoff, that the system of international investment to Third World countries is "a system characterized by and tending to perpetuate an international division of labor in production corresponding to the needs of the advanced capitalist world." As his proof Warren offers Hollis Chenery's study of the relationship between Third World imports of foreign capital and independence-dependence ratios, which seems to show that, after a decade of borrowing, those countries which borrowed most achieved most independence. Warren rejects the sociological theory that simply compares "inward capital flows with the resulting outward flow of interest and profit" but ignores "what exactly has been done with the capital in-between." Even when

> a large excess of outward flow of funds over inward investment can be shown (as it frequently can) this proves nothing whatsoever, either about a drain of foreign exchange (because the investment may expand capacity which produces exports or saves imports) or about a drain of surplus value (the investment may expand productive investment and thus the surplus, but in a form which is not readily convertible into foreign exchange). The so-called drain may merely be the foreign exchange price paid for the establishment of productive facilities. Such foreign investment is a sensible path for capitalist (and indeed socialist) economic development provided that the productive facilities established are worth the price paid."

But Warren carefully qualifies his endorsement by arguing that such foreign direct investment is not valuable to the Third World (or, implicitly, socialist) country if it "suffocates indigenous investment, rather than supplements it . . . since there would be an outflow of profits which need not otherwise have taken place." Warren further argues that "the view that exploitation caused by foreign investment can be equaled with stagnation is absurd." He also emphasizes that "imperialist countries since the war have themselves adopted a positive policy of *favouring* Third World industrialization." Clearly Warren's use of the term "imperialism" rejects the view inherent in Luxemburg, Lenin, and to some extent Kautsky, that trade between advanced and less developed nations is *per se* "imperialist." This interpretation springs from the mercantilist conception (to the effect that "trade equals war"), carried into socialist literature by Luxemburg.[26]

The issue of parasitism is itself a complex phenomenon. For instance, prior to 1910 United States political leaders—and for the most part business leaders also—favored a kind of foreign investment which would be largely complementary to the internal American economy. The State Department invariably opposed the establishment of American (manufacturing) branch plants abroad to utilize cheap foreign labor, a phenomenon which would result in the export of jobs and increase the rate of profit of American domestic capital investment. From the standpoint of the foreign nation this would restrict the development of its manufacturing industry, and tend to confine development to labor-intensive industries, designed to supply primary materials for the industrially developed nation.

But the major obstacle to the development process as a whole in Third World areas was the lack of an infrastructure base for development. This infrastructure is a network of interacting economic and cultural phenomena. For instance, for development to take place there must be a modernized labor force habituated to intensive labor in mines and factories on a continuous basis. Development of the means of transport and the economic infrastructure—railroads, canals, roads, power plants, coal mines, internal and coastwise steam shipping—tended to also create such a labor force. This economic infrastructure historically returns only a long-term and low profit, but it is the basis for subsequent profitable investment in manufacturing.

The unwillingness of the United States government to encourage investment in manufacturing in "agrarian zones" at least prior to 1910 worked to provide the techniques needed for modernization while leaving ownership of manufacturing industry (in China, for instance) in the hands of the indigenous population. On the other hand, British and Japanese capital were already entering manufacturing in China. In this specific sense much of the nonmanufacturing infrastructure investment has a developmental effect. It may be the desire of American State Department leaders that no manufacturing take place, but the objective reality is that, over time, more and more capital-intensive development will take place. As D. C. M. Platt has shown, the most significant determinant of the degree to which foreign investment in a Third World country is developmental is whether the recipient is politically independent. If it is, it is able to force a competitive relationship among rival foreign investors and so bargain for more and more of its national interest, as Latin American nations and businessmen did in the nineteenth century.[27]

Indeed Rosa Luxemburg's assertion that imperialism is nondevelopmental can only apply to areas which do not have tariff autonomy, and in which manufactured goods are dumped. The major example would seem to be the colonies of the major European empires, particularly the British and French colonies of southeast Asia, and most especially British India. American imperialist leaders such as Theodore Roosevelt and General Leonard Wood regarded European imperialism as exploitative and implicitly parasitic, although they regarded the British Empire as the least parasitic and most developmental. Their definition of developmental imperialism was that the indigenous peoples had a stake in the development process sufficiently large to seem worth fighting for in the event of external aggression. Roosevelt and Wood both believed that none of the Europeans had attained this degree of cooperative development, but that the United States was in the process of achieving it in the Philippines, and had achieved it in Cuba.[28]

On the issue of parasitism there was a contradiction between Lenin's politics and his acceptance of Hobson's moralistic critique. As head of the Soviet government after 1917, Lenin sought foreign aid. With his enthusiastic approval, the Soviet regime signed agreements with the Rockefeller banking and industrial network through Frank A. Vanderlip, President of the National City Bank of New York. It is true that these agreements were repudiated almost immediately by the American side, very probably because of pressure from the government. But it is important to note that the agreements were not repudiated by Lenin. The overwhelming weight of evidence is that he would have happily worked with American private capital. Subsequent to the repudiation of the agreements by the US side, and more especially after Lenin's death, the autarchic model of development seemed to get moral emphasis. But the Bolsheviks were simply making a virtue of necessity. It seems clear that Lenin would have accepted foreign investment, but that he would have tried to insist that it function as part of the Soviet Union's developing planned system of modernization with publicly-owned industrial enterprises. The implication is that the government of the country receiving capital can prevent foreign investment from having parasitic effects, if the elites managing the modernization program are imbued with a consciousness of national goals and are willing to pursue those goals without fear or favor. Although he may have endorsed the Hobsonian concept of parasitism, Lenin acted on the basis that such parasitic tendencies could be blunted. In this respect, Lenin was quite close to Warren's analysis and very distant from the Third World assumptions which Rosa Luxemburg made, and which Samir Amin developed.[29]

III

In recent years since the Keynesian revolution and monetarist counter-revolution the argument that there can be no surplus capital has gained wide currency. Keynes himself developed a rather sophisticated version of this argument. In an exchange with J. A. Hobson between February 3 and 14 of 1936 Keynes outlined his differences with Hobson's surplus-capital theory. "What you have described as overinvestment," Keynes explained, "I regard as pushing of investment to a point where capital is so abundant that further investment cannot for the time being compete in its respective returns with the rate of interest. But this is not absolute overinvestment. The capital is still capable of yielding something in conditions of full employment, but not as much as the current rate of interest requires." But, Keynes argued, "the apparent failure of consumption in such circumstances is not really due to the consuming power being absent, but to the falling off of incomes. The falling off of incomes is due to the decline in investment occasioned by the insufficiency of the return to new investment compared with the rate of interest."

Keynes assumed new investment by individual entrepreneurs who, prior to investing, would have to borrow from the banks at the prevailing rate of interest. If the prevailing rate of interest was higher than the prospective rate of return potential entrepreneurs would not borrow from the banks and hence would not invest. Keynes also assumed that "if steps are taken to increase investment, the effect of this on incomes will increase demand up to a point where the apparent redundancy disappears." But by Keynes's own assumptions the markets will not yield the required investment because the rate of interest exceeds the prospective rate of profit. Hence Keynes implied that the state must intervene to invest the capital at rates of return lower than the rate of interest. Conant knew that option to be open but rejected it because he thought that it would tend to drive the system toward socialism.

The differences between Conant and Keynes are therefore seen to dissolve into different assumptions about whether or not the state would undertake an investment program, with Keynes assuming that it would largely because it ought to, and Conant assuming that it ought not, and hence would not. They are agreed on the problem: that more capital is seeking investment than can be profitably placed. They disagree on the solution. In Conant's view, in the absence of new investment outlets foreign investment empires must be built jointly by the state and private enterprise. On the other hand Keynes's view, in 1936, was that domestic/economy government investment programs were needed to invest capital at rates of return below the rate of interest.[30]

The non-Keynesian or neoclassical theory which asserts an equality between savings and investment is based on a network of assumptions. It assumes that the relationship between the supply of capital and the demand for capital is roughly analogous to the relationship between supply and demand for commodities in general. This in turn is based on an acceptance of the assertions in Say's law of markets, which states that the purchasing power created by the production of commodities will be used to purchase commodities. If this assumption is accepted, whatever capital is invested results in the production of consumer's goods (or services), or producer's goods which are almost immediately consumed while all income is either spent for consumer's goods or producer's goods. That portion which is spent for producer's goods is the automatic equivalent to savings. Perhaps the key assumption is that differences in the rate of interest create more or less savings, and keep the relationship between savings and investment in equilibrium. This is in turn based on further assumptions: *(1)* that there is no hoarding within a given investment market, and *(2)* that investors feel that there is reasonable security for their investment. We know that there always is some hoarding even in the most modernized industrial nations, but we do not know that there is enough to interfere with a rough equivalence between savings and investment. Yet we do know that throughout most of the industrial capitalist epoch many investments have been exceedingly risky, due to, for instance, wars and exchange risks due to conflicting monetary standards. For much of recorded history the assumption of an equivalence between savings and investment, *via* the free play of market forces—supply and demand yielding equilibrium—has not been a reality; consequently surplus capital did exist, although this reality was frequently obscured by enormously wasteful defense and/or foreign aid expenditure, dissipating capital in unproductive ventures abroad.

Surplus capital has not disappeared, and neither Keynesian nor neoclassical theoretical arguments based on assumptions contradicted by history have been able to define it away.[31]

Much of the literature on imperialism since 1945 (perhaps since 1935) has focused on the wrong questions. This is partly because the issues have had momentous implications for the international contestants for power and wealth. The Cold War has increased the misconceptions of the significant issues involved. Leninist theorists insist that imperialism is an inevitable sociological stage, a natural outgrowth of the postcompetitive capitalist economies, and of the development of surplus capital. They further insist that investment by capitalist nations results in a parasitic and illegitimate use of the natural resources and labor power of developing nations.

Most theorists in capitalist states react defensively to these Leninist assertions. They largely deny that economic imperialism and surplus capitalism exist. They insist that capitalist investment in developing areas is the best and most rapid way to develop Third World resources. They also imply that such investment has the character of disinterested economic aid and is therefore purely benevolent.

This paper has attempted to sort out rival claims and tries to make some tentative propositions about economic imperialism which relate more closely to the actual literature of the study of economic imperialism. In this connection, it seems highly probable that theorists and policy makers such as Charles A. Conant were right when they asserted the existence of surplus capital when investors measured prospective return against risk. It also seems highly likely that, as risks fluctuate, surplus capital becomes a recurring phenomenon in the industrial capitalist states. Consequently, capitalist investment in modernizing nations cannot be purely disinterested, at least during much of the period in which such investments have been made. On the other hand, Third World nations need foreign capital, technology, and technicians, and the most abundant source of these is located in the industrial capitalist nations. It is also clear that there is nothing inherently exploitive nor parasitic in the foreign investment relationship *per se*. In this connection, the construction of the International Monetary Fund and the International Bank for Reconstruction and Development have prevented any single industrial nation from exclusively controlling Third World investment outlets. This in turn has provided developing nations with bargaining leverage to obtain capital, technology, and technicians on a generally more advantageous basis than was the case when industrial nations had exclusive colonial or semicolonial empires. Karl Kautsky was correct in two of his predictions: the Bretton Woods system has clearly functioned as an ultraimperial mechanism, damping down the economic factors leading toward war among the industrial states. Lenin's prediction of rivalry and war among the industrial states has not been the rule since the perfection of these institutions. Of equal influence in muting rivalry and war has been the system of tariff reductions since World War II, which reduced protectionist policies which were often the cause of tension. Hence the argument which Lenin and subsequent Leninists have advanced—that economic imperialism was an inevitable stage before the disintegration of capitalism—has proved to be wide of the mark.

Both Leninist (as well as neo-Leninist) and most nonsocialist scholars working on the imperialism problem have missed researching the most fruitful kinds of questions relating to economic imperialism. The intrusion of Cold War issues is probably the chief inhibiting factor preventing more fruitful research. The prospects for the National Endowment for the Humanities and/or the Social Science Research Council funding, on any adequate scale, the kind of research necessary to uncover the changes in economic empire since 1900 are remote unless and until the Cold War ends.

The Foreign Policy of Antislavery, 1833-1846

Edward P. Crapol

Few historians have recognized that the antislavery enterprise possessed a distinct foreign policy. Nor have they understood that this foreign policy formed an integral part of a movement ideology. Premised on a belief that the slave power controlled national policy, the antislavery ideology that emerged in the 1830s included, among other things, a view of America's future role in the world that incorporated a mix of idealism and self-interest. Slavery was a blot on the nation's republican honor. To purify the republic the abolitionists urged a new direction in the nation's diplomacy that accorded with their romantic vision of America as the beacon of liberty and the wellspring of republican principles. In attempting to halt the expansion of slavery and the slave power, they also recommended foreign policy initiatives that protected the future of free institutions by opening new markets to the products of free labor. For thousands of nineteenth century American men and women who entered the abolitionist ranks, the idea of a slave power in control of the federal government undermining their cherished liberties and limiting their economic options reflected political reality and spurred their campaign to emancipate the slave and end the reign of the "slavocracy."

Perhaps the reason why an abolitionist foreign policy has gone unnoticed by historians is to be found in their tendency to question the validity of conspiracy theories as explanations of power relationships in American history. All too frequently in the dock of historical inquiry abolitionists have been judged guilty of seeing conspiracy where none existed. Recently a few historians have acknowledged the importance of the slave power thesis. Eric Foner, for one, has argued that the slave power idea "was a way of ordering and interpreting history, assigning clear causes to inexplicable events" and that it became "the ideological glue of the Republican Party" in the 1850s.[1] To date, however, the origins of the slave power thesis have not been pinpointed and historians generally have ignored the foreign policy of antislavery and its crucial importance to the development of an abolitionist ideology.[2] It should be recognized as well that whether or not the slave power analysis was totally valid and objectively true in all its particulars is essentially irrelevant to an understanding of the abolitionists' ideology and the foreign policy that flowed from it. Their experience in the movement produced their perception of the slave power, which in turn governed their behavior and political response.

The initial intellectual formulation of what became the slave power thesis was provided by Lydia Maria Child. In 1833 this popular young novelist cast aside a budding literary career to announce her conversion to the cause of immediate emancipation. The occasion of her antislavery debut was the publication of *An Appeal in Favor of That Class of Americans Called Africans*. In this highly influential and widely read tract Child focused on the evils of slavery as an institution, asserting that it "is the system, not the men, on which we ought to bestow the full measure of abhorrence." True republicans throughout the nation, argued Child, should favor the common good over "all other considerations" by seeking an end to this inhumane system of bondage. While attempting to arouse the moral indignation and moral virtue of all Americans, including slaveholders, Child wisely directed her appeal primarily to the interests of nonslaveholders of the North.[3] In the process she successively laid the ideological underpinnings for a coherent abolitionist critique of the nation's diplomacy. Her analysis foreshadowed a full-scale abolitionist campaign in the 1840s to redirect American foreign policy by offering an alternative to the nation's existing proslavery behavior in international affairs.

It was the nullification crisis of 1832-33 that served as the immediate backdrop for Child's original statement of the slave power thesis. In framing her trailblazing synthesis she relied heavily on the political thought and analysis of former president John Quincy Adams. Then a representative from Massachusetts, Adams was deeply involved in the nullification crisis which arose when South Carolina challenged federal authority on grounds of "states rights." Adams joined other northerners in the Congressional debates who fought to save the Union by scotching South Carolina's challenge. In the course of the debate Adams placed the nullifiers on the defensive by charging it was they as representatives of the slaveholding interest who held an unfair advantage in the existing union. Betraying his Federalist heritage, Adams identified the three-fifths clause of the Constitution (which allowed for five slaves to be counted as three free white persons in calculating membership in the House of Representatives) as the source of the slaveholding interest's grip on national power. The history of the Union, Adams proclaimed, "has afforded a continual proof that this representation of property, which they enjoy as well in the election of President and Vice President of the United States as upon the floor of the House of Representatives, has secured to the slaveholding states the entire control of national policy, and, almost without exception, the possession of the highest executive office of the Union."[4] In the view of the Massachusetts representative it was the nonslave states that truly were aggrieved, and not the slave states as the nullifiers would have it.

Child's argument in the *Appeal* closely followed that of Adams. She too identified the three-fifths clause as the vehicle for southern domination. That despised clause granted the South twenty undeserved representatives in the House. It guaranteed the South "a controlling power," a "ruling power in this government." Repeating Adams's already sweeping charges of southern domination throughout the nation's brief history, Child cited that region's sustained control of the presidency, the vice presidency, the federal judiciary, and the Congress. In this scheme of things northern interests were at best being ignored and at worst totally suppressed. Child concluded that the South virtually had a stranglehold on the federal government, a grasp so tight as to assure "the preservation and extension of slave power." At first glance her analysis appeared to have been merely derivative of the Adams/Federalist argument. This was true to a point. But only to a point, as Child pushed the critique several steps further by shrewdly coining the phrase "slave power" and directing abolitionist thought along the path to a full-scale ideology.

Maria Child did not stop at labeling southern control of the national government as the handiwork of slave power. She proceeded to originate an antislavery critique of American diplomacy. To begin with, Child denounced the United States' longstanding refusal to grant formal diplomatic recognition to Haiti. Although the United States initially had aided Toussaint L'Overture, the black liberator of Haiti, by concluding a secret trade agreement with him in 1799, official diplomatic recognition was withheld. American trade with the black republic continued until 1806, when the Jefferson administration, under pressure from Napoleon, instituted a formal trade ban. Trade with Haiti eventually resumed, but diplomatic recognition remained out of the question, continually blocked by a skittish South fearful of granting approval to a government that had come to power via a successful slave revolt.

For Child, official American recognition was long overdue as well as politically and commercially justified. In the three decades since Haiti won its independence from France the island nation had prospered and was "fast increasing its wealth, intelligence, and refinement." While total American trade with Haiti in the early 1830s approached the not inconsiderable level of $3,000,000 even without the aid of formal diplomatic ties, Child once again displayed her political sensitivity by emphasizing that recognition undoubtedly would lead to an expanded northern commerce with the black republic.[5] But without sustained antislavery lobbying in Congress and abolitionist pressure on the Andrew Jackson administration, Haitian recognition appeared doomed. Not only did the "existence of slavery among us" prevent it but, as Child bitterly observed, "our northern representatives have never even made an effort to have her independence acknowledged, because a colored ambassador would be so disagreeable to our prejudices."[6]

Within a few years after the publication of Child's *Appeal* the demand for Haitian recognition became a staple in the abolitionist diplomatic agenda. Why did such a trivial diplomatic matter become a key issue and gain widespread support among the antislavery faithful? Primarily because Maria Child brilliantly used the issue to expose with unmistakable clarity what many considered to be the central paradox of antebellum America. A republic supposedly dedicated to the principles of human liberty and freedom condoned and defended racial inequality, and allowed several million human beings to be owned as property within a system of chattel slavery. The Haitian issue confronted Americans with the choice of accepting or rejecting black equality, and indirectly acknowledging the humanity of American slaves, which explained why the recognition question invariably sparked an angry and hostile response from slavery's defenders.

Texas was the other foreign policy concern explicitly dealt with in the *Appeal,* as Maria Child warned readers of the dangers accompanying the territorial "extension of slave power." "The purchase or the conquest of Texas is a favorite scheme with Southerners," she maintained, "because it would occasion such an inexhaustible demand for slaves." In this instance Child was gratified that at least up to the present moment, "the jealousy of the Mexican government places a barrier in that direction."[7] By identifying and labeling the slave power, and by pinpointing its designs on Texas and exposing its implacable resistance to the diplomatic recognition of Haiti, Child formally had inaugurated both an abolitionist ideology and its corollary, what was quickly to become a full-blown abolitionist foreign policy.

Less than three years later the accuracy of Child's slave power analysis, with its warning of the threat of slavery's extension into adjacent territories, appeared confirmed. In March 1836 Texas revolted from Mexico and declared its independence as the Lone Star Republic. Many abolitionists, including such veterans as Benjamin Lundy and Child's husband, David Lee Child, saw the hand of the slavocracy at work behind the scenes in Texas. Lundy, on the verge of establishing a free labor colony in Mexican territory claimed by the insurrectionists, immediately responded by issuing two broadsides charging southern slaveowners with complicity in the uprising. To Lundy's mind the revolution was unjustified; Mexico may have abolished slavery in the province, but it had not oppressed the Texans. Quite the contrary, the Mexican government repeatedly had endeavored to accommodate the colonists in any number of ways. Hence, Lundy believed the true goal of the revolution was to reestablish and perpetuate the institution of slavery. Southern slaveholders and northern land speculators "cheerfully cooperate" in support of this venture, he said, for what they and the Texans ultimately desired was the annexation of this extended slave market to the United States.[8] What Lundy revealed was taking place in Texas was no theoretical abstraction; it was a clear and concrete example of the slave power on the move to extend its domain.

To prevent the annexation of Texas and thwart the ambitions of the slave power, Benjamin Lundy suggested an alliance to Congressman John Quincy Adams. The Quaker abolitionist offered to supply Adams information on the Texas issue as ammunition for his antiannexation campaign in the House of Representatives. Adams accepted Lundy's offer, graciously noting "it will be a favour to me," and, making clear his allegiance to antislavery was unwavering, the former president confidently predicted that their collaboration "may promote the cause in which you take so much interest, and to which probably more than anything else, the remainder of my political life will be devoted."[9] True to his word, Adams adopted and expanded upon Lundy's views in his public and private battle against Texas annexation. According to Adams the Jackson administration had been "breeding" this project since it first took office, but it was "not ready to proclaim its yet secret labours for the double purpose of enlarging the dominion and riveting forever the Slave holding domination of the Union."[10] The administration's political reluctance to act quickly on annexation reflected a fairly widespread northern uneasiness that taking Texas would add a number of new slave states to the Union and upset the congressional balance. It was also confronted directly by a vigorous antiannexation petition campaign aimed at Congress by the antislavery forces. The annexation movement stalled and by early 1838, after Martin Van Buren had entered the White House, Adams happily wrote Lundy that he saw no impending move for annexation during the present Congressional session, although he acknowledged the situation might change drastically in the future.

An abolitionist foreign policy definitely had taken shape by the late 1830s. It had been fused in the crucible of the Texas controversy and the ensuing petition campaigns opposing annexation. It was tempered in a second great petition campaign during the winters of 1838-39, when for the first time a call for Haitian recognition was included. At the end of the decade, when William Jay, son of Founding Father John Jay, published *A View of the Action of the Federal Government, in Behalf of Slavery,* the overall structure of abolitionist ideology and an accompanying foreign policy was firmly in place. With meticulous care Jay put the finishing touches on the ideological framework as he detailed how the federal government was in thrall to the slave interests. For Jay, as well as for his intellectual predecessors John Quincy Adams and Maria Child, the ratio of federal representation mandated by the three-fifths clause was the crux of the problem. This provision in the Constitution allowing for five slaves to be counted as three free white persons meant that "the slave-holding interest," according to Jay's calculations, had in the lower branch of Congress a representation of twenty-five members "in addition to the fair and equal representation of the free inhabitants." From the very beginning in 1789 this unfair ratio had "given the slave-holders an undue weight in the national councils" and constituted the basis of the slave power's current hegemony in Washington.[11]

Prominent among Jay's litany of slave power abuses were illustrations of its virtual monopoly of the nation's foreign policy. "Even American diplomacy must be made subservient to the interests of the slaveholders," he complained, as "republican ambassadors must bear to foreign courts the wailings of our government for the escape of human property." Another galling example of the slave power's influence was evident in Washington's continual refusal to recognize Haiti. Jay cited trade figures that suggested that, while imports from the black republic to the United States were substantial, American exports to the island were "subjected to severe discriminating duties." The explanation for this disparity between exports and imports was the policy of nonrecognition. To lift the existing restrictions diplomatic recognition must be granted, which of course Jay recommended to open a lucrative market to American goods and allow for a "greatly extended" commerce with Haiti.[12]

As further testimony to the slave power's political sway in the "national councils," Jay noted that Texas, unlike Haiti, had been granted recognition very shortly after its announcement of independence. Haiti had been "independent both in name and in fact for thirty-seven years," yet the United States continued to withhold recognition. In contrast, "twelve months after Texas declared her independence, she was received by us into the family of nations, and honored by an interchange of diplomatic agents." Such "indecent haste" for Texas recognition was evidence of the slave power's desire for annexation. In addition, this diplomatic double standard was the consequence of a southern fear that official sanction for the black republic of Haiti might prompt a slave insurrection in the United States.[13] By exposing Washington's double standard concerning its recognition policy toward Texas and Haiti, William Jay capped what for many Americans was a powerful and persuasive indictment of the slave power's role in shaping the nation's diplomatic priorities. As such, his *View* represented what amounted to the final milestone on the path of a full-fledged abolitionist ideology.

Undoubtedly Maria Child's *Appeal,* John Quincy Adams's writings and speeches, Benjamin Lundy's broadsides, and William Jay's *View* were the beginnings of an antislavery ideology premised on a belief in the validity of the slave power thesis. During the 1830s reality increasingly confirmed analysis as the ideology took shape on the battlefield of antislavery protest. When the rank and file of the antislavery enterprise sought domestic and foreign redemption for the "sinful republic" their quest inevitably led them into the political arena. The moral suasion of pulpit and lectern, of pamphlet and mail campaign to enlighten southern brethren, quickly gave way to the political act of petitioning state legislatures and the United States Congress. That in turn led to the tactic of "questioning" political candidates to elicit formal support for one or more of the goals of the antislavery cause. Each action, whether one of moral suasion or political activism, invariably evoked reaction from their foes. Abolitionist speakers were attacked, their meetings violently disrupted, and southern post offices were burned to prevent delivery of antislavery literature, while abolitionist petitions to representatives in Washington were routinely tabled after 1836 as mandated by a Congressional "gag rule." More often than not, the pattern of response to antislavery activity gave substance to the slave power analysis and reinforced a movement ideology.

This abolitionist ideology blossomed outside the narrow confines of the organizational structures of national and state antislavery societies; it was neither constrained by organizational control nor exclusively shaped by the leading lights of the enterprise. Intellectuals and activists such as the Childs, Adams, Lundy, and Jay may have launched and sustained the process, but many other men and women, some prominent, some less so, helped forge a culture of resistance to the evils of chattel slavery. The process of creating an abolitionist ideology would appear to be an example of Gordon Wood's observation that ideas and ideology can emerge and develop without reliance on great thinkers to dispense intellectual guidance to a movement. Building a movement culture involves more than a one-way transaction in which an intellectual elite provides the requisite ideology and network of ideas for the rank and file of the reform or revolutionary enterprise.[14] This was perhaps most vividly illustrated in the lobbying, petitioning, and lecturing activities of the abolitionists. It was a truly democratic enterprise in which men and women, black and white—gender-free and color-blind—participated in what may be said to have been the first organized pressure group in American history that attempted to influence and change the direction of the nation's foreign policy.

But having developed a comprehensive ideology the abolitionists rather quickly faced a dilemma that ultimately split the organized sector of the movement into two groups. Should they continue with their current level of political activity which was essentially that of a pressure group and which, with the exception of blocking Texas annexation, seemed to be having only a marginal impact? Or should they organize a separate political party dedicated to ending slavery and eradicating the slave power? For many in the antislavery enterprise the next logical step, dictated in good part by their acceptance of the ideology itself, was independent political action via a separate abolitionist party. This cadre of abolitionists believed that as a pressure group they had gone about as far as they could go. Neither of the two national political parties was responsive to the slave power analysis nor to the abolitionists' mounting concern about the protection of the civil rights and personal liberties of members of the movement.

During the years 1838-40 the columns of several of the major antislavery newspapers reflected a noticeable restlessness. This was especially true among such stalwarts as William Goodell, James G. Birney and Henry B. Stanton. Goodell was perhaps the first to broach the subject of forming a political party with two articles that appeared in the late summer of 1838 entitled "Political Action Against Slavery." Although he believed an abolitionist political party was justified, Goodell hedged, saying that the time was not yet right. Perhaps initially even more cautious about the necessity of independent political action was Birney, a former slaveowner and future presidential candidate of the Liberty Party. In a public exchange with F. H. Elmore, a member of the House of Representatives from South Carolina, Birney employed the slave power analysis while only hinting at the viability of an independent party. It was Henry B. Stanton at the 1839 annual meeting of the American Anti-Slavery Society who first explicitly recommended an independent abolitionist party and perceptively observed that the Northwest was the region that held the key to abolitionism's success. "Here, Sir," he argued, "is our hope for the final extermination of slavery" because the free Northwest shall provide six or eight large states "to yet march into the Union." Stanton's advice to organize and capture the votes of the Northwest became one of the guiding principles of the Liberty Party, the first third party in the nation's history.[15]

While the political abolitionists proceeded to organize a separate antislavery party, "Senex," an anonymous correspondent to the *Emancipator,* and Joshua Leavitt, the newspaper's editor, utilized Stanton's insights to formulate an antislavery foreign policy alternative. This aimed at opening the British market to the surplus wheat and corn of the Northwest by actively seeking the repeal of the British Corn Laws, which placed restrictive duties on imports of foreign grain. "Senex" and Leavitt argued that an American campaign to force England to repeal or modify the Corn Laws would boost the price of grain and relieve the stagnation in the flour trade brought on by the depression that had plagued the country since the Panic of 1837. Leavitt pushed the antislavery phase of the argument further by claiming that repeal of the Corn Laws "will strike one of the heaviest blows at slavery by relieving the free states from the dependency on cotton as the only means of paying their foreign debt."[16] Over the next five years, until the Corn Laws were repealed in 1846, Leavitt would hammer away at the need for an end to their iniquitious restriction in order to promote economic prosperity in the Northwest and to undercut the slave power's grip on the nation's foreign economic policy.

At an antislavery convention in Albany, New York in the spring of 1840 the "Friends of Immediate Emancipation" nominated James G. Birney for President and Thomas Earle of Pennsylvania for Vice President. In accepting the nomination Birney outlined a political program for what became the Liberty Party that not only was premised on the movement ideology but also was designed to activate an abolitionist foreign policy. "The truth is," Birney stated, "the government of the country is in the hands of the slave power." He believed this had been the case since 1820 when "that power" triumphed on the "Missouri question" and gained the ascendency "in direct antagonism to the free institutions everywhere." The slave power's hostility to commerce was evident in the policy of nonrecognition of Haiti. The island republic, "teeming with the most valuable products, and wanting what we can furnish," was ready to supply "us a valuable trade" but only if "commercial intercourse can be conducted on terms of mutual benefit and dignity."[17] Such hostility was not surprising to the native southerner and former slaveowner:

> For what can a free, republican and commercial state look for, but confusion and ruin, when they entrust their affairs to a people without commerce, without manufactures, without arts, without industry, whose whole system of management is one of expense, waste, credit and procrastination.[18]

Slavery and the slave power were defined by the presidential candidate as fetters on national progress; to unfetter the American republic Birney announced that the Liberty Party's primary goals were "the rescue of the country from the domination of the Slave Power and for the emancipation of the slaves." His order of priority in stating these goals foreshadowed a clear change in emphasis that had been predicted by those abolitionists who opposed independent political action for just that reason.[19] As the movement became increasingly political in the 1840s, it also became more concerned with economic and social issues that directly affected northern white Americans, and less committed to black freedom and racial equality.

Shortly after Birney accepted the party's nomination he sailed for England with Stanton to attend the first World's Anti-Slavery Convention in London. Joshua Leavitt, who became the party's self-appointed campaign manager, wrote Birney about the political and economic virtues of the Corn Law scheme, suggesting the London Convention should "appoint a committee to consider the bearing of the Corn Laws on the question of slavery." With the 1840 and future Liberty Party campaigns in mind, Leavitt instructed Birney: "If you can be instrumental in opening a market for Western flour, it will be of the greatest advantage—even the attempt will be regarded with favor in our N.W. states." Apparently Leavitt was still working out the details of the Corn Law strategy and was trying to keep

Birney abreast of matters so that he might speak in behalf of the proposal to the leaders of the British antislavery movement. Whether or not Birney and Stanton went out on the circuit in England that summer and fall preaching for a joint Anglo-American effort to repeal the Corn Laws is unclear. What is clear, however, is that Leavitt continued to refine the argument, all the while forwarding additional information to Birney and Stanton and looking for a way to sail to Britain to deliver personally the anti-Corn Law message.[20]

Although Leavitt failed to reach England that summer, he did serve as the Liberty Party's chief campaigner during its first presidential canvass. In the fall of 1840 he traveled to Ohio, then the nation's top wheat-producing state, to deliver a series of speeches on the slave power theme and the news that Corn Law repeal would open a huge market for American wheat exports. In the course of stumping for the Birney-Earle ticket Leavitt offered Ohio voters an alternative approach to foreign policy that succinctly articulated the diplomatic goals of antislavery. To begin with, he assumed that "the people of the great grain-growing West know and feel that our present slavocratic democratic administration have done nothing, have attempted nothing, have thought of nothing, towards opening a market for the immense products of their farms." If they wanted to change and broaden the nation's diplomacy then "only an anti-slavery administration can open the market, first in Haiti, and then in Great Britain, Ireland, France, which will be adequate to the exigencies of the North West, and aid in diffusing the blessings of commerce, peace, civilization and liberty over the globe."[21]

The 1840 Liberty effort drew little support from the American electorate as the Whig victory led by William Henry Harrison over the Democratic incumbent Martin Van Buren occupied center stage for American voters. But for Liberty supporters the overriding impact of the campaign was as an educational process, for the leadership as well as the rank and file. Steadily and surely the abolitionist ideology was being transformed into a coherent political program. Leavitt perfected his Corn Law argument in two "Wheat Memorials" that he publicly circulated and submitted to the United States Congress and the New York State legislature. In these memorials the editor of the *Emancipator* presented exhaustive evidence to demonstrate the benefits that would result for the United States if the British Corn Laws were repealed. Leavitt made no reference in his tracts to the connection of repeal to antislavery nor did he employ the slave power theme. While the antislavery implications of his scheme were clear to informed abolitionists, and probably just as evident to the proslavery forces, he apparently felt it necessary to bring the project before a national audience to gain legitimacy. Leavitt was playing a dangerous game. Stressing the national benefits may have appeared to be sound strategy, but in the end it backfired.[22]

In May 1841 the Liberty Party met in New York City to complete the transformation of abolitionist ideology into political practice. The delegates raised policy to a more sophisticated level, moving from a purely reactive policy to offering an official alternative to existing diplomacy. Tired of witnessing "the reign of the Slave Power over this nation" and of seeing "the national diplomacy and treaty making power uniformly and efficiently subservient to the interests of slavery at the expense of national interests, and the national honor," they promised a Liberty administration would vigorously pursue foreign markets for the products of free labor. Presumably the quickest path to this goal was the one suggested by Joshua Leavitt. The convention wholeheartedly endorsed his remedy and formally thanked him for his memorial to the 22nd Congress "praying the adoption of measures to secure an equitable and adequate market for American wheat."[23] And one of their top priorities in this quest for markets would be to establish an immediate working alliance with the antislavery and anti-Corn Law forces in Great Britain.

The belief that repeal of the Corn Laws would bring economic prosperity to the free farmers of the North while simultaneously undermining the slave power's grip on national policy won widespread approval among the antislavery faithful by the end of 1841. It remained a staple in the program of political abolitionists until Great Britain finally removed the restrictions in 1846. During that period of less than five years the Corn Law argument was repeated incessantly in abolitionist speeches, resolutions, and pamphlets, in the pages of antislavery newspapers affiliated with the Liberty Party, and even in nonpartisan agricultural journals such as the *Genesee Farmer*. It would be quite accurate to say that the Corn Law scheme became a virtual panacea for the antislavery enterprise from the time of Leavitt's first wheat memorial until actual repeal. It represented an early example of what was to become normal, accepted practice in the American political experience: the seduction of seeking a foreign policy solution to a seemingly insoluble domestic problem.

Obviously for abolitionists it was Great Britain that held the key. If only that nation could be persuaded to open its "great markets" to American "breadstuffs" then according to adherents of this foreign policy panacea "the industry of free labor *must* and will control the action of government in five years more and mould our policy for its own advantage."[24] Of course, it was assumed by Leavitt and the bulk of the Liberty Party that Britain could be convinced to relinquish its grain restrictions because it stood to benefit enormously from such action. That was the beauty of the plan. It seemed a perfect illustration of free trade orthodoxy. Both parties to the transaction would prosper and eliminate troublesome problems. Increased American wheat exports to Britain would relieve hunger among the English lower classes by providing cheap bread; it would also provide the foreign exchange for the farmers of the Northwest to purchase British manufactured goods on a grand scale. Great Britain would be able to feed its people cheaply and find a vast new market for its manufactures, which in turn would alleviate industrial unemployment. If the Corn Law scheme appeared a panacea for American abolitionists, it seemed no less so for British reformers.

Though other aspects of abolitionist foreign policy were not forgotten—the recognition of Haiti was still demanded and the annexation of Texas stoutly resisted—the Corn Law remedy took top billing on the agenda in the early 1840s. The strategy for victory over the slave power became economic expansion and free trade via Corn Law repeal. To cement the requisite alliance between American political abolitionists and British reformers there was an informal exchange of emissaries of good will. In the summer of 1841 John Curtis of Ohio sailed for England as a "missionary" of antislavery who "goes out to aid the Anti-Corn Law League."[25] Prior to his departure Curtis met Joseph Sturge, a British Quaker on an antislavery mission to America, in Buffalo, New York enroute to Niagara Falls. This symbolic crossing of paths characterized the budding Anglo-American reform partnership and began an intellectual exchange between the two men that led to Sturge's total conversion to the American position on the tie between antislavery and Corn Law repeal.[26]

Upon his arrival in England John Curtis immediately went on the circuit spreading the abolitionist gospel on the need for repeal of the Corn Laws. He toured the industrial midlands speaking at Manchester (where he was introduced by Richard Cobden), Leeds, Blackburn, and Birmingham (where his friend Sturge, recently returned from his visit to the United States, presided over the meeting). Curtis's speeches to English audiences included a discussion, complete with statistics, of the American Northwest's vast agricultural capacity to meet Britain's demands for wheat and foodstuffs. In Manchester he boldly contended it was in England's power by opening trade in corn to release the American North of its "vassalage" to the slave power and to "strike a death-blow to American slavery." Within a few months after his arrival Curtis also published a pamphlet for the National Anti-Corn Law League entitled "America and the Corn Laws."[27] His lecture tour received extensive coverage in the London *Morning Chronicle* and in the United States the *National Intelligencer* as well as Leavitt's *Emancipator* kept the American public informed of Curtis's activities.[28]

The accounts of Curtis's lectures in the *National Intelligencer,* submitted by its Paris correspondent Robert Walsh, were mildly critical and openly skeptical about some features of his argument. Walsh doubted whether England's taking large additional supplies of northwestern grain would automatically lead to a reciprocal purchase of British manufactures by American consumers. If that did occur it might be an unfavorable development because it would mean American producers would be displaced and "the ground we have gained in manufactures" sacrificed for what at best was a questionable scheme. The correspondent also ridiculed Curtis's faith in "cheap bread as the panacea for national ills, without reflecting how many countries of Europe possess it, and yet are lamentably wretched and backward in general domestic condition." Presumably irritated by the antislavery spokesman's cocksure attitude about the validity of his proposals, Walsh caustically questioned Curtis's authority to speak for the American people and American interests.[29]

There were other Americans who wondered as well on what authority not only Curtis but all antislavery representatives were speaking for the United States and its interests. This definitely was a question raised by President Tyler and supporters of his proslavery administration. To say the least, it was politically worrisome for the administration to see abolitionists supporting free trade principles at home and abroad in an effort to gain ultimate control of the federal government and eradicate the slave interest. In the fall of 1841 Tyler sent Duff Green to England as his secret executive agent. He was to serve as an ambassador of slavery to counteract the impact of Birney, Stanton, and Curtis. Arriving in London in early December, Green quickly went on the offensive addressing letters to the press and establishing contacts with prominent Englishmen in finance and business. He also employed the carrot-and-stick approach with his hosts. The carrot was the offer of a commercial treaty with the United States that was favorable to Southern cotton and Northwestern grain and that would protect Britain's raw material sources and its global commercial supremacy. The stick, usually applied anonymously in the columns of English newspapers and journals, involved a denunciation of Great Britain's hostility to slavery and support for the emancipation crusade. Britain's support for antislavery was not, according to Green, motivated by philanthropic or altruistic concerns; its true goal was to enhance Britain's economic power in the world. This would be accomplished by destroying slavery in Brazil, Cuba, Texas, and the United States, leaving British possessions with a monopoly of basic raw materials.[30]

Other administration supporters charged that the Liberal Party was England's mouthpiece, serving British interests, not American. Henry A. Wise of Virginia in a lengthy speech before the House of Representatives identified Leavitt and Birney as foreign agents in the pay of Britain. The entire antislavery enterprise was characterized by Representative Wise as an operation directed and financed by Britain. In a speech before the Virginia Legislature, Thomas Gilmer made a similar observation about the designated Liberty ticket of Birney and Morris. The blatantly clear political and economic connections between American abolitionists and British reformers were cited as evidence to support these charges. In attempting to discredit abolitionism and cast doubt on its legitimacy as a domestic reform movement, the Tyler forces appealed to the American public's residual Anglophobia. It was extremely doubtful that the charges were true. But the abolitionists' reliance on the Corn Law panacea and their cultivation of an Anglo-American reform coalition made them vulnerable to such attacks on their patriotism.

Leavitt and his cohorts were undaunted by the assault launched and led by Green, Wise, and Gilmer. The abolitionists tried to maintain the offensive by charging that "the peculiar institution" endangered American security in time of national peril. An attack on the United States by a naval enemy undoubtedly would be directed against Southern shores in anticipation that a slave insurrection would ensue, thus placing the defense of the entire country in jeopardy. Slavery was the nation's Achilles heel according to Leavitt and he asserted that the Tyler administration recognized America's vulnerability on this score. Why else, asked Leavitt in the *Emancipator,* had Secretary of the Navy Abel P. Upshur, a fellow Virginian and close confidant of President Tyler, recommended a naval buildup in his recent annual report? It may have been that Upshur wanted a larger navy to protect American commerce, which Leavitt would favor if that indeed were the primary motive. The *Emancipator* editor suspected otherwise; Upshur's report heavily emphasized the need for improved coastal defenses as the reason for increased naval expenditures. He concluded that Upshur and Tyler intended "the services of the navy for the defense of slavery."[31] Once again national interests were to be subsumed to the interest of the slave power.

The question of the annexation of Texas remained a concern for abolitionists especially with slaveholder John Tyler in the White House. The Tyler administration avoided exciting public opinion on the issue until early 1843 when Gilmer published a letter in the *Madisonian* recommending immediate annexation of Texas. Although the former Governor of Virginia attempted to emphasize national, not sectional, advantage, the reaction in the North was unfavorable. Nothing much came of Gilmer's trial balloon, but editor Leavitt remained vigilant by warning his readers that the annexation "issue never will be abandoned until the leading politicians of the South abandon slavery itself."[32] That summer Leavitt attended the second World Anti-Slavery Convention in London and in a series of meetings with leading British abolitionists, including Joseph Sturge, solicited their support on the Texas issue. He made clear to convention delegates his belief that continued Texan independence would be a major blow to the designs of American slavery.

However, the main objective of Leavitt's trip to England in 1843 was to present personally to the British public the virtues of his Corn Law scheme. His analysis had undergone some refinement in the three years since he had first proposed the plan. On the anti-Corn Law circuit in England after the Anti-Slavery Convention had ended, Leavitt now attacked the British aristocracy as a main obstacle to repeal. As beneficiaries of the discriminating grain duties, the landed aristocracy resisted all efforts to alter the *status quo.* To overcome this opposition to repeal, Leavitt supported the Chartist campaign for extended suffrage. In late July at a large Anti-Corn Law League meeting in London Leavitt appeared on the platform with Richard Cobden and John Bright. In his speech before the assembly he claimed a conspiracy against Corn Law repeal existed among British aristocrats and American slaveholders. This charge shortly would be rendered absurd as Leavitt belatedly realized that his opponents also understood that repeal might operate to their political benefit. Next on Leavitt's English agenda was a private audience with British Foreign Secretary Lord Aberdeen to discuss British and American tariff policy.[33] This exercise in private diplomacy stirred critics at home and set in motion another more sweeping counteroffensive by the administration.

Upon his return to the United States in August Joshua Leavitt proceeded to Buffalo, New York to attend the Liberty Party convention. Candidates for the party's 1844 ticket were chosen at the meeting and an official party platform was adopted. Despite opposition from Salmon P. Chase of Ohio—who favored men of greater national political prominence— the delegates strongly endorsed James Birney and Thomas Morris as the Liberty candidates for President and Vice President. The Liberty Party platform affirmed its members' belief in the antislavery ideology that had emerged over the past decade. The familiar litany of slave power abuses, originally exposed by Maria Child, John Quincy Adams, and William Jay, was reiterated as justification for their demand that "the National Government be rescued from the grasp of the slave power." The foreign policy plank of the platform, while not mentioning or recommending Leavitt's Corn Law scheme, deplored a national policy that "strains every effort of negotiation, to secure the markets of the world for the products of slave labor" while ignoring the needs of free labor. In order to insure the "permanent prosperity" of the entire nation the Liberty platform insisted that government "exert its utmost energies to extend the markets for the products of free labor."[34] In preparing for the 1844 campaign the Liberty Party had converted an ideology into a formal political program. The slave power analysis had become the ideological cement of political abolitionism.

The Tyler administration's response to Leavitt's private diplomacy and the Liberty Party's sustained attack on the slave power was a series of foreign policy initiatives designed to outmaneuver the abolitionists while stifling the antislavery challenge posed by Great Britain. Earlier, during his first trip to England, Duff Green had realized that Britain essentially had two options for retaining worldwide commercial supremacy. The British might continue to pursue their current course, which Green considered one of universal hostility to slavery and the slave trade. This policy was predicated on the belief that destruction of slavery in its remaining strongholds of Brazil, Cuba, Texas, and the United States would increase the cost of raw materials to Britain's manufacturing rivals, allowing the British to retain a competitive edge in world markets. Green believed the British were also working to establish a monopoly of the oceans, particularly in the Pacific. The other option involved a move toward free trade, including repeal of the Corn Laws, to lower the cost of production for British industry and open new markets for British exports. Given those choices, Green not surprisingly favored the second option as less threatening to an American administration intent on preserving its peculiar institution. As he wrote to Secretary of State Daniel Webster in early 1842, the trick was to compel England "to fall back on the principles of free trade. She will, in that event, open her ports to our corn, and having abandoned her warfare on our manufactures, will cease to annoy our domestic institutions."[35]

Ironically both Leavitt and Green came to favor repeal of the Corn Laws. Obviously they did so for different reasons and in anticipation of different results. Both expected to kill two birds—one foreign and one domestic—with a single stone. Leavitt advocated repeal as the way to loosen the slave power's grip on foreign policy by opening a vast market for American grain, which in turn would knit an antislavery political alliance between the Northeast and the Northwest. Green saw repeal primarily as the way to have Britain abandon its antislavery crusade and its threat to American slavery. He also hoped a complementary result would be the forging of a South-Northwest political coalition that might propel Tyler, or another proslavery Southerner such as John C. Calhoun, to victory in 1844.

While Tyler and his chosen advisors, particularly Upshur, did not feel compelled to act on Green's version of the benefits of Corn Law repeal, they did mount a foreign policy blitz that included the free trade objective of a liberalized commercial treaty with Britain. They also pushed for a stronger navy to promote and protect overseas commercial expansion, and not merely for coastal defense. To allow for American trade expansion in the Pacific the Tyler administration contemplated annexation of the Hawaiian islands and, more importantly, in 1844 succeeded in negotiating the United States' first treaty with China. On the expansionist agenda as well were concerted and secret diplomatic attempts to annex Texas and the strategy of securing Oregon for the North as a trade-off for Texas. All of these diplomatic initiatives were intended to outmaneuver Anglo-American abolitionism and to create a national political alignment that would allow Tyler, on the strength of his foreign policy record and the restoration of economic prosperity, to win election to a second term on his own merit.

Tyler's activist foreign policy did not win him another term in the White House. But his efforts did lay the groundwork for his successor James K. Polk, a fellow proslavery Southerner, to consummate his foreign policy strategy. Polk had openly employed the Texas-for-Oregon ploy in his victory over Henry Clay, a victory many argued had been made possible by the Liberty Party's strong showing in New York, denying Clay the electoral votes of that crucial state. Spurred by what he perceived to be the electorate's approval of Polk's call for annexation, and wishing to take credit for bringing Texas into the Union, Tyler pushed through annexation by joint resolution of Congress in the last weeks of his presidency. That bit of constitutional sleight of hand outraged abolitionists and confirmed their belief in the evil machinations of the slave power. When Polk formalized the process in December he administered the *coup de grace* to the antislavery opponents of annexation.

To fulfill the Oregon portion of its expansionist platform, the Polk administration took up the anti-Corn Law argument perfected by Leavitt and propagated by the Liberty Party in the previous five years. Implicitly acknowledging the validity of Duff Green's argument that repeal could be turned to the South's advantage, the Polk Democrats appealed to the Northwest's need for a foreign market for its foodstuffs, and in turn expected that region's Congressional support for reduced tariffs and a move toward free trade. To sweeten the economic pie, the westerners were led to believe their call for waterway improvements would receive the administration's support through the passage of a federal rivers and harbors bill.

The Democratic strategy proved successful, at least in the short run. Support for tariff reduction came from the Northwest in 1846 with the passage of the Walker tariff. In conjunction with the American action, Great Britain repealed the Corn Laws. Although the evidence for some sort of free trade bargain between the United States and Britain leading to the Oregon compromise is inconclusive, the governments of both nations by 1846 had come to accept the view that mutual tariff reduction would lead to mutual economic benefits. In that Anglo-American diplomatic climate a compromise on territorial issues was possible as well. The peaceful settlement of the Oregon dispute at the 49th parallel was the result. The Polk package, deftly uniting foreign policy objectives and domestic political objectives, seemed complete. Certainly the political abolitionists recognized they had been outmaneuvered: two could play the same game in using the Corn Law scheme for political ends. But Polk and his supporters failed to follow up on their foreign policy victories. The hopes for a Democratic ascendancy based on a political alliance between the South and Northwest were dashed when President Polk vetoed the rivers and harbors bill in the summer of 1846.

To their credit some of the Liberty Party editors, especially the *Emancipator*'s Joshua Leavitt, had seen what was happening to their Corn Law scheme. They backed off, and by early 1846 were cautioning the Northwest that the promised bonanza of the British market might be mere illusion. Leavitt approved a "wait and see" approach.[36] But there was no escaping the fact the Liberty men had been coopted. One of their most important foreign policy planks had been absorbed by the opposition—an all too familiar pattern in American politics. It was a bitter pill to swallow and the initial reaction was to deny the validity of their own analysis, which over the past five years had been so forcefully presented as the key to ending the slave power's dominance of the nation's foreign policy. Of course, as one prominent economic historian has pointed out, repeal "signaled the emergence of a large scale international wheat market with England as its center," which in the long run brought the economic benefits to the American Northwest that Leavitt and others had predicted.[37] But it did not bring the promised immediate demise of the slave power and in that sense the strategy had been oversold politically. The slave power ideology remained intact. The abolitionist challenge after 1846 was to find other political and diplomatic strategies to combat and ultimately destroy the slave power.

In the wake of the annexation of Texas and the repeal of the British Corn Laws the abolitionist search for a new foreign policy strategy was brief. The question of territorial expansion was quickly reinstated as a paramount concern of the antislavery forces after the United States declared war on Mexico in May 1846. The Polk administration, apparently not satisfied with Texas, greedily sought more Mexican territory for the extension of slavery and slave power. Birney, Chase, and Leavitt, to name but a few of the more prominent Liberty leaders, did not share either former President Tyler's or Polk's confidence that the extension of the sphere guaranteed the nation's future. Ambivalent at best about territorial expansion during the heyday of "manifest destiny," most Liberty Party members questioned Tyler's claim that "there exists nothing in the extension of our Empire over our acknowledged possessions to excite the alarm of the patriot for the safety of our institutions."[38] For them the extension of the sphere was synonymous with the extension of slavery, and Tyler's self-imposed limitation of "acknowledged possessions" was a meaningless phrase if the administration's territorial ambitions in reality were boundless. At stake, as the Wilmot Proviso symbolized, was the future direction of the nation: would it be slave or free? For Liberty Party members as for all antislavery Americans, slavery and the slave power must not be allowed to monopolize America's future. With the appearance of the Texas controversy and the outbreak of the Mexican War, the question of territorial expansion, as Stanley Elkins has observed, became the moral metaphor for the future in the antebellum United States. At issue was whether new territory "would be dominated by one total ideological configuration or by the other."[39]

The antislavery identification of territorial expansion as the moral metaphor for the nation's future dominated the movement ideology in the years between the Mexican War and the Civil War. Translated almost immediately into the political rallying cry of "free soil," this foreign policy component of the ideology displaced the earlier emphasis on a "free diplomacy" unfettered by the slave power and dedicated to commercial expansion for the products of free labor. The concept of a "free diplomacy" formed an integral part of the slave power idea that evolved into an abolitionist ideology. When it emerged in the 1830s antislavery foreign policy also prompted the first truly democratic, grass-roots lobbying effort to restructure American diplomacy. It failed in that mission, but the legacy of the original antislavery foreign policy, which sought to "aid in diffusing the blessings of commerce, peace, civilization and liberty over the globe," would be evident in the ideology of the Republican Party and would reappear as one of the pervasive themes of post-Civil War American diplomacy.

"Europe First" and its Consequences for the Far Eastern Policy of the United States

Fred Harvey Harrington

In December 1941 the United States was attacked in the Pacific by an Asian power, Japan, and suffered the most humiliating defeat in the nation's history. Whereupon the military and political decision makers in the American government decided that our top priority was defeating a European power, Germany.

Shocked as they were by the Pearl Harbor catastrophe, most Americans if polled at that time would probably have favored designating Japan as Enemy Target Number One. The Europe First choice, however, was in line with the position most officials, and most citizens, had held for a century and a half: that in calculating the national interest of the United States Europe and the Atlantic were clearly more important than eastern Asia and the Pacific.

It could hardly have been otherwise, given the European background of the American republic, and our many transatlantic ties. Unfortunately, this approach carried with it a tendency to think of the Far East in European rather than Asian terms. Most members of the American public and their official representatives neglected the Far East. They made little effort to understand the problems and aspirations of the people of China, Japan, and Korea, or the people of south and southeast Asia and the Pacific Islands. On the contrary, they regarded Asians with indifference or hostility, not the best basis for building policy.

Economic, strategic, and other forces modified the situation somewhat late in the nineteenth century, as the United States became aware of its strength on the Pacific and new status as a world power. Some then toyed with thoughts of Asia First. But there soon followed a retreat from the Far East, under way even before World War I firmly reestablished Europe First, for a full thirty years.

There have been cataclysmic changes in Asia in the decades since World War II. Beaten in battle, Japan has come back as an extraordinarily strong exporter of goods and capital. China, long impotent, has been united and strengthened under communist rule. India, Indonesia, and other independent nations have replaced the European colonies in south and southeast Asia and the Pacific.

Inevitably, the United States has been affected by these developments. American trade with the region has grown dramatically, and now exceeds our trade with Europe. We have become heavily involved in Far East diplomacy, increasing commitments as western European powers have reduced theirs. American blood, a great deal of American blood, has been shed on Asian soil. News coverage of the Far East has expanded, as has travel to that area; and the United States now has a fair number of scholars with expertise on Asia.

Has this brought an end to the Europe First theme in foreign policy? Attitudes and policies can change. Altered circumstances have more than once persuaded policy makers to abandon long-cherished positions (defense of neutral rights, for instance, and no entangling alliances, both once considered "fundamental principles of American foreign policy"). Have the new developments across the Pacific caused the United States government to forge new policies based on an understanding of Asian nationalism and the special problems of east, southeast, and south Asia—poverty, overpopulation, ethnic, linguistic and religious friction, political repression and human rights, and conflicts within the region?

Well, these matters have received some attention. But the Cold War has overshadowed everything else in the years since 1945. Presidents from Harry S. Truman to Ronald Reagan have weighed world problems in terms of "stop-the-Russians." This has meant subordinating—really, neglecting—important local and regional questions in the developing world. It has also meant the survival of Europe First. For the Soviet Union is more a European than an Asian power; and in its competition with the Russians, the United States government knows that it must have the support of western European allies.

President Reagan's trip to Europe in the spring of 1985 will be remembered chiefly for his ill-advised visit to the Bitburg cemetery. One leading commentator, though, noted that the tour also had a Europe First flavor. "It demonstrated that the United States still gives prime concern to its Atlantic partners even though the Pacific links are greatly expanded."[1]

Europe First: The Basic Pattern

In their first century of independence Americans made much of the uniqueness of their mission. They contrasted their democratic institutions with what they termed the decadence of monarchical Europe. Linked with this was pride in their republic's ability to avoid involvement in Europe's power struggles. Actually, however, the United States was for all practical purposes a part of the European system. Economic requirements, national origins and culture, and diplomatic necessity bound Americans to Europe— and there were no comparable ties to the Far East.

Economic: As a developing nation, the United States obtained needed investment capital from London and the Continent, for the First Bank of the United States, for the purchase of Louisiana, the Erie Canal, railroads, and western land development. The young republic also looked to Europe for the imports and exports required for economic growth. Expansion of the domestic market eventually reduced the near-total dependency, but the European connection remained an absolutely essential element in the American economy.

Economic ties with the Far East were far less important. Whalers and traders in tea and opium did establish the United States on the Pacific early in the nineteenth century. This helped with the international balance of payments and familiarized Americans with oriental bric-a-brac. But these shipowners touched only the rim of Asia, and they did not try to understand the inhabitants of that continent. Their single-minded interest was in profit. ("Go where you please," wrote one owner to his captain, "but for God's sake don't lose anything."[2])

National Origins and Culture: European links, important in economic matters, were even more impressive on the cultural side. In the early days of the republic, most Americans were of British descent. They spoke English, and only English. Their legal, political, educational, and religious institutions had English roots. They read English books, relied on the mother country for technological innovations. They followed British leadership in many areas of social reform. And newcomers from England and Scotland adjusted quickly to life in the United States; they were the "invisible immigrants."

Along with the British ties there were many other transatlantic influences. Immigrants poured in from Ireland, Germany, and Scandinavia, later from southern and eastern Europe. In science, music, theater and painting, the United States was virtually a European colony, with Americans studying in Europe and Europeans touring on this side of the Atlantic. Well-to-do Americans vacationed in Europe, or went there on business and diplomatic assignments. Their libraries were stocked with books from England and the Continent.

Europe, always Europe. When they referred to the Old World, Americans meant Europe, not the older world beyond. History outside of the American experience meant Europe and the Mediterranean, with the Far East included only when it was "discovered" by European explorers. There was lively interest in the French Revolution and Napoleon, the Greek War of Independence, Europe's 1848 revolutions, Fenian activities. But the Indian Mutiny of 1857 won only minor notice, and that because it was a revolt against the British. The long and bloody Taiping Rebellion, which shook China to its foundations, received almost no attention in the United States.

Immigrants from Europe met with discrimination when they crossed the Atlantic; but their reception was gentle compared to the treatment accorded the first arrivals from eastern Asia. Racism, language and religious barriers, dislike for unfamiliar social customs all played a part, as did nativism and economic competition among workers. What followed could fill volumes in the history of prejudice. Featured were discriminatory laws, outright exclusion, longtime denial of citizenship to those of Asian ancestry. Not to mention horrors, from the Rock Springs massacre of Chinese laborers in 1885 to World War II concentration camp imprisonment of Japanese- (but not German- or Italian-) Americans.

Lack of understanding and contrasts in attitudes were also apparent on the cultural level. A few Americans, notably the transcendentalists, were influenced by India's literary and religious classics. Generally, though, Americans learned about the Far East from the Protestant missionaries, who saw eastern and southern Asia as prime mission fields. These Christian agents learned Eastern languages, mixed with Asians and turned out many books. But they went out to instruct, not to learn. Most of them looked down on Orientals and their "heathen" cultures; and they passed their prejudices on to their compatriots back home.

Diplomacy: It was much the same in international relations. Europe was of central concern to the United States, the Far East much less so.

Granted, the American republic sometimes resorted to bluster during disagreements with European nations (the Monroe Doctrine, "Fifty-Four Forty or Fight," the Ostend Manifesto). Yet in the main American officials proceeded with caution when dealing with the European powers, preferred diplomacy to force, and chose distinguished citizens to handle negotiations with them.

In contrast, few prominent Americans were involved in transpacific diplomacy. The best known of those who went to eastern Asia, Caleb Cushing and Anson Burlingame, did so only after they were rejected for posts in Washington and Europe. Far Eastern assignments often went to naval officers and second-level politicians who were uninformed about the Far East and thought of Asians as inferior. Consequently they saw no impropriety and little risk in using force or the threat of force in dealing with Asian governments.

Often this meant joining Britain and Continental powers in threats or action. Working with Europeans in a "cooperative policy" seemed natural to Americans who saw "civilized people" lining up against the "unenlightened," Christians against "heathens" or "savages." Josiah Tattnall, of the United States Navy, echoed this view when he gave naval assistance to the British against the Chinese in 1859. "Blood is thicker than water," said the commodore, adding that he would "be damned if he'd stand by and see white men butchered before his eyes."[3] An earlier example was John Quincy Adams's trader-inspired defense of the British position during the Opium War.

Sometimes representatives of the United States acted independently of the Europeans. Minor trade disputes in which Americans were not without fault led the United States Navy to destroy a Sumatran village in 1832 and, with diplomatic encouragement, to slaughter over two hundred Koreans in 1871. Threat of force was a factor in the opening of Japan and Korea to outside commerce, though these nations yielded to the Americans in part out of fear of attacks from stronger western nations.

Officials back in Washington authorized all this activity. It fitted in with a desire to support trade, missionary effort, and the national honor. But, rating the Far East as an area of secondary importance, the policy makers were reluctant to go further. Time after time in the middle of the nineteenth century they rejected or ignored suggestions that the United States add to its diplomatic and naval strength in the western Pacific, and acquire territory there. The proposals to take colonies came from Matthew C. Perry, a naval officer; from businessmen like Gideon Nye; from Peter Parker, a missionary-diplomat.

These annexation possibilities came when internal conflicts were driving Americans toward civil war. The domestic crisis left little time for international adventures. Europe still demanded attention, since England and the Continental powers were factors in the American sectional controversy (European aid to the Confederacy, French invasion of Mexico). But who could think of distant Asia?

Nor did the situation change immediately after the Civil War. Whaling and the carrying trade declined, reducing America's economic stake in the Pacific and eastern Asia. The last of the great China traders, Russell and Company, closed its doors in 1891. Meanwhile, missionary efforts to persuade Americans to show sympathetic interest in Asia were offset by mounting opposition to immigration from the Orient.

Rising Interest in the Pacific and Eastern Asia

Late in the nineteenth century and early in the twentieth there was an increase in American interest and activity in the Pacific and eastern Asia. The United States acquired colonies in the mid- and western Pacific; sought a naval base in China; joined European powers and Japan in the Boxer military expedition on the Asian mainland; pressed for trade and investment opportunities alone and in an international consortium; supported stepped-up missionary endeavors; bid for diplomatic leadership with the Open Door notes, with mediation in the Russo-Japanese war and with a neutralization proposal for Manchuria.

This burst of imperialist activity caused some speculation as to a possible shift of priorities away from Europe. Then the situation changed again, with an American retreat from the Far East. But what happened is worth examining, in view of the present-day importance of Asia to the United States.

One of the major reasons for this upsurge of interest in a region that had received so little emphasis was a search for foreign markets.

Promoting exports had always been important to the United States; perhaps it was the "most consistent theme in American foreign policy."[4] Securing outlets for farm products was the central problem during the first century after independence; and the outlets were mainly in Europe. Continuing strong in agriculture after the Civil War, the United States added strength in manufacturing. Although the expanding domestic market absorbed many of these products, many producers depended heavily on foreign sales. And during the cruel depressions of the 1870s and 1890s observers noted that American ability to produce was far outrunning home demand. As Robert W. Shufeldt stated in 1878: "At least one-third of our mechanical and agricultural products are now in excess of own wants, and we *must* export these products."[5]

Export where? The American government did try to protect traditional transatlantic markets by opposing European moves to discriminate against American farm products. At the same time, politicians, businessmen, and others looked east to Europe for new markets for agricultural and industrial goods, north to Canada, south to Latin America—and west across the Pacific.

Commodore Shufeldt, just quoted, was one of those who had his eye on the Far East; he knew Asian waters as a naval officer instructed to protect trade, and he would presently handle negotiations for the opening of Korea to foreign commerce. Secretaries of State from William H. Seward to James G. Blaine to John Hay were intrigued by the possibilities, and gave encouragement to exporters (State Department publications on trade opportunities, published annually before 1880, were brought out daily before the end of the century). Businessmen, editors, and politicians saw "vast undeveloped fields" for sales in the Far East, opportunities "such as were never presented to any nation." There would be "new, large and increasing markets" for "our surplus meat and bread, cotton goods . . . and other products," a chance to solve the "serious problem" posed by "our prospective surplus of manufactures."[6]

Navy spokesmen joined in predicting a great future for exports to the Orient. This fitted in with their service's traditional role as protector of American merchants overseas, and with their successful late nineteenth century drive for a world navy. Alfred T. Mahan's sea power doctrines, unveiled in these years, also emphasized Far Eastern trade.

So did the missionaries, most of whom believed that the flow of western goods helped them introduce Christianity and democracy (the Bible and the ballot box) into non-Christian lands. The post-Civil War years saw a major increase in mission effort; and hopes for success were centered on eastern and southern Asia.

Tying all this together was a mounting interest in the Pacific Ocean. At the time of independence the United States hugged the Atlantic; settlements were on the coast and near rivers flowing into that ocean. In the decades that followed, westward expansion moved Americans across the continent. This excited the national imagination—if the Atlantic was a European lake, the Pacific was "our ocean." Acquisition of Russian Alaska and increasing American influence in Hawaii strengthened this feeling, which suited the American expansionist philosophy and the imperialist ideas then building up in Europe.

Time brought disappointment, especially in trade. Ignorance of Asian conditions had produced extravagant expectations. Americans interested in export operations hopelessly overestimated the purchasing power of the residents of the Far East. At the same time they underestimated the difficulties of trading with the Orient and the strength of the competition (chiefly from Britain, though also from Continental Europe and, later, from Japan). So Americans found modest rather than spectacular markets in China, Korea, and Japan. They did less well there than in Canada, Latin America, and Europe and in their expanding home market.

But although these dreams of great success across the Pacific failed of realization, they had long-term influence on American foreign policy.

To cite four examples:

1) Plunging into a Cuban war with Spain in 1898, the United States crushed a Spanish fleet in Manila Bay and won a foothold in the Philippines. Desire to capture Far East trade, notably in China, played a significant part in the decision to "keep" (really, to purchase) the islands. This gave the United States a distant possession difficult to defend, a distressing three-year war with Filipino freedom fighters, and many subsequent complications.

2) The same interest in increased trade was behind John Hay's Open Door notes of 1899. These notes, and their 1900 sequel, had next to no impact on the troubled China scene when they were issued. Yet they were well received at home, for John Hay understood the value of catchwords. Almost immediately the Open Door became a permanent part of the American diplomatic vocabulary. Successive generations of officials would use it to suggest that the United States had higher motives than other powers; and to justify United States intervention in eastern Asia and elsewhere.

3) Investment and trade go hand in hand in developing countries. Hence in encouraging exports to eastern Asia Americans joined in the scramble for concessions and other investment opportunities. Wall Street and Washington were not fully prepared for this, since the United States was still a debtor nation and its financiers had little surplus capital to send abroad. Still, they tried, the bankers operating with government guidance and support for a generation from 1890 to the Taft-Knox dollar diplomacy days.

The results were catastrophically bad. In Korea American concession-aires sold out to the Japanese, to the distress of the Korean government. China projects failed to get off the ground. An American-sponsored neutralization proposal for Manchuria drove Russia and Japan together, to the disadvantage of China. The first Consortium, in which the United States played a leading role, was little more than a six-power effort to control China; it helped to bring on the Chinese revolution of 1911.

4) In going after Far Eastern business, Americans learned a little, though not much, about the people who lived across the Pacific. They did not, however, learn to like Orientals, or to accept them as equals. Asians still encountered hostility and discrimination in the United States. The situation was made worse in these imperialist days as Americans were deluged by a flood of literature extolling the superiority of their Anglo-Saxon heritage and their "duty" as white people to control and guide the "inferior" colored races. Although military victories won respect for the Japanese, that respect was soon mixed with suspicion, even a touch of fear.

Inevitably, Americans operating in the Orient felt closer to their European competitors than to their Asian customers. There was friction sometimes, most frequently with the Russians; but the United States government often worked with combinations of the European powers (or the European powers and Japan) in seeking solutions to the China question such as the Open Door, the Boxer Protocol, or the Chinese Consortium. Here again was the "cooperative policy," offering Western approaches to Eastern problems.

Retreat from the Far East

Disappointment at many levels led to an American pullback from the Far East in the years before World War I. Trade and investment developed too slowly to satisfy business or the State Department. Passage of new immigration restrictions led to a Chinese boycott of American goods. Other powers paid only lip service, if that, to the Open Door (for that matter, the United States was not generous in applying that doctrine in the Philippines). Russia and China cooperated to check American thrusts into Manchuria; and after Washington used strongarm tactics to force its way into the Chinese Consortium, neither Wall Street nor the American government was happy with the results. Few grieved when President Woodrow Wilson pulled the United States out of the Consortium in 1913.

The military picture was even more discouraging. The Navy failed to get either its base in China or adequate funds for Philippine defense, so it pulled back to Pearl Harbor. Japan, considered a friend during the Russo-Japanese war, seemed less so later, as she absorbed Korea (without protest from the United States) and became more active in China and on the Pacific. By then it was apparent that the Philippines, at first thought of as a strategic asset, were the opposite, an Achilles heel. And President Theodore Roosevelt, for all his earlier enthusiasm about our Far East future, came to the conclusion that it would be unwise to risk a land war in Asia to defend the Open Door.

The missionaries also fell short of their objective of christianizing the Orient. Pressing for conversions and opposing Asian religions yielded only a small return, except perhaps in Korea; and there was opposition from rural people, as in the Boxer rising, and from young urban nationalists. The influential world missionary conference in Edinburgh in 1910 therefore recommended cutting back on evangelical work and concentrating on providing medical and educational assistance to developing countries.

Meantime, European prospects were improving. Despite their fears, American manufacturers found that they could compete with Europeans on their home ground, that American iron and steel could undersell the British on the London market. Farm exports to Europe held up, too, in spite of predictions that it would be necessary to dispose of both industrial and agricultural surpluses in new markets.

That was just the beginning. After 1914, World War I gave unlimited opportunities in Europe to American farmers, manufacturers, and investment bankers. This much reduced the importance of other areas. In fact, in tightening ties with Europe, United States business missed some promising openings in the Far East and Latin America.

For the American public and for President Wilson World War I was almost totally a European affair. Entering the war as a belligerent in 1917, the United States fought in Europe against a European enemy, the Kaiser's Germany. Our soldiers served side by side with French and British partners. The public back home saw the war as a struggle to save democracy and civilization, defined in American and European terms; and in Europe, at Versailles, our President and three European leaders dominated the peace negotiations.

The war did have a Pacific and east Asian side, with Japan taking over German holdings and increasing its influence in China. Like other Americans, Wilson suspected that the Japanese advance posed a threat to United States interests. But, absorbed in Europe (no one was more Europe First than he), he did little to check the Japanese. Rather, he gave way to Japan in the Lansing-Ishii agreement and, after pressure from the European Allies, in the Versailles treaty. He did organize a new Consortium in an effort to prevent Japan from monopolizing loans to China; and he sent troops to northeast Asia when it seemed that the Japanese might take advantage of the confusion that followed the Russian Revolution. Neither move was especially effective; and in yielding to Japan, Wilson disappointed the Chinese, the more so since their government had declared war on Germany to please the United States.

Even so, while playing his European hand, Wilson raised Asian hopes. His Fourteen Point peace plan did emphasize Europe and the adjacent Near East; but it also sounded a general call for national self-determination. The word was spread worldwide by the Committee on Public Information, an American propaganda agency. It struck a responsive chord in Asia. People under pressure, like the Chinese, found it appealing; and it appeared to hold out hope for colonial populations from Korea to the Philippines and British India. The United States, however, failed to take advantage of the resulting good will, just as it would miss opportunities to capitalize on American popularity at the close of World War II.

Europe First was under a strain in the years after World War I. High idealism faded when the war to end wars ended in an old-fashioned peace settlement; when the defeat of hated Germany was followed by the rise of a no less hated Bolshevik Russia. After the Senate failed to accept the Versailles treaty few practical politicians dared to favor American membership in the European-based League of Nations. Difficulties over repayment of war debts increased anti-European feeling; such politicians as Big Bill Thompson of Chicago were able to make political capital out of anti-British utterances.

The wisdom of keeping out of European wars was a recurring theme on into the 1930s, with humorist Will Rogers saying, "We have never lost a war or won a peace." The peace movement, crushed by World War I hysteria, staged a comeback; and a disillusioned public bought books that stated or suggested that the United States should not have fought in Europe in 1917, and should avoid European wars in the future. As George Washington had advised.

And yet, despite these strong reactions, Europe retained top priority in the view of most Americans. Economic bonds were tightened as the western world moved toward the age of multinational enterprise. Transatlantic travel and communication improved, as did cultural exchange. Britain and the United States continued the naval cooperation that had developed in World War I; and the State Department was consistently Europe First.

Relations with the Far East continued to be considered of secondary importance. Naval strategists dissented, stating that Japan rather than any European power was the "most probable enemy."[7] But few Americans were concerned, for the Japanese government was conciliatory in the 1920s, and Japan was a good trading partner. The Japanese did, however, make it difficult for Americans to do business in Korea and Manchuria. That was distressing. So was the discovery that the once-prized Philippines were in some ways an economic as well as a strategic liability. And the old desire to build up China as a center of American activity in eastern Asia ran into all sorts of obstacles: divisions within the Chinese republic, Russian influence for a while, rising nationalism, and anti-missionary, anti-Consortium, anti-foreign feeling.

The Far East remained a low priority throughout the 1930s, the decade before Pearl Harbor. During those ten years of Sino-Japanese hostilities the United States limited its opposition to Japanese aggression to a few public comments plus nonrecognition of military conquest. Until war in Europe took a critical turn there was no official boycott, no freezing of Japanese credits, no military response to such incidents as the sinking of the *Panay;* and there was little meaningful assistance to the Chinese.

By contrast, the American government moved much more quickly when the war in Europe began. Within two years the United States, still technically neutral, was providing military assistance to Hitler's opponents, had joined Britain in a statement of principles embodied in the Atlantic Charter (the name itself is significant), and was having naval encounters with German submarines.

Why the difference? There were of course special reasons for holding back when Japan seized Manchuria in 1931. The United States was wallowing in depression, and looking inward. The American military was not ready for combat, and a cautious president was in the White House. Besides, then and later China promised to be a feeble partner in any military action. And the Japanese militarists, perceived as nasty potential foes, still did not arouse the bitter antagonism that Americans would feel toward Adolf Hitler.

Feeling against Japan increased as the decade of the 1930s wore on; but the great majority of Americans were much more interested in the European developments that followed the rise of Hitler. A lifelong Europe Firster, Franklin D. Roosevelt, was in the White House. The newspapers, movies, books, ethnic groups, academic and political discussions all concentrated on the European theater. There was a rise in interventionist sentiment after the outbreak of hostilities in 1939, and especially after the fall of France and the beginning of the Battle of Britain. But even those who wanted the United States to stay out of the European troubles—the America Firsters, for example—had their eyes on Europe, not on Asia.

In the year before Pearl Harbor, polls showed that most of the public wanted to stay out of the war. Yet those same pollsters also found that Americans wanted to help England, even at the risk of war. Here one can see the force of Europe First. No one asked whether the United States should help China at the risk of war.

American participation as an acknowledged belligerent in World War II began and ended with dramatic events in the Pacific and Far East—Pearl Harbor and the dropping of the atomic bomb. During the conflict, however, it was the

> preponderance of judgment among those responsible for American strategy that the main effort of the United States in the war with the Axis Powers of Europe and Asia should be made in the European theater and that Germany must be defeated first. This . . . stands as the most important single strategic concept of the war. . . .
> Not once during the course of the war was this decision successfully challenged.[8]

It was also decided that the main assault on Japan would be from the sea rather than from the mainland of Asia. This was a sensible decision, given China's weakness and the logistical problems involved in Asian operations (which would become clear later, in Korea and Vietnam). It meant, though, that Americans at home learned quite a bit about the Pacific islands during World War II, but very little about the Asian mainland, which would be the theater of so much action after 1945.

Bypassed here, the Chinese were left out of the major policy decisions of the war. The United States did insist that China be recognized as a great power during the conflict and in the United Nations at war's end. But, meeting at Teheran and Yalta, Roosevelt, Churchill, and Stalin reached agreement on war and peace plans for eastern Asia without consulting Chiang Kai-shek. Granting all of Chiang's shortcomings (apparent even then) this nevertheless was a case of Europe First outsiders cavalierly deciding Far East questions by themselves, as they had been doing for a hundred years.

After World War II

The five years after the end of World War II saw tremendous change in east, southeast, and south Asia. The world's two most populous countries changed their forms of government, India becoming an independent republic while China turned communist. Other Asians, released from Japanese occupation, managed also to win independence from their former American, British, Dutch, and French colonial masters.

During that half decade the United States was involved in a variety of ways: as the occupying power in South Korea and Japan; by mixing, rather unhappily, in Chinese politics; by supplying aid to and establishing contact with the newly independent countries (though in the transitional period the American government tended to side with the European colonial powers).

In its priorities, however, the United States still looked to Europe. It had done so throughout World War II, in the FDR "get along with the Russians" days. It did so still as policies shifted to "check the spread of Soviet Communism." Nearly all the major thrusts of the late 1940s oriented toward Europe—the Marshall Plan, the Truman Doctrine, the Berlin blockade, creation of the North Atlantic Treaty Organization.

There was nothing really comparable in the Far East. Instead, the Truman administration considered a strategic pullback from the Asian mainland after Mao Tse-tung took over China. American troops were withdrawn from newly independent South Korea in 1949. Then, early in 1950, in a famous Press Club speech, Secretary of State Dean Acheson defined the "defense perimeter" of the United States as covering Japan and the Philippines, but not Formosa or anything on the Asian mainland, even South Korea.

However ill advised (and it was that), the Acheson statement fitted in with much that had gone before. The secretary was designating as the United States defense zone the Pacific Ocean area in which Americans had fought in World War II; and, in line with the thinking of many of his predecessors, he was indicating a desire to avoid complications on the mainland of Asia. While of course maintaining total interest in the mainland of Europe.

Truman, however, had to abandon the proposed pullback a few months after Acheson spoke. When communist North Korea moved south in June 1950, the President immediately rushed military aid to South Korea. Communist China joined on North Korea's side; and American and Allied troops were involved in a land war on the Asian mainland.

Thereafter there could be no thought of an offshore defense perimeter. President Truman, however, refused to abandon his Europe First position. He would not allow his theater commander Douglas MacArthur to broaden the Korean conflict by striking into China; nor did he seek United Nations military sanctions against that enemy. He assured his European allies that he "had no intention of widening the conflict or abandoning our commitments in Europe for new entanglements in Asia." In the developing struggle with the Soviet Union, he was convinced that "Europe . . . is still the key."[9]

Others disagreed. The communist takeover in China and the Korean War persuaded many Americans that their government had given too much attention to Europe, too little to the Far East. Longtime advocates of Asia First, missionaries and others, spoke out more boldly than before. Republicans, long in the minority, saw a good issue here. Moderates like Clare

117

Boothe Luce said somewhat inaccurately that the Republican party had favored a strong Far Eastern policy ever since the days of John Hay and the Open Door. Others followed Chiang Kai-shek's China lobby in demanding stepped-up military action across the Pacific. Senator Joseph McCarthy wildly charged that the Far Eastern policies of the Truman Democrats and the State Department smacked of communist influence and treason.

As debate heated up, the two sides seemed far apart. They were agreed, however, on one point: that the major goal of American foreign policy must be to check the spread of Soviet communism. All of Truman's European efforts had that emphasis; and when the Korean crisis broke he was sure that the Russians were behind it all. His critics did not disagree with that conclusion; they wanted more attention paid to the Far East as the best way of combating Soviet expansion. Both sides assumed for some time that the People's Republic of China was Moscow's tool.

Obviously it would have been improper to ignore the question of Soviet influence in the Far East during the 1950s. But there were other factors, too, such as Asian nationalism and regional rivalries. By almost totally concentrating on the threat of Russian communism the American government and its critics misinterpreted some Asian developments and missed important opportunities. Worse than that; the emphasis contributed to a Red Scare in the United States that lasted on into the 1960s. "Soft on communism" charges—a McCarthy specialty but indulged in by White House officials also—deprived the American government of the services of many of its best experts on the Orient. And made politicians reluctant to discuss possible alternatives in Far East policy.

Most of the seven presidents since Truman have continued to think of the Far East more in Russian than in Asian terms. The domino theory and the formation of the Southeast Asian Treaty Organization, preoccupations of Secretary of State John Foster Dulles in the Eisenhower administration, fit this pattern. So do the Vietnam troubles, which still haunt us, and attitudes toward communist China, viewed as an enemy when close to Moscow, as a possible friend after breaking with the Soviet Union. Japan was told to disarm in 1945, then was urged to rebuild her military strength as the United States became concerned about the Russian threat. The American government has appeared to excuse corruption and authoritarianism in anti-Soviet countries like the Philippines; and it has been unhappy about India's close links with the Soviet Union though India is considerably more democratic than the Philippines. The seventh post-Truman occupant of the White House, Ronald Reagan, sees the hand of what he calls the "evil empire" everywhere.

How to check Soviet Communism? With a strong Far East policy, said Asia Firsters; drive to victory in Korean and other conflicts; switch priorities from Europe. They pressed their views on Dwight Eisenhower when he succeeded Truman in 1953.

Unsuccessfully. The incoming president said he was neither Europe First nor Asia First—he did not think in such terms. His military career, however, had reached its climax in Europe, where he had served as theater commander in World War II, and as head of NATO later. He therefore closed out the Korean war as a draw—not a solution he would have found acceptable in Europe.

Yet Eisenhower took the Far East seriously, as a vital if secondary region. He went there when president, establishing a precedent since followed by all presidents, vice presidents and presidential hopefuls. Accepting the domino theory, he applied it to southeast Asia in 1954. His successors, following the theory a decade later, took the United States into the most unpopular war in American history, in Vietnam.

The fighting in Vietman turned attention to the Far East as never before; but it did not build support for Asia First. Anti-Communist though they were, most Americans saw little point in this war; eventually they regarded it with repugnance. Protests at home and lack of success in the field led President Johnson to give up thoughts of seeking reelection. And when the end came, in 1975, the general consensus was that the United States should not again send troops to fight in a land war in Asia.

In the years since Vietnam the Far East has become more important than ever to the United States. There remains the unfortunate tendency to think of Russia as the key to Asia (particularly in the Reagan era). But changing circumstances have forced Americans to give some attention to other matters also: the emergence of the Far East as our major trading partner; the troubling adverse trade balance with Japan; economic and cultural relations with a changing China; the impact of Asian students and immigrants on the United States; the beginnings of significant tourist travel across the Pacific; encouraging prospects for cultural exchange. Media coverage has improved (though mostly, but not altogether, about calamities). There are more experts on Asia in the United States than ever before. They are in the government, on campuses, and in business; and some of them have had impact on the public. Although one could hardly call Americans knowledgeable about matters Asian, the situation is a little less appalling than it was a few short years ago.

As of now, European ties are still considered more important than connections with the Far East. We may assume that Europe First has years to go. We may assume also that for some time policy makers will put the heaviest emphasis on the Soviet threat, both in Europe and in Asia. There are indications, however, that other factors, such as the Japanese economic threat, may figure in the making of Far Eastern policy in the future. And that Americans will continue to learn more about the people of Asia and their many problems.

One further point. Those of us who take economic matters seriously note with interest the rapidly rising economic ties of the United States with eastern Asia. Such ties with Europe have contributed toward the long dominance of Europe First. Perhaps out of the changing trends will come a growing interest in Asia First.

Not soon. Later, who can tell?

The Evolution of the Monroe Doctrine from Monroe to Reagan

Walter LaFeber

From its early years, and certainly since the 1840 to 1900 era when an awesomely industrializing United States became a great world power, American diplomacy has constantly had to make choices—often tragic choices—between two stark alternatives: open competition with other leading powers and working with revolutions in the areas where the competition was to occur, or the acceptance of a system of spheres of influence. Indeed, as William Appleman Williams pointed out in *The Tragedy of American Diplomacy*, US diplomatic history can be defined as the two-century-old quest for a world shaped by open competition (not, however, by working with revolutionaries), a competition that can replace the usual world of colonialism, stifling economic restrictions, and the warfare that such restrictions have produced.[1] This quest, the argument ran, was symbolized and encapsulated by John Hay's Open Door Notes of 1899-1900 that demanded "a fair field and no favor" for growing North American interests in Asia. Those notes, moreover, had been anticipated a half-century before by Washington's policies that opened China and Japan to more Western trade, and seventy-five years before that by John Adams's Model Treaty.

Throughout the quest, however, North Americans frequently ran up against—and were even seduced by—the advantages of a sphere of influence arrangement. A brief working definition is that "a sphere of influence is a determinate region within which a single power exerts a predominant influence, which limits the independence or freedom of action of political entities within it."[2] One scholar has usefully divided such spheres into "hard" and "soft." In "hard spheres" the dominant power "reduces the independence of states to the point where the will of the hegemon is pervasive and seemingly permanent." In "soft spheres" the hegemonic power is more indirect, allows a greater degree of independence, and may even be exerted by mutual acceptance, although both sides clearly understand who has the whiphand and can make final decisions.[3] Third party influence is systematically excluded to the benefit of the hegemon, and certainly no "fair field and no favor" policy exists in the sphere.

With few exceptions, US diplomacy has proceeded from the dual assumptions that the open-door approach is good (in part because it supposedly meshes with such traditional North American beliefs as market competition and political self-determination), and that the United States can condemn the spheres of other powers because it has followed the virtues of the open door. Not even that historic cornerstone of US diplomacy, the Monroe Doctrine, has been viewed by key officials as an exception to the long search for an open door for all. Williams can define the Doctrine as "clearly the manifesto of the American empire."[4] Two conclusions reached by top officials give another view and even serve as benchmarks for the five decades (1900 to 1945) in which North Americans transformed themselves into the world's greatest power.

The first quotation appeared in a 1901 letter from the new US President, Theodore Roosevelt, to his close and highly knowledgeable friend, Hermann Speck von Sternberg:

> I regard the Monroe Doctrine as being equivalent to the open door in South America. That is, I do not want the United States or any European power to get territorial possessions in South America but to let South America gradually develop on its own lines, with an open door to all outside nations, save as the individual countries enter into individual treaties with one another. Of course this would not anywhere interfere with transitory intervention on the part of any State outside of South America, when there was a row with some State in South America. I wish that the same policy could be pursued in China.[5]

The second set of conclusions was reached in early 1944 by the State Department's Subcommittee on European Organization. Because the Monroe Doctrine had been produced by a liberal ideology, had not simply been imposed on small states, and had not been used for exploitative purposes by the senior power, the Subcommittee concluded that the use of the Doctrine to establish a sphere of influence had been "moderate and limited."[6]

Ten years later, the most distinguished historian of the Monroe Doctrine, Dexter Perkins, reached a quite different conclusion. Perkins bluntly lamented that the "Protean idea could not be made extinct," but suggested that North Americans place the Doctrine on the discard pile of history because the principles conveyed "a definite impression of hegemony, of supercilious arrogance, of interference."[7] As the twentieth century struggled to a close, high US officials dissented from Perkins's conclusion and made the issue less academic. For about a quarter-century, from the mid-1950s until 1981, the Doctrine had largely disappeared from the language of US policy makers. Then, in 1980-82, leading conservative spokesmen resurrected Monroe's message (or, more exactly, what they believed the 1823 message meant), and in November 1984 Secretary of Defense Caspar Weinberger publicly and directly used the Doctrine to justify US policy in Central America.[8] A leading historian could conclude a few years earlier that "The doctrine is so vulnerable, so far removed from realities, that it becomes an easy target for ridicule or contempt,"[9] but this did not inhibit the Reagan administration as it set out to enforce the Doctrine with military force.

This essay briefly traces the development of the Monroe Doctrine after 1823 and suggests that, far from being an "open door" policy as Roosevelt hoped, the Doctrine's ideas have been transformed into an ideological justification for a separate if usually "soft" US sphere of interest. The pivotal stage in that transformation occurred between 1895 and 1905 when the Monroe Doctrine actually became the Roosevelt Doctrine (and not a mere "Roosevelt Corollary," as textbooks have it). Americans throughout the hemisphere have since been living with the Roosevelt Doctrine, although— for purposes of public relations as well as their own denial of history—US officials have continued to invoke the name of Monroe's Doctrine. Some of the results of that invocation have been momentous and ominous: a belief that nineteenth century successes justify continued use of force; a "domino theory" that appeared in the original Doctrine and was later simply assumed by Americans; an assumption that the Doctrine can work in the Latin America of the late twentieth century because it worked in the Latin America of 1895 to the 1960s; and, overall, that because the Monroe Doctrine's origins were "liberal," and its results beneficent, it does not resemble a sphere of influence either "hard" or "soft."

The North American understanding of the Monroe Doctrine in the twentieth century bears little resemblance to the original declaration. One scholar, Kenneth Coleman, has drawn policy implications from that ignorance. The Doctrine, Coleman has argued, becomes whatever a president says it is, and given North Americans' traditional willingness to defer to the president on foreign policy issues, the malleability of the Doctrine allows a president to draw a conditioned response of acceptance from most Americans whenever he covers a policy—however threadbare—with the mantle of Monroe's declaration.[10] In US diplomacy the Doctrine has become the equivalent of the Emperor's new clothes.

In his seventh Annual Message of December 2, 1823, President Monroe made a number of points (not merely the three traditionally associated with the Doctrine) that have enjoyed long lives, if in somewhat mutant form as they have aged. He began the foreign policy analysis not by warning about imminent European encroachments or falling dominoes, but by stressing that any differences with Great Britain or Russia—the two powers whose policies had triggered US concern—could be worked out by "amicable negotiation." Monroe knew that his Secretary of State, John Quincy Adams, had already come to a satisfactory understanding with the Russians about their overzealous claims to the western coasts of the North American continent. Confident that the Russians had already backed off and that England had no intention of either planting further colonies in North America or allowing the French and Spanish to plant new claims, Monroe—with, to use Mark Twain's later phrase, "the calm confidence of a Christian holding four aces"—announced that "the American continents . . . are henceforth not to be considered as subjects for future colonization by any European powers."[11]

That statement opened the continent to colonization by the leading American power, that is, the United States. Monroe thus followed this section with a mention of the growing US Navy, and then, most notably, with a lengthy analysis of how an extensive internal improvements system was creating the roads and canals that provided ambitious North Americans new access to "very fertile country." Freed of the immediate dangers of further European colonization, a separate New World continental empire was taking shape.

Monroe then discussed the revolution in Greece and expressed "our most ardent wishes" that the Greeks would again "become an independent nation." He interjected himself no further in that war. When in a cabinet meeting the President expressed the desire to go farther, Adams had pulled him back with the argument that such a declaration "would be a summons to arms—to arms against all Europe, and for objects of policy exclusively European. . . ." Russia might even break off "diplomatic intercourse with us." Adams preferred "to disclaim all interference on our part with Europe; to make an American cause, and adhere inflexibly to that. . . ."[12] Adam's argument resulted in the most misunderstood line in Monroe's message.[13] The President backed down from his original position and declared that, while North Americans sympathized with liberty-seeking Europeans, "in the wars of the European powers *in matters relating to themselves* we have never taken any part, nor does it comport with our policy to do so" (emphasis added). The qualification in midsentence severely limited any conception that Europe and America comprised two separate spheres that seldom if ever would meet. Monroe instead argued that when an issue related to North Americans arose in Europe they could become involved in Old World affairs. It would have been strange if Monroe had not made such a qualification. He had been Secretary of State in 1811-14 when the United States became fully and bloodily involved in Europe's Napoleonic Wars because the conflict threatened important North American interests.

By inserting that crucial qualification, therefore, Monroe and Adams had it both ways: they announced in the same paragraph that Europeans should not interfere in American affairs (the so-called "noninterference" and "two spheres" principles of the Doctrine), but that under certain circumstances—which the United States could define on its own—Americans could interfere in European affairs. There is a straight line from this section of Monroe's message to the claims by US officials in 1919 and especially in 1944-45 that, in Secretary of War Henry Stimson's view, the United States could act in Eastern Europe because it was in American interest to balance Soviet power in that region, but could also assert full control over the Western Hemisphere because the Russians possessed no interests in the region. Stimson's top assistant, John McCloy, summarized this prevailing Washington assumption: the United States "ought to have [its] cake and eat it too."[14]

In considerably more diplomatic language, Monroe anticipated McCloy's conclusion, then underlined the point by repeating that while the United States wanted to stay out of Europe's quarrels (but "submitting to injuries from none"), in the Americas

> circumstances are eminently and conspicuously different. It is impossible that the allied powers should extend their political system to any portion of either continent without endangering our peace and happiness; nor can anyone believe that our southern brethren, if left to themselves, would adopt it of their own accord. It is equally impossible, therefore, that we should behold such interposition in any form with indifference.

Another straight line seems to run between these words of 1823 and Defense Secretary Weinberger's remarks on November 17, 1984, that one of the Monroe Doctrine's "facets, one of its phases, was that there should be no interference, no sponsorship of any kind of military activity in this hemisphere by countries in other hemispheres."[15] Monroe, however, never went out on such a limb, nor even questioned military aid given by the British to Latin American revolutionaries in Peru and Chile. Neither he nor Adams (who followed him into the Executive Mansion) ever acted upon the assumption that they should attempt to block military activity, so long as it remained that. True, Monroe warned against the extension of any European "political system" to the American hemisphere, but he understood that while Latin or North Americans might choose such a system, he doubted that such a thing would happen. And, given his own close association in the 1780s with the nation's founders, he agreed with their emphasis on the right of self-determination. Weinberger, on the other hand, elevated (and narrowed) the issue to military aid, and ignored Monroe's loophole in regard to self-determination. Having satisfied itself that the Doctrine was being violated, moreover, the Reagan administration even attacked the Nicaraguan elections of 1984 as a charade that bore little resemblance to self-determination. That charge has been countered, if not undermined, by reports of US experts on Latin America who observed the elections.[16]

But that is not even the crucial issue; at least it was not for President Monroe. Monroe wisely refrained from defining methods for self-determination. The President, and especially his Secretary of State, did not believe Latin Americans were prepared by either their history or contemporary circumstances to choose their governments through North American methods. Adams was outspoken. He told Henry Clay that he saw "no prospect that they would establish free or liberal institutions of government. . . They have not the first elements of good or free government. Arbitrary power, military and ecclesiastical, was stamped upon their education, upon their habits, and upon all their institutions."[17] That Adams's words revealed a self-righteous New Englander is indisputable. That they revealed a *realpolitiker* who understood that North American political categories could not be used to measure Latin American political realities is also indisputable. Adams had warned in 1821 that any attempt to impose such categories abroad could lead to US intervention "in search of monsters to destroy," and that process, he feared, could transform the North American system from one based on "liberty" to one based on "force."[18] Monroe's and Adams's categories of 1823 bore little resemblance to Weinberger's concerns of 1984, and their assumptions had even less similarity. Having thought through the essentials that separated the political systems of the nations of the Western Hemisphere (as well as those separating those of the Old and New Worlds), Monroe and Adams were able to define a policy that protected their nation's interest while not violating its principles or undercutting the "fundamental maxims" (to use Adams's words) of US government.

The Monroe Doctrine turned out to be a cutting edge for North American intervention throughout the Western Hemisphere, but it did not begin that way. In its first manifestation it attempted to define a system in which ambitious and increasingly powerful US merchants and shipowners could conquer new markets by competing in a true open-door world in decolonized Latin America and—of special importance—in which the rapidly growing population of the US could expand until, in Adams's words, "Europe shall find it a settled geographical element that the United States and North America are identical."[19]

Adams, the co-author of the Doctrine, felt strongest about the question of peaceful expansion. He had not always held that view. Before 1820 he successfully defended Andrew Jackson's use of force and drumhead justice to seize Florida. Adams also exhibited few qualms in forcefully removing Native Americans from lands desired by white farmers and speculators. The turn seemed to come during the explosive debates over Missouri's entry into the Union as a slave state in 1820. With clarity, Adams suddenly understood that expansion could mean expansion of a slave system whose "evils" taint "the very sources of moral principle. . . It perverts human reason." Rather than allowing slavery to expand farther, especially through the use of force, he agonizingly concluded that the free states might secede and establish a "new Union . . . unpolluted with slavery," whose example would then attract the other states into a slave-free association.[20] His July 4, 1821, address discussed these points, especially the danger of using force to extend American interests, more abstractly, but with great power. From 1821 until his death in 1848, brought on by a stroke suffered as he damned the use of US military power to seize parts of Mexico, the chief theoretician of the Monroe Doctrine generally opposed the use of force to expand a North American sphere of influence. Cuba, for example, must fall naturally like an "apple" and "gravitate only to the North American Union."[21] Adams felt so strongly about Cuba ultimately joining his nation that he virtually single-handedly convinced Monroe to issue the Doctrine unilaterally and not (as the British, Thomas Jefferson, and James Madison advised) issue it jointly with Great Britain because the British wanted a mutual "hands-off" pledge inserted that would apply to the entire hemisphere. Adams condemned any tying of US hands. Nor is there any evidence that he found any fault with the remarkable final section of Monroe's 1823 message that paraphrased Madison's *Federalist #10* by arguing that continued expansion could only strengthen the Union. But Adams believed the empire could be achieved slowly, naturally, with minimum or no force, and without slavery.

The transformation of the intentions and principles of 1823 to the rationalizations and justification for the use of force in the twentieth century occurred over more than three-quarters of a century. Between 1823 and 1826, Latin American nations who read Monroe's message too casually made five direct requests that the United States help them protect their independence. All were turned down. When the French or British fleets made demands of Latin American governments, or when England seized the Malvinas in 1833, no sound of protest seeped out of Washington.[22]

When, however, southern slave expansionists coveted Texas between 1842 and 1845, commercial and agrarian interests targeted the Pacific coast of the continent in 1844-45, and British influence in both regions threatened to blunt US expansion. Presidents John Tyler and James K. Polk resurrected "Monroe's Doctrine" that had been all but forgotten for nearly two decades. When Tyler waved the Doctrine in 1842 to justify the seizing of Texas, a leading Venezuelan newspaper warned that Mexico and then other nations could follow: "Words like these should open the eyes of all the Hispanic republics. Do you want to be under the fatherly tutelage of Washington? Beware, brothers, the wolf approaches the lambs."[23] A year later the Democrats, in national convention, justified their claim to "all" of Oregon (that is, up to 54′40°) by declaring that sole British control in the region would be "dangerous to peace and a repudiation of Monroe's doctrine that the American continents are closed to European colonization."[24] In his Annual Message of December 1845, Polk adopted the convention's position as his own. He privately told Democratic Senator Thomas Hart Benton of Missouri that he meant to target "Mr. Monroe's doctrine against permitting foreign colonization, and . . . had California and the fine bay of San Francisco as much in view as Oregon."[25]

Polk's declarations foreshadowed the Doctrine of the twentieth century. He intended to force the pace of expansion as the rampaging "manifest destiny" spirit of the 1840s dictated, even if it meant seizing areas (such as the land north of the Columbia River, or most of California) where there were no or few North Americans. Moreover, he indicated a willingness to use force to impose Monroe's principles. In reality, he quickly backed down and compromised when the British threatened to mobilize their fleet along the northwest coast, and his justification for going to war against Mexico and annexing California was debt and indemnity claims against the Mexicans, not the principles of Monroe. At the moment Polk revived those principles, the British and French fleets were freely interfering in South American affairs but he paid no attention—despite a strong plea from the US Chargé in Buenos Aires to point Monroe's warnings toward Argentina.[26] Polk instead explicitly distinguished between the two New World continents by declaring that the Doctrine applied "with greatly increased force" to any new colonization attempted in North America.

When he tried to widen the application in early 1848, the president met with one of the fiercest and most effective attacks ever launched against the Doctrine. The encounter began when Polk heard that the British or Spanish might use an Indian civil war in Yucatan as an excuse to seize the peninsula, and do so even at the invitation of the Yucatan officials who were under siege. Polk told Congress that the Monroe Doctrine, as well as danger to US "security," justified direct intervention in Yucatan. Led by John Calhoun (D.-SC), Congress humiliated the president. The South Carolinian raised the central questions about such use of the 1823 principles: it was an "absurdity" to claim that European intervention in an Indian war in Yucatan threatened US security, and it was unconstitutional for the president to force the country into war through a unilateral application of the Doctrine. Behind these two questions lay the most profound point of all. Polk's reasoning, Calhoun charged, "puts it in the power of other countries on this continent to make us a party to all their wars; and hence I say, if this broad interpretation be given to these declarations, we shall forever be involved in wars."[27] Calhoun's words carried weight. He had been in Monroe's cabinet in 1823.

The results of the Doctrine's resurrection in the 1840s were therefore not incompatible with its birth in 1823. By applying the principles to the North American continent, Polk went along with Adams's preferences and even more sharply defined and limited Monroe's generalization. That Tyler and Polk unleashed a war with Mexico that carried the seeds of the North

American Civil War is clear. But the conflict with Mexico was neither caused nor justified by the Monroe Doctrine. The self-interests, irrationalities, mythologies, and political payoffs in "manifest destiny" propelled the country into the war of 1846-48. When Polk tried to extend the Doctrine into Yucatan for purposes of outright "imperialism" (Dexter Perkins's word[28]), the Senate attack threatened to restrict the principles permanently to, in Calhoun's phrase, "declarations—nothing more." There was "not one word in any of them in reference to [US] resistance." When the Yucatan conflict quieted, Polk with relief withdrew his request from Congress.

Throughout at least the mid-1860s, US officials interpreted the Doctrine conservatively and restrictively for the most part.[29] They focused on the North American continent. They backed away from using force to back such general principles. In a fashion striking when compared with twentieth century policies, Washington policy makers acted in Latin America often by supporting revolutionaries. They refused to use force because, as men as ideologically different as Adams and Calhoun agreed, such use could lead to the undermining of crucial US political and constitutional principles.

After the Civil War, however, a slow transformation began to occur. The Doctrine evolved as US power developed. The Grant administration officially added a new principle to the Doctrine (although its roots went back at least to 1811): the United States would not countenance the transfer of one European holding in the Western Hemisphere to another non-American nation. Washington took it upon itself to declare not only that Europeans could not acquire new colonies, but that they could not dispose of old colonies except under US guidelines. Meanwhile the long economic depression that set in during 1873 led many North Americans to look southward for markets to consume the overproduction of the nation's incredibly productive industrial and agricultural complexes. One result was the birth of the Pan-American movement in the 1880s. Resembling the Monroe Doctrine, Pan-Americanism aimed at creating a Western Hemispheric system separated from the European system, but, unlike the 1823 principles, it sought to achieve this goal multilaterally.[30] For that reason, among others, Pan-Americanism remained an ideal more talked about than realized, while US officials continued to deal with Latin-American problems unilaterally and with increasing insensitivity.

In 1895-96 Grover Cleveland's second administration dramatically wheeled out the Doctrine and aimed at the world's leading power. Great Britain vigorously supported British Guiana's claim against Venezuela for territory along the Orinoco River. It was a critical area because the river controlled trade access to much of the northern part of the South American continent. Acting unilaterally (Cleveland never consulted in any detail even with the Venezuelans), the United States told the British to back down and send the dispute to international arbitration. With other crises brewing, and realizing that a growing Anglo-American relationship was too vital to be threatened by such an issue, the London government acquiesced to Cleveland's demands.

The Venezuelan episode of 1895-96 marked the point when the United States government extended its power under the Doctrine far beyond the region of the North American continent, the Caribbean, and Central America and proclaimed a sphere of influence over a vast area to the south. When Secretary of State Richard Olney invoked the Doctrine and told the British in his note of July 20, 1895, that United States' "honor and its interests are involved," Monroe's 1823 principles were projected directly on the South American continent. When Olney wrote the famous lines that "Today the United States is practically sovereign on this continent and its fiat is law upon the subjects to which it confines its interposition" because "its infinite resources combined with its isolated position render it master of the situation and practically invulnerable as against any or all other powers,"³¹ he announced that the United States could extend its sphere of influence as far as its power could reach. Since its power was "invulnerable," it could reach far indeed. Observers in Mexico and Chile quickly understood and protested Olney's claim. Many doubters were quieted by England's virtual surrender to it.³²

Over the next decade the 1895 principles were given a new definition (and military claws) by Theodore Roosevelt. As Assistant Secretary of the Navy in 1897-98, Roosevelt believed the Monroe Doctrine required that the Navy must "back up diplomacy with force," and that the new US fleet could now fulfill this mission.³³ He also understood that the Venezuelan crisis and the war of 1898 had made the United States one of the world's great powers, certainly the dominant power in the Western Hemisphere. Like many leaders of great powers in recorded history, Roosevelt wanted no disturbance of the *status quo* in regions his people could or did dominate. He came to the presidency in 1901 at precisely the point when his generation understood that four hundred years of North American landed expansionism was ending, and that their next historical epoch would probably be characterized by maintaining peace on their borders and influence in neighboring markets and security check points.³⁴

Roosevelt's view changed radically, however, on the tactics needed to maintain that peace and influence. In 1901 he had told von Sternberg that the Monroe Doctrine was "equivalent to an open door in South America."³⁵ In 1903 the Germans and British took him at his word. They threatened the use of force to collect debts from Venezuela. As the implications of Europeans landing in Venezuela filtered through Roosevelt's mind, he came to understand that, although "these wretched republics cause me a great deal of trouble," another European attempt to collect debts through force "would simply not be tolerated here. I often think that a sort of protectorate over

South and Central America is the only way out." He personally disliked such an idea ("I would even be ready to sponsor a retrocession of New Mexico and Arizona" to avoid it[36]), or so he claimed, but no acceptable alternative appeared. Having learned the lesson in 1895-96, the Europeans were ready to play the game of spheres. Before moving against Venezuela, they carefully gave Roosevelt advance notice, asked his approval, welcomed his services as a mediator, allowed the US minister to act as an agent for Venezuela, and assured Roosevelt they did not wish to challenge the Monroe Doctrine.[37] In this age of imperialism and colonialism, few spheres were treated with such understanding by the great powers.

In his annual messages of 1904 and 1905, Roosevelt took European deference out of the realm of chance and ensured that henceforth all parties would understand that the United States accepted the responsibilities, as well as rewards, of acting as the sole policeman in the enforcement of the Doctrine. The direct cause of the announcement was a threatened French intervention in Santo Domingo, an intervention that could have resulted in diminshed US control of that country's finances and a possible revolution that would make the Caribbean region more unpredictable. To Roosevelt, who valued order as one of the highest virtues, the only policy could be the use of US naval power to quiet the unrest followed by a takeover by Washington officials of the Santo Domingo customs houses and treasury. "All that this country desires," Roosevelt declared, "is that the other republics on this continent shall be happy and prosperous; and they cannot be happy and prosperous unless they maintain order within their boundaries and behave with a just regard for their obligations toward outsiders." The United States obviously reserved the right to define "order" and "just regard." The most revealing line of the 1905 Annual Message was Roosevelt's claim that "the proposed method will give the people of Santo Domingo the same chance to move onward and upward which we have already given to the people of Cuba."[38] Under the Platt Amendment, which Roosevelt had insisted be inserted in the Cuban Constitution itself, the United States had the right to control Cuban finances and intervene whenever US officials wished.

The use of the Monroe Doctrine as an extensive, indeed open-ended, sphere of interest could not have been more publicly defined. A large number of US senators refused to approve Roosevelt's treaty with Santo Domingo on the grounds that US naval vessels should not be the main legitimacy for other governments. Roosevelt circumvented the Senate by making an executive agreement with his Santo Domingo regime.[39] With his power to define and enforce his version of the Monroe Doctrine triumphant both at home and in neighboring areas, Roosevelt no longer equated the 1823 principles with the open door. He now saw them as a guarantee that "Latin American republics" could not use the Doctrine as a "warrant" for remaining "as small bandit nests of a wicked and inefficient type." He privately added to a close friend, "We may possibly have to chastise Venezuela, though I hope not."[40]

Roosevelt's "Corollary" to the Doctrine clearly did not limit its reach to the Caribbean or the access routes to the newly building Panama Canal. It reached as far as US police power could extend. Given the growth of the Great White Fleet, the reach was far. Such force could be used not according to some commonly understood legal justification, but according to criteria (an appropriate "moral order," or an inappropriate "revolution") that the United States president unilaterally defined. The *Providence Journal* had overwhelming evidence on its side when the newspaper editorialized that Roosevelt's policy tended toward "an essential suzerainty, latent if not always active, of the United States over all the countries to the south of us."[41] International law and Pan-Americanism were fine ideals, but as Roosevelt's Secretary of State, Elihu Root, stated with his usual clarity, "Since the Monroe Doctrine is a declaration based upon the nation's right of self-protection, it can not be transmuted into a joint or common declaration by American States or any number of them."[42] This determination and ability to go it alone (which is actually the best and most historically based definition of "isolationism" in US diplomacy) introduced the Monroe Doctrine to the twentieth century.

When these three criteria of the Roosevelt "Corollary"—criteria unilaterally defined that can be used to justify using US military power throughout much of the hemisphere—were applied by Roosevelt in Santo Domingo, and then by presidents William Howard Taft, Woodrow Wilson, Warren G. Harding, and Calvin Coolidge in a half-dozen other nations over the next quarter-century, it becomes clear that Roosevelt did not add a mere "corollary." He transformed the meaning of the Monroe Doctrine. When US officials from John Foster Dulles in 1954 to Caspar Weinberger in 1984 used the Doctrine as justification for their use, or proposed use, of US force, they were unconsciously referring to Theodore Roosevelt's precedent, not James Monroe's. The earlier president had declared in favor of the Latin American revolutions; after Roosevelt, US officials opposed and even tried to crush such revolutions. Monroe foreswore US involvement in the revolutions and demanded that other powers follow the North American example; after Roosevelt, the United States, using both overt military and covert political and economic tactics, became deeply involved in the internal affairs of countries that ranged from Mexico and Nicaragua to Brazil (in 1964) and Chile (1964 to 1973). With the Roosevelt Doctrine as a guide, US troops entered the territory of Caribbean states on no fewer than twenty occasions between 1898 and 1920.

This historic switch in the Doctrine's targets, from attacking European states that would interfere with Latin American revolutions to attacking the revolutions themselves, was acknowledged when Secretary of State Charles

Evans Hughes marked the centenary of Monroe's message. The "great republics" to the south, he observed, have been "safeguarded by the historic doctrine," and no longer fear "European powers, but look with apprehension at the expansion . . . and formidable strength of the Republic of the North."[43] Hiram Bingham, a scholar of the Doctrine and later a US senator, had published a book in 1913 that pinpointed when the change occurred and then precisely defined that change, although he mistakenly limited its geographical scope:

> Our policy toward the republics of Central America has undergone a startling development since the beginning of President Roosevelt's administration. In the words of a recent minister in Honduras, our policy has changed "from simple mediation and scrupulous non-intervention, to a policy of active, direct intervention in their internal affairs; and secondly, these interventions have become as startlingly frequent as they have become increasingly embarrassing in character."

With equal insight, Bingham issued a warning that turned out to be prophetic. Carried out to its logical conclusion, the "new Monroe Doctrine," as Bingham called it,

> means a policy of suzerainty and interference which will earn us the increasing hatred of our neighbors, the dissatisfaction of Europe, the loss of commercial opportunities, and the forfeiture of time and attention which would much better be given to settling our own difficult internal problems. . .
> If we persist in maintaining the [new] Monroe Doctrine, we shall find that its legitimate, rational, and logical growth will lead us to an increasing number of large expenditures, where American treasure and American blood will be sacrificed in efforts to remove the mote from our neighbor's eye while overlooking the beam in our own.[44]

An apparent exception in the "logical growth" of the new Doctrine occurred during the 1930s, but that decade also produced its most dangerous challenges. The exception occurred when President Franklin D. Roosevelt replaced "Monroe Doctrine" with "Good Neighbor Policy" as the characterization for his Western Hemisphere policy. The Good Neighbor foreswore armed intervention, and in Pan-American conferences of 1933, 1936, 1938, and 1940, the American countries, north and south, pledged multilateral consultation and application of the original 1823 principles.[45] The State Department had meanwhile explicitly dropped the Roosevelt "Corollary" in 1929-30, although it carefully added that the change in no way detracted from the US right to protect its interests as it saw fit in the Western Hemisphere. Taken together, the 1929 to 1940 developments marked the one decade of the twentieth century when US officials publicly backed off from declaring a right to stop Latin American revolutions unilaterally and, if need be, by force.

Privately and indirectly, however, the Roosevelt administration acted unilaterally to enforce the 1823 principles and, at times, threatened to enforce those of 1904-05. US power had reached a level that allowed Washington officials to protect their nation's interests merely by displaying their military strength or quietly exercising the leverage exerted by their markets and exports. As they watched the Axis threat approach the hemisphere, Washington policy makers used currency, commodity, and customs regulations to tie Latin Americans closer to them, and—while praising free trade and reciprocity—moved to build a cartel trading system under their own control.[46] The Roosevelt administration used diplomatic and economic pressures in an attempt to discipline and then modify Mexico's decision to nationalize its oil production. After noting this US pressure, and observing how Washington used a combination of "military, economic, and diplomatic levers" to keep in power such "clients" as Somoza in Nicaragua, Hernández Martinez in El Salvador, Trujillo in the Dominican Republic, and Batista in Cuba, historian Clayton Knoppes concluded that "the Good Neighbor policy was United States hemispheric hegemony pursued by other means."[47] Certainly FDR was both aware of his power and not reluctant to use it. When senators expressed concern in early 1939 that Central America might be ripe for Axis influence, the president remarked, "Central America? Properly equipped and with the knowledge of how to get the right people to do it for us, we could stage a revolution in any Central American government for between a million and four million dollars. In other words, it is a matter of price."[48]

Nor did the supposed multilateralization or the nonintervention emphasis of the Good Neighbor policy stop what Bingham had called the "logical growth" of the Doctrine. It grew, as usual, along with US power and Washington's view of threats to its national interest in the hemisphere. Indeed during the late 1930s FDR, instead of dropping the Doctrine, made it more global. During 1917-20 Woodrow Wilson had asked that Monroe's principles be accepted before the world. (Wilson quickly discovered, however, that the outside world mistrusted the US and that North Americans refused to dilute and expose Monroe's principles in the uncontrollable global arena.) By 1941 Roosevelt brought North Americans a long way to accepting a part of Wilson's original vision: to think of the Doctrine as intertwined with a global responsibility they would have to assume. Many officials and patriotic citizens would have liked to have simply sealed off the American continents against Axis incursions or suspicious instability, but they had learned they could not live alone. As top US Treasury official Harry Dexter White observed, "A totally self-sufficient isolated hemisphere trade bloc might cost the United States up to two-thirds of its normal foreign trade revenues."[49]

The trick would be sealing off the hemisphere into a *de facto* US sphere while ensuring that other parts of the world remained open. It was a preview of the dilemma facing Truman, Stimson, and McCloy six years later. Axis aggression rolled on in Europe and Asia during 1938-40 and Roosevelt moved to seal off the hemisphere. He first extended US defense lines "hundreds of miles away from our continental limits," implied that Canada now fell under the Monroe Doctrine's protection, extended the Doctrine to Greenland in 1940, and the next year applied it to Iceland and—in blanket fashion—"to other island outposts of the New World." Privately he believed the principles stretched to the Canaries, Azores, and even West Africa because these points occupied strategic accessways to the Western Hemisphere.[50]

The policy of spheres had led to a fear of falling dominoes, but that fear had been anticipated at least as early as Tyler's and Polk's terms in the 1840s. The Doctrine, as Woodrow Wilson had hoped, moved out beyond the New World, although it moved largely only in the minds and policies of North Americans. They were nevertheless learning to think, during the so-called "isolationism" of the late 1930s, as they would think as the world's greatest superpower after 1945: the Western Hemisphere must be impervious to Old World (or Japanese) influences, while more and more outlying areas were to be open to US control in order to protect the New World. Nor was this view undercut by the geopolitical pioneering of Nicholas Spykman and others who warned after 1941 that maps should be studied from a polar perspective, not Theodore Roosevelt's, to understand that the United States was more susceptible to upheavals in London, Berlin, or even Moscow than in Rio or Santiago.[51] US officials saw no reason why Spykman and Monroe could not be reconciled. Even as FDR peered at the Canaries and West Africa, he ordered the US military to prepare to move 100,000 men into northeast Brazil in case rumors were true that 6,000 German soldiers were traveling to Brazil hidden in merchant ships. The War Department's plan, POT OF GOLD, rested on the twin beliefs that England would fall and the Brazilians would welcome North American troops. Neither belief was true, and British grittiness, in the words of a Brazilian historian, saved FDR from "a politically irreparable error,"[52] because German propagandists and the many Latin Americans who feared the United States would have set back the Monroe Doctrine many decades.

As Germany threatened the 1823 principles directly, so Japan threatened to undercut them more indirectly but perhaps even more dangerously. The German drive aimed at relatively close-by areas that the United States Navy (or, in the case of attempted subversion, the Federal Bureau of Investigation) could protect. The Japanese danger, however, placed North American interests in both Latin America and Asia in jeopardy, and in Asia Washington officials had little effective recourse other than going to war with the Japanese empire 8,000 miles away. Tokyo officials triggered the danger by claiming that their policies for sealing off and exploiting Manchuria in 1931-32, northern China in 1937-38, and Southeast Asia between 1938 and 1940 were only a Monroe Doctrine for Asia. Throughout the 1930s US specialists tried to destroy the analogy, but they labored under major handicaps. As early as 1905, Theodore Roosevelt had apparently told the Japanese, fresh from their stunning victories over the Russian fleet, that they should establish a Monroe Doctrine over Asia. Roosevelt no doubt meant that they should exclude European, particularly Russian, colonialists while allowing in such staunch supporters of the open door as North Americans. But the Japanese never forgot his advice.[53] Nor did they forget the admission by secretaries of state William Jennings Bryan and Robert Lansing between 1914 and 1917, or US Ambassador William Castle in 1930, that Japan had special rights in Asia. Castle expressly compared these rights to the Monroe Doctrine.[54]

As it became clear in 1933 that Japan took the comparison seriously, George Blakeslee, a leading scholar of Asia and sometime State Department official, argued that the two applications of the 1823 principles were unalike because North Americans used theirs "solely" for "self-defense," wanted only the *status quo,* and claimed no "special interests, hegemony, or economic privileges." The Japanese, however, used military aggression "to overthrow the *status quo* in Manchuria to Japan's own advantage," and then effectively colonized the conquered areas. As Blakeslee probed deeper, however, he found some disturbing parallels. The US relationship to the Caribbean region since 1900 did resemble that of Japan to Manchuria. Both were

> strong Powers facing countries which are weak in political organization and military strength and which are torn by frequent civil war. Both are capitalistic and industrialized, in contrast with their neighboring lands which are essentially agricultural. Both have shown administrative and organizing ability of a high order. Both have national interests, strategic and commercial, which they regard as vital—the United States, the Panama Canal; Japan, the South Manchuria Railway. Both have very large investments: the United States approximately $3,293,000,000 (1929) in Mexico and the republics of the Caribbean (not including Venezuela or Colombia); Japan between $800,000,000 and $1,000,000,000 (the yen reckoned at par) in Manchuria.[55]

Blakeslee then drew a key distinction: the United States had the comfort of proclaiming an open door in neighboring regions but reaping the benefits of an actual sphere of interest—in other words, it could have it both ways—because of geopolitical and demographic realities that the Japanese did not enjoy:

> The United States is a vast territory with a great population *vis-a-vis* a dozen Caribbean republics, each with a relatively small area and population. Japan, on the other hand, is a country with a relatively small area and population *vis-à-vis* the vast territory and great population of China. An attitude which therefore appears natural for the United States to take

toward the Caribbean states does not appear natural for Japan to take toward China. . . .

The United States does not need to use military force to induce the Caribbean republics to permit American capital to find profitable investment. The doors are voluntarily wide open. . .[56]

The "doors" were "voluntarily wide open" only after many US interventions between the Civil War and 1933 had propped them open.[57] Japan's problems were that it was a half-century behind the United States in using force to secure neighboring areas; and that no Japanese interests were located in the Caribbean-Central American region, but the United States believed open access to China, Manchuria, and Southeast Asia to be critical for the West's economic survival.

Washington and Tokyo finally went to war over that issue of access. When the struggle ended, Monroe's two worlds literally appeared in 1945-47. The Monroe Doctrine did not have to be again proclaimed because the "two camp" division of the world (as the Soviets termed it), and the *de facto* economic and military hegemony of the United States over the Western Hemisphere allowed North American officials to assume the validity of the Doctrine. Harry Dexter White's desire to create an integrated capitalist international economic system, and FDR's policy of extending US military power far beyond the boundaries of the New World had been plans in the 1930s, then became realities in the 1940s. But throughout these years the evolving principles of Monroe were not questioned, just extended. The principles received even more multilateral support at the 1945 Chapultepec Conference, the 1947 Rio Treaty meetings, and the 1948 gathering that created the Organization of American States. The United States, however, consistently emphasized that it had not surrendered its unilateral right to move in the hemisphere. As long as that right existed, Dexter Perkins observed in 1955, "in a sense, the Monroe Doctrine will exist also."[58]

The year before Perkins made his observation, the Eisenhower administration used the Central Intelligence Agency and CIA-controlled Guatemalan exiles to overthrow a constitutionally elected, reform-minded government in Guatemala. The government had, among other policies, moved rapidly towards a land reform program that endangered major US corporate holdings. When Secretary of State John Foster Dulles threatened reprisals, the Guatemalan officials imported a boatload of Soviet-bloc arms. After the overthrow occurred, Dulles, in a nationwide radio broadcast, said nothing of the CIA involvement and argued that the *golpe* was merely Guatemalan democracy at work, but he emphasized that the Soviets had chosen Guatemala as a base from which "to breed subversion which would extend to other republics. The intrusion of Soviet despotism was, of course, a direct challenge to our Monroe Doctrine, the first and most fundamental of our foreign policies."[59]

The CIA's operation, and Dulles's justification, explicitly moved the Doctrine into a new realm of its history. Henceforth the principles would apply against internal subversion as well as external threat. In a real sense, the Doctrine had been used against internal subversives, as Washington officials defined them, as early as 1909-12 when the United States forcefully removed an overly nationalist (and overly anti-US) ruler of Nicaragua; in 1927 to 1933 when US troops fought Nicaraguan guerrilla leader Augusto Sandino; and in the 1930s when Washington officials feared that Axis ideological penetration would result in Axis political and economic bases.

Dulles's use of "Soviet subversion" as a justification for intervention against a legitimate government within the sphere gained new potency in 1959 when Fidel Castro's guerrillas conquered Havana, then moved slowly over the next two years into the Soviet economic bloc. An attempted CIA-led invasion at the Bay of Pigs failed tragically, and President John F. Kennedy's Alliance for Progress, even with its $100 billion for development in a single decade, failed to isolate or seduce the Cubans. During the 1962 Missile Crisis, Kennedy refused to mention the Monroe Doctrine because of its reputation in Latin America. He also apparently understood that its meaning had been twisted and extended out of shape in the twentieth century. When Justice Department officials suggested that the Doctrine conferred certain rights on the United States, the President retorted, "The Monroe doctrine. What the hell is that?"[60] But as one of his closest advisors, Undersecretary of State George Ball, recalled, the "national credo" continued to live because "we regarded [the hemisphere]—though we avoided stating it in those terms—as our exclusive sphere of interest and influence." Ball noted that during the Missile Crisis former Secretary of State Dean Acheson used the Doctrine to urge Kennedy to strike the missile sites directly. Immediately after the crisis ended, leading conservatives William F. Buckley and Edward Rickenbacker (President of Eastern Airlines) attacked Kennedy's deal with the Russians and formed The Committee for the Monroe Doctrine whose objectives included destroying Castro and restoring the 1823 principles as the committee defined them.[61] In 1966 President Lyndon Johnson landed 22,000 US and OAS troops in the Dominican Republic. In his public explanation, he did not mention the Doctrine, but the president declared that Cuban and other "evil forces" were the targets of his action. He pinpointed the new subversive threat, and also provided a precedent and rationale for protecting the sphere against such threats.[62]

During the decade after Johnson's action in the Dominican Republic, talk about the Doctrine subsided. Concern over Latin America, which seemed to be unnaturally stable, gave way to consuming debates over Vietnam and the Middle East. In 1975 the United States even signed a Protocol of Amendment to the Rio Treaty that accepted the principle of "ideological pluralism," pledged nonintervention, and recognized the right of every state "to choose freely their political, economic, and social organizations." The US Senate ratified this historic clause in 1979.[63] But as it acted, revolutions erupted in Nicaragua, El Salvador, Guatemala, Peru, and Colombia that aroused North Americans to focus once again on Latin America, and to resurrect the Monroe Doctrine as a justification for an escalating interventionism.

When President Ronald Reagan referred to the Doctrine early in his first term, William Buckley declared that this "re-baptism . . . is nothing less than a spiritual experience." Richard Nixon continued his own personal political resurrection by using the Doctrine to justify strong action against "the Soviet Union . . . in Latin America." Senator Steven Symms (R.-Id.) proposed a resolution in 1982 that "arms" should be used if necessary to stop Marxism-Leninism in the Americas. His spokesman said that Symms aimed at "reinstituting the 1823 Monroe Doctrine." Despite many qualms that it gave a blank check to President Reagan, the resolution passed both houses of Congress by large margins.[64] The US invasion of Grenada in 1983 and the refusal to accept any World Court ruling on the CIA's mining of Nicaraguan harbors in 1984 fit perfectly into the movement to reinstitute the Doctrine. Then Weinberger defined the principles as meaning "that there should be no interference, no sponsorship of any kind of military activity in this hemisphere by countries in other hemispheres." He directly referred to the Soviet supplying of Nicaragua's military forces.[65]

The 1823 Doctrine actually could not be defined in those terms. It differed in at least three respects from Weinberger's view. First, Monroe and Adams wanted to prevent European nations from forcing Latin Americans to act against their will (as, for example, becoming recolonized). Weinberger objected to Latin Americans acting according to their own will if he perceived those actions as dangerous to US interests. Monroe objected to outside threats. Weinberger was willing to intervene against internal, domestic activities. Second, Monroe sided with the Latin American revolutions and wisely refrained from setting up criteria to measure the wholesomeness of their political procedures. Weinberger and the Reagan administration opposed revolution and established their own criteria, based largely on an atypical North American experience, to measure the acceptability of the revolutionaries. Third, Monroe and Adms had no desire to become involved in internal Latin American affairs. Weinberger and other Reagan administration officials took the United States directly into the heart of societies in (among other places) El Salvador, Nicaragua, Honduras, and Jamaica.

That in the late twentieth century US power and Latin American conditions, as well as the Doctrine's principles, bear little resemblance to the 1820s is obvious. But more important, that power and those conditions also bear little similarity to 1904-05, and it is the Roosevelt Doctrine, not Monroe's, that Dulles, Acheson, Johnson, Reagan, and Weinberger had in mind when they justified unilateral US intervention in the internal affairs of

Latin American states. As their history was skewed, so was their political science. For Theodore Roosevelt's world had disappeared by the 1950s and 1960s. He and his successors had forcefully controlled many Latin American governments by using US troops to depose an uncooperative leader and replace him with one more cooperative. No native force could withstand the troops, and if it could, the native contingents (as in Guatemala during June 1954) deserted the government to join the invaders. Ernesto "Che" Guevara had personally witnessed that desertion,[66] and the experience reinforced lessons taught by Marxist-Leninist dogma: the army and the government should be one. Castro applied that lesson and the Bay of Pigs became a synonym for US policy failure. In Chile, President Salvador Allende did not apply the lesson and was the victim of a *golpe* pulled by his own army and supported by the United States. The Sandinistas learned the lesson and withstood immense US pressure that aimed to splinter the Nicaraguan government.

Nor is the Latin American theater like that of eighty years ago. Such regional powers as Venezuela and Mexico (with their oil wealth), Brazil, Argentina, and Colombia can exercise influence and block US actions more effectively than they could even in the 1930s. US officials historically have been able to deal easily with the elites of Latin American countries, but rapid political and economic changes, the communications-technology revolution, the example of Castro, and the incredible urbanization in much of Latin America have transformed those societies, made the political systems more complex, and have required that the elites listen closely to their own people. At the same time, US trade, investment, and even military ties and influence have declined dramatically between the United States and many Latin American nations. The southern peoples have meanwhile moved rapidly towards Japanese and West European products, markets, and military supplies.[67]

US policy, moreover, must operate in these evolving, increasingly complicated theaters even as it tries to resolve the contradiction that has confronted it since World War I and especially during the 1930s and 1940s: maintaining its own sphere of interest, even through the use of military intervention into the domestic affairs of sovereign states, while protesting and trying to undercut the Soviet sphere. One way to deal with the contradiction would be to discard the Monroe Doctrine. As early as 1853 the British Minister to the United States, John F. Crampton, observed that "By eternal repetition this so-called doctrine is gradually becoming in the minds of the Democracy here one of those habitual maxims which are no longer reasoned upon but felt."[68] A century and a quarter later, a leading scholar worried that as a "Doctrine" the principles by definition are "binding upon the faithful" (that is, on all North Americans), and are "like canon law" with the United States acting as "the medieval papacy reserving to itself the claim of infallibility."[69] By dropping the Doctrine and dispersing the fog that has gathered around it (a fog that allows US officials to justify Theodore Roosevelt's military interventionism with James Monroe's noninterventionist principles), policy makers would at least have to justify their plans more rationally and specifically instead of using the Doctrine to short-circuit debate.

One other alternative does exist: to repudiate the Roosevelt Doctrine and return to Monroe's principles of noninterference in the internal affairs of Latin American nations. Such a feat would require the kind of historical understanding that many North Americans find difficult and US officials often find inconvenient. But this alternative is preferable to the danger that in a world marked by the inevitable decline of North American hegemony those officials will attempt to use force to maintain a misunderstood Doctrine over resisting people for ill-defined purposes.

Herbert C. Hoover and the
Dream of Capitalism in One Country

Patrick Hearden

Herbert C. Hoover was a leading American proponent of economic nationalism. Reared in a Quaker family in rural Iowa, he quickly acquired a respect for communal values and a dislike for violent behavior. Both of his parents died while he was still a young boy, but Hoover worked hard as a mining engineer and became a millionaire by age forty. His early religious experience, combined with his later vocational success, conditioned his basic outlook on life. Hoover viewed himself as a Christian capitalist dedicated to resolving the inherent tension between the profit motive and the golden rule. He believed that, while people should be free to pursue their own individual interests, they also should be willing to join together to promote the common good. Hence he preferred to employ persuasion rather than coercion in attempting to maintain harmonious relations among social classes and between countries. In short, Hoover was an idealist who hoped that the principle of voluntary cooperation would generate domestic prosperity as well as world peace.[1]

As secretary of commerce between 1921 and 1928, Hoover advocated the establishment of an American System which would function success- fully as a self-contained economic unit. The fact that farmers in the United States were producing more food and fiber than the domestic market could absorb did little to dampen his zeal for a nationalist economic agenda. Neither did the sharp drop in American agricultural prices caused by the sudden decline in European demand for farm commodities when World War I ended. Hoover boldly asserted in 1922 that the United States could "reestablish its material prosperity and comfort without European trade."[2] He hoped that in the long run migration from rural areas to urban centers would reduce the domestic supply of farm staples and thereby relieve the country from the problem of agricultural overproduction. "Generally," Hoover argued in 1924, "the fundamental need is the balancing of agricultural production to our home demand."[3]

Hoover used his position in the Commerce Department to champion the cause of an American System. He became a vigorous advocate of high tariffs to protect the home market for American farms and factories, and he urged business executives to raise real wages in order to increase the purchasing power of the domestic labor force. At the same time, Hoover opposed McNarry-Haugen schemes calling for the subsidized dumping of American agricultural surpluses abroad. Instead he favored the voluntary organization of farm cooperatives designed to help members market their crops in the United States. Noting that Americans were utilizing about 90 percent of their total output, Hoover argued that the level of domestic consumption could be increased to 97 percent of national production. He thought that production accords and protective tariffs would enable the United States to become less and less dependent upon foreign commerce.

Although his enthusiasm for economic nationalism never waned, Hoover remained staunchly opposed to centralized planning to facilitate the creation of a self-sufficient American System. As an unbending devotee of economic liberty, he believed that each person must have an equal opportunity to improve his or her position in the marketplace. Hoover feared that governmental regimentation would not only stifle individual initiative but also undermine entrepreneural freedom. He therefore relied upon voluntary cooperation in the private sector rather than federal regulation in order to achieve an internal balance between supply and demand. While serving as secretary of commerce, Hoover encouraged trade associations and farm organizations to make a concerted effort to match domestic production with the requirements of the home market. He also sponsored a propaganda campaign designed to inspire a basic shift in American values away from an emphasis on personal wealth and toward a commitment to social welfare. Such a moral regeneration, he concluded, would help preserve the essentials of free enterprise in the United States.

Hoover wanted to steer the United States along a middle course which would avoid the extreme forms of individualism and collectivism. Accordingly he worked hard to induce competitive interests to join together in cooperative associations. Hoover believed that the principle of self-regulation, combined with the practice of scientific management and the use of new agricultural methods, would enable businessmen and farmers to increase efficiency, raise living standards, and maintain a balanced economy. He also thought that enlightened cooperation between industrial leaders and labor unions could increase productivity, eliminate waste, and reduce class antagonism. Hoover wanted the government to sponsor and coordinate voluntary programs which would stimulate individual initiative within the framework of collective endeavors. In this way, he explained, the United States could create a "new economic system based neither on the capitalism of Adam Smith nor upon the socialism of Karl Marx." Consequently Hoover said that he favored a "third alternative" dedicated to the principle of "cooperative competition."[4]

Hoover was the prophet of the New Era during the Indian Summer of capitalism. While stock prices were soaring toward dizzying heights on Wall Street, he became the Republican candidate for president, and the speculative boom only confirmed his confidence in the free enterprise system. "We in America today," Hoover exclaimed in his acceptance speech in August 1928, "are nearer to the final triumph over poverty than ever before in the history of any land."[5] Then, after his sweeping victory, the new Chief Executive promised that the United States would continue to bask in the sunshine of prosperity. "I have no fears for the future of our country," Hoover declared in his inaugural address in March 1929. "It is bright with hope."[6] Yet, as the hours of sunlight grew shorter in October 1929, the Great Crash on Wall Street brought the bull market to an abrupt close. And, when stock prices continued to plummet, Hoover's dream of a golden destiny for America turned into the nightmare of a global depression. Soon the dual scourges of want and war threatened the very existence of free enterprise throughout the world.

The crisis of capitalism had its roots in the political economy of the roaring twenties. Although the United States was enjoying a period of swift business expansion at this time, it was not long before the country began to suffer from the ills of industrial overproduction. Technological innovation and scientific management made factories more efficient and workers more productive. But reductions in manufacturing costs were not translated into lower prices for American consumers. Nor did the rise in real wages keep pace with the rapid increase in earnings for big businesses. Consequently, as corporate profits were plowed back into plant construction, the ability of the United States to produce outstripped its capacity to consume. The federal tax policy, which provided relief for the rich but not the poor, only reinforced the maldistribution of income and intensified the twin problems of underconsumption and oversaving. Thus the prosperity of the United States became increasingly dependent upon the exportation of surplus capital and surplus commodities.

The international market structure, however, rested upon shaky foundations. The billions of dollars that Americans loaned the Allies during World War I had transformed the United States from a debtor into a creditor nation. But Republican political leaders, while insisting on collecting the obligations due the country, refused to lower the tariff and accept payment in goods. Instead they sponsored the Fordney-McCumber Act of

1922 which raised import duties to the delight of distressed farmers and small manufacturers interested in safeguarding the domestic market. The Republicans supported a policy of credit extension rather than a program of tariff reduction. Private American loans permitted European countries to buy more merchandise than they sold when trading with the United States. These loans likewise enabled Germany to make reparation payments to the Allies and in turn allowed England and France to pay their debts to the United States. The maintenance of these intergovernmental payments as well as the shipment of American commodities across the Atlantic depended upon the continued flow of dollars abroad. But after the Great Crash of 1929, the export of capital from the United States slowed to a trickle. And, as the financial arrangements which had buttressed world trade collapsed, overseas outlets for surplus American products dried up.[7]

During his years in the Commerce Department, Hoover had hoped that private American investment would help promote the postwar economic reconstruction of Europe. He wanted the Allies to moderate their reparation demands so that American bankers would be willing to invest in the revitalization of Germany. While he advocated reproductive loans which would stimulate European economic rehabilitation, Hoover did not want the American financial community to underwrite European military spending. He not only believed that military expenditures would undermine European economic recovery but he also feared that an arms race would lead to another world war. In a memorandum prepared in January 1922, Hoover called for a European disarmament agreement and a reparation settlement based upon the capacity of Germany to pay. He also advocated private American loans to help promote monetary stability in Europe and thereby protect the American market from European commodities that were subsidized by depreciated currencies. Thus his program for European economic reconstruction dovetailed with his desire to establish a self-sufficient American System.[8]

Hoover hoped that private bankers would cooperate voluntarily with government officials in establishing an enlightened foreign investment policy. Admitting that loans for unreproductive purposes might provide American financial interests with immediate rewards, he warned that unsound investments mighty lead to defaults and thereby embroil the American government in dangerous diplomatic controversies. Rather than making wasteful and speculative loans in hopes of reaping quick profits, Hoover argued, American bankers should invest in projects which would improve living conditions and contribute to international friendship. He wanted to use informal loan control procedures to encourage bankers to comply voluntarily with his high investment standards. Despite his exhortations, however, the masters of capital refused to act in accord with his wishes. Hoover thereupon recommended formal government supervision of foreign loans. But since the State Department opposed his recommendation, Hoover could only continue to urge bankers to behave in a more responsible fashion.[9]

Hoover also demonstrated his desire to promote international harmony by his commitment to the Good Neighbor policy. A few weeks after winning the presidential election in November 1928, he embarked upon a good-will tour of Latin America. During his journey, Hoover gave various addresses and interviews which provided a clear indication of the policy that his administration would pursue toward the countries south of the Rio Grande. "I have come to pay a call of friendship," he declared. "I would wish to symbolize the friendly visit of one good neighbor to another." Hoover completely rejected the idea that the United States should play the role of a big brother who had a duty to act as a tutor and policeman for his Latin American siblings. "There are no older and younger brothers on the American continent," he insisted. "All are the same age from a political and spiritual viewpoint." Thus Hoover promised that after he took office the United States would "abstain from further intervention in the internal affairs of Latin America." During his trip, Hoover constantly stressed the need for respect, friendship, and mutual helpfulness among the family of nations in the Western Hemisphere.[10]

Soon after he entered the White House, Hoover began to act like a Good Neighbor by extending a helping hand in hopes of settling several territorial disputes in Latin America. The Hoover administration succeeded in June 1929 in helping Chile and Peru to reach a peaceful reconciliation of their longstanding boundary controversy. A few years later, Hoover was equally successful in using his good offices to help solve a territorial dispute between Guatemala and Honduras. President Hoover and his State Department aides also tried to keep the peace by lending good offices to Bolivia and Paraguay in an effort to resolve the Chaco affair and to Peru and Columbia in hopes of ending the Leticia controversy. Although neither boundary dispute was settled until later, the Hoover administration did make persistent attempts to diffuse these two explosive issues. Thus, by doing everything in his power to help maintain peaceful relations in Latin America, Hoover made good on his promise that the United States would work to promote friendship among the nations of the Western Hemisphere.[11]

President Hoover also kept his word that his administration would refrain from intervening in the internal affairs of Latin American countries. Shortly after his inauguration, he made it clear that the government in Washington would not enforce private concessions in Latin America or collect debts by military operations. Hoover declared in May 1929 that the United States should not "intervene by force to secure or maintain contracts between our citizens and foreign states or their citizens." In other words, he wanted Yankee businessmen who were investing in Latin American countries to understand that they were doing so at their own risk. And when rebellions broke out in Panama and Honduras Hoover refused to interfere in order to safeguard the economic interests of his countrymen. Hoover not only practiced a noninterventionist policy in Latin America but he also reduced the number of troops that the United States had stationed in the Caribbean. During his administration, all of the Marines in Nicaragua were removed. Hoover similarly prepared the way for the eventual withdrawal of occupational forces in Haiti.[12]

But the response Hoover made to the severe political and economic problems caused by the Great Depression revealed the limits of his conception of what it meant to be a Good Neighbor. A wave of revolutions swept across Latin America following the onset of hard times. Unlike Woodrow Wilson who had withheld recognition from any government which achieved power by means of the bullet rather than the ballot, President Hoover followed the traditional policy of recognizing all governments that exercised *de facto* control regardless of how they obtained power. But the new Latin American governments needed more than official recognition from Washington. They also required foreign markets for their agricultural commodities and raw materials so that they could acquire dollar exchange to service debts due foreigners and to pay for industrial goods purchased from abroad. The Latin Americans therefore hoped that the United States would buy large quantities of their surplus products. Yet, despite their pleas for commercial concessions, Hoover refused to lower the high tariff wall surrounding the United States. Hence his determination to build a self-contained American System narrowly circumscribed his efforts to behave like a Good Neighbor.[13]

Big bankers and large manufacturers interested in foreign commerce vigorously opposed the nationalist economic program sponsored by Hoover. These business internationalists objected to the high American tariff policy because it ran counter to the postwar creditor status of the United States. They pointed out that trade barriers erected to protect the domestic market would make it difficult for European countries to obtain the necessary foreign exchange either to repay their war debts or to purchase American products. Many sophisticated business leaders likewise advocated the reduction of Allied debts and German reparations. American financiers extended large loans to the Weimar Republic to help underwrite the Dawes and Young plan designed to scale down reparations to Germany's capacity to pay. In addition, the members of the corporate community with the most internationalist outlook advanced schemes to refund the Allied debts in an attempt to lighten the burden of payment on England and France. But their efforts were in vain, and the day of reckoning marked the beginning of a decade of depression.[14]

President Hoover's initial response to the Great Depression remained true to his commitment to build an autonomous American System. Shortly after the stock market panic in October 1929, he declared that the United

States could "make a very large degree of recovery independently of what may happen elsewhere." And, despite strong criticism from business internationalists, Hoover supported the Hawley-Smoot Act of 1930 which raised tariff rates to record levels. The president had convinced himself that Americans could solve their own problems, and he boasted that the United States was "remarkably self-contained."[15] His confidence that internal adjustments would be sufficient to restore American prosperity rested upon his faith that enlightened businessmen would put their concern for national welfare before their desire for personal wealth. Thus, hoping to nip the depression in the bud, Hoover optimistically launched a domestic recovery program based upon the principle of voluntary cooperation.

Hoover placed the major burden for promoting economic recuperation on the back of the business community. In a series of dramatic White House conferences, he secured from corporate leaders pledges not only to maintain production, wages, and employment but also to expand construction to create additional jobs. Then the president directed the Federal Reserve System to loosen its credit requirements in order to make money available for capital investment. He also authorized increased federal spending on public works to complement the anticipated rise in private construction. Yet, while Hoover exhorted business leaders not to retrench but to expand their operations, they did just the opposite. Businessmen cut back production, reduced wages, laid off workers, and curtailed construction. Furthermore, while the Federal Reserve System maintained an easy credit policy, member banks used the additional funds to improve their liquidity rather than to make money available for business investment. So Hoover's initial recovery program failed in every detail.[16]

Unwilling to admit failure, however, Hoover began to blame Europe for delaying economic rehabilitation in America. A European financial crisis, commencing in April 1931 when Austria's largest bank closed its doors, led to large withdrawals of foreign gold on deposit in the United States. The particularly severe financial problems in Germany, moreover, threatened the stability of the entire American credit system. If German banks defaulted on the huge notes held in the United States, American banks would be even less willing to make loans at home. President Hoover, hoping to isolate the United States from European financial shocks, proposed a one-year moratorium on all payment of Allied debts and German reparations. "The purpose of this action," he explained in June 1931, "is to give the forthcoming year to the economic recovery of the world and to help free the recuperative forces already in motion in the United States from retarding influences abroad."[17] Although the president blamed European financial disturbances for prolonging the depression, he continued to believe that the restoration of American prosperity need not await European recovery. The United States, Hoover declared in December 1931, could insulate itself from Europe and "make a large measure of recovery independent of the rest of the world." Thus he argued that the "action needed is in the home field and it is urgent."[18]

Hoover moved quickly on the domestic front to strengthen the country's credit structure. As the number of bank failures reached alarming proportions, he persuaded Wall Street financiers in October 1931 to establish the National Credit Corporation. But, when strong banks refused to jeopardize their own position by accepting the slow assets of weak banks, Hoover reluctantly concluded that the government would have to come to the rescue. The Reconstruction Finance Corporation, created in January 1932, was authorized to lend federal funds to railroads, banks, and other financial institutions. The president then pleaded with bankers to extend more credit and with businessmen to borrow more cash to expand their operations. But once again the principle of voluntary cooperation proved inadequate. Although the government made money available, the prevailing pessimism in the business community meant that it would not be used. Hoover had failed to inspire a basic change in American values, and his dream of a corporate Christian commonwealth never became real. "You know," he complained privately, "the only trouble with capitalism is capitalists; they're too damn greedy."[19]

Still Hoover remained hopeful that a renewal of optimism would provide the psychological incentive necessary for overcoming the depression. He subscribed to the prevailing view which held that business confidence depended upon a balanced budget. Yet, because spending on public works was increasing while tax collections were decreasing, the federal government had accumulated the largest peacetime deficit in American history. Believing that fiscal integrity was a prerequisite for economic recovery, Hoover tried to reduce the national debt in 1932 by cutting public works spending and calling for an increase in taxes. But this drive to achieve a balanced budget made it more difficult for Hoover to provide jobs for the unemployed. His commitment to fiscal orthodoxy also made him more reluctant to reduce the war debts and thereby lose an additional source of revenue.

Business internationalists, while agreeing with Hoover on the need to balance the budget, believed that the restoration of American prosperity depended upon the revival of foreign commerce. "It ought to be apparent to every thinking person," declared Will Clayton in April 1930, "that the productive capacity of the United States, both in agriculture and in manufactures, is far in excess of domestic requirements."[20] Business internationalists like Clayton advocated a comprehensive program designed to help make European countries become good customers for surplus American commodities. First and foremost, they wanted to lower the tariff wall which was blocking the flow of trade between Europe and the United States. Second, they desired a drastic reduction in intergovernmental payments to help the former European belligerents put their financial houses in order.

Third, they wanted to induce European countries to cut the military spending which was contributing to their economic instability. Hence business internationalists called for a reduction in American tariffs and Allied debts in exchange for disarmament agreements, currency stabilization, and trade concessions.

The House of Morgan represented the wishes of the internationalists when in the spring of 1932 it made a concerted effort to resolve the reparations-debt tangle. Thomas W. Lamont, S. Parker Gilbert, and Russell C. Leffingwell, all Morgan partners, told French officials that, if the Allies worked out a reasonable and permanent arrangement with Germany, congressional attitudes toward the debts would probably mellow after the autumn elections.[21] The Morgans feared that England and France would use the forthcoming Lausanne Conference to abolish reparations in an attempt to pressure the United States to do the same to their debts. They worried that such a tactic would "harden public opinion in America at the very moment when every proper means should be adopted to soften it."[22] Lamont worked closely with Norman H. Davis to deter the British from taking any action that might suggest that the Allies were preparing to repudiate their debts to the United States. "If at Lausanne," they warned, "there should be a complete cancellation of German Reparations the first impression given in America would be the Governments over here had not attempted to reach the best settlement with Germany that could be arrived at, but simply had addressed themselves to lying down on America to take care of the German default."[23]

Nevertheless, at the Lausanne Conference in June 1932, England and France agreed to terminate reparation demands against Germany, but only on the condition that the United States should similarly renounce its claims regarding war debts. Although disappointed by the British and French, Secretary of State Henry L. Stimson concurred with business internationalists like Lamont who believed that a settlement of the question was "of vital importance to our own economy and to any revival of our export trade."[24] Stimson thus thought that the United States should acquiesce in the Allied maneuver to repudiate their financial obligations. President Hoover disagreed. He complained to Stimson in July 1932 that "the European nations were all in an iniquitous combine against us," and he insisted that "the debts to us could and should be paid." Stimson replied that, if he and Hoover differed so fundamentally, he "couldn't give him much good advice" and therefore he "ought not to be his advisor."[25]

This issue remained dormant for several months only to explode like a bombshell in Hoover's face. Almost immediately after the election in November 1932, Great Britain asked the defeated Hoover administration for a suspension of its debt payments including the installment due in the next month. Other nations soon made similar requests. "The quicker we get these damn debts out of the way," Stimson noted, "in some settlement, in which I hope we may be able to get some *quid pro quo* for our concessions, the better off we will be.''[26] He cautioned Hoover that, although the United States should try to get the best bargain it could, he "didn't expect that we were going to save much of the debt." Hoover retorted that Stimson was "ten millions of miles away from his position," and he reiterated his belief that the debts could be paid because they were "merely a chip on the current ordinary prosperity.''[27] Hoover was adamant because he did not accept the internationalist argument that American recovery depended upon a revival of European trade which in turn depended on debt cancellation.

During his last months in the White House, however, Hoover decided to pursue a *quid pro quo* policy. Great Britain had abandoned the gold standard in September 1931, and Hoover feared that cheap European goods would flood the American market if other countries followed England off gold and devalued their currencies. He also fretted that the American credit system would be undermined if massive military spending produced a financial collapse in Europe. Desiring to protect American banks and markets from further shocks from abroad, Hoover wanted to trade debt reduction for monetary stabilization and arms limitation. His willingness in effect to make the moratorium on intergovernmental payments permanent was consistent with his high tariff position. Both revealed his firm belief that the United States could, if given the chance, pull itself up by its own bootstraps.

Japanese officials, in stark contrast, did not think that their narrow chain of home islands could operate successfully as a self-sustained economic system. During the last third of the nineteenth century, Japan had embarked upon an ambitious modernization program which stimulated visions of imperial grandeur. The swift pace of industrial development enabled Japan to export finished goods in exchange for raw materials and foodstuffs imported from abroad. The rapid expansion of overseas commerce, in turn, made it possible for Japan to support a growing urban work force on a limited natural resource base. As the country experienced a dramatic population explosion, it became increasingly dependent upon foreign trade. Japanese leaders, realizing the vital importance of export outlets, soon began casting covetous eyes on the potentially vast markets in the Orient. They hoped, in particular, to obtain exclusive business concessions in China.[28]

But Americans insisted that the Open Door policy should prevail in China. At the beginning of the twentieth century, the United States had extracted from the leading European and Asian powers pledges to respect the territorial integrity of the Chinese Empire and the principle of equal commercial opportunity in each Chinese province. American businessmen believed that, given a fair field and no favor, they would be able to capture a large share of the China market.[29] But Japanese diplomats, hoping to take advantage of European distresses during World War I, demanded special economic privileges in China. The United States responded in 1922 by sponsoring the Washington Conference, and the American delegation succeeded in getting the Japanese to renew their promises to abide by the traditional rules of the game in the Orient. And this new order for the Far East remained intact as long as Japan continued to enjoy prosperity within the framework of the Open Door policy.[30]

The onset of global depression and the resurgence of Chinese nationalism, however, presented a serious threat to the Land of the Rising Sun. The hard times caused a drastic decline in western demand for Japanese goods. The United States, which had been the largest consumer of Japanese exports, reduced its purchases from Japan by more than 40 percent between 1929 and 1930. To make matters worse, Europeans joined with Americans in erecting high tariff walls against Japan. The Chinese nationalists, in the meantime, began to boycott Japanese products and to undermine Japanese interests in the province of Manchuria. As a result, in 1931, the United States replaced Japan as the biggest shipper of commodities to China. Japanese leaders, faced with the loss of Oriental as well as Occidental markets, concluded that the principle of equal commercial treatment had failed to meet the needs of their country. Thus, after the Japanese army seized Manchuria in September 1931, civilian authorities in Tokyo decided to set up Manchukuo as a puppet state whose doors would be closed to American trade.[31]

American officials differed in their response to the Japanese move to carve out an exclusive sphere of economic influence in Manchuria. Secretary of State Stimson wanted to suspend trade with Japan. He believed that the Japanese industrial structure would quickly collapse if it were denied access to export markets and raw materials from across the seas. But President Hoover ruled out the option of economic sanctions. He feared that any attempt to badger Japan into withdrawing from Manchuria might lead to a military conflict in the Pacific. In line with his predilection for economic isolation and his Quaker dislike of violent confrontation, Hoover believed that the United States should employ moral suasion rather than physical coercion against Japan. The president hoped that public condemnation would ultimately persuade the Japanese to cooperate voluntarily with the United States in upholding the principle of nondiscriminatory trade in the Orient. Stimson yielded to Hoover, and in January 1932 the secretary announced that the United States would not admit the legality of any forceful change in the territorial integrity of China. By refusing to recognize Manchukuo, the Hoover administration reaffirmed American economic interests in Asia without risking war with Japan.[32]

The League of Nations, led by Great Britain, remained equally cautious. Meeting at Geneva in December 1931, the League established a commission under Lord Lytton to investigate the Sino-Japanese conflict, and in March 1932 the powers assembled at Geneva adopted the nonrecognition policy.

Britain refused to go farther and impose sanctions of any kind against Japan. The British were willing to acquiesce in the establishment of Japanese hegemony in Manchuria if Japan would respect Britain's imperial concerns elsewhere in the Far East. London therefore applauded in October 1932 when the Lytton Commission recommended the creation in Manchuria of an autonomous regime which would remain under China's sovereignty and yet safeguard Japan's special interests. But the Japanese were infuriated when the League endorsed the mild Lytton report, and in February 1933 they withdrew from Geneva. Then the Japanese promptly consolidated their position in Manchuria and extended their control into other provinces in northern China.[33]

Secretary of State Stimson became increasingly concerned about the Japanese menace to American commerce in Asia. Unlike President Hoover, he never subscribed to the notion that capitalism could work within the confines of a single nation. "Our foreign trade has now become an indispensable cog in the economic machinery of our country," Stimson asserted in November 1932. "It is essential to the successful and profitable functioning of our whole nation."[34] For that reason, he concluded, the American government should exert its influence to keep the door into China open. Stimson reiterated his internationalist outlook a few months later. "Our trade with the Far East has stood the test of the depression more satisfactorily than has our trade with any other region abroad," he declared in March 1933. "It is thus apparent that our policy and action in the Far East are matters of great practical importance to the present and future welfare of the United States."[35]

Stimson had already taken it upon himself to urge President-elect Franklin D. Roosevelt to look after American commercial interests in Asia. During a visit with Roosevelt at Hyde Park in January 1933, the retiring secretary of state spoke at length about the situation in the Orient. Stimson expressed confidence that the Chinese would eventually succeed in resisting the Japanese penetration of their northern provinces. Roosevelt agreed with Stimson that "Japan would ultimately fail through the economic pressure against the job she had undertaken in Manchuria."[36] A week later, Stimson informed the League of Nations that there would be no break in American policy toward the Far East after the new administration took command. Stimson also let it be known in Washington that Roosevelt would support the nonrecognition doctrine when he entered the White House.[37]

Roosevelt made it clear from the very outset that his administration would sustain the American commitment to the Open Door in China. Some members of Roosevelt's famous advisory group, the Brains Trust, were dismayed. Hoping to promote domestic recovery through internal economic experimentation rather than external commercial expansion, Rexford Tugwell and Raymond Moley warned Roosevelt in January 1933 that the continuation of the nonrecognition policy toward Manchukuo might result in a war with Japan. Roosevelt admitted the possibility of a military confrontation in the Pacific, but he told Tugwell and Moley that he had no intention of abandoning American interests in China.[38] Neither did Cordell Hull. After replacing Stimson as secretary of state, Hull told one of his subordinates that "we would fight if Japan tried to tell us that we would not be allowed to trade in China."[39] Thus, while Tugwell and Moley were preparing to launch the New Deal at home, Roosevelt and Hull were looking ahead toward development of New Frontiers abroad.

Before the decade came to an end, however, American leaders would be haunted by the nightmare of a closed world. The Germans were intent on establishing economic hegemony over the entire European continent, and the Japanese aimed to build a huge Asian trade bloc under their suzerainty. Yet Hoover still clung to his noninterventionist position. Rather than favoring the deployment of military force to keep the world open for American exports, Hoover remained committed to his utopian vision of capitalism in one country. But the Roosevelt administration refused to acquiesce in the Axis attempt to partition the planet into exclusive spheres of economic influence. Believing that free enterprise depended upon foreign commerce, President Roosevelt decided to create a war cabinet, and in June 1940 he appropriately selected Stimson to serve as secretary of war. Then Roosevelt, aided and encouraged by the internationalists in his cabinet, gradually maneuvered the United States toward involvement in World War II.

Freda Kirchwey: Cold War Critic

Margaret Morley

In her role as editor and publisher of the liberal journal, *The Nation,*
Freda Kirchwey was one of the Truman administration's most persistent
critics during the early Cold War years. While Kirchwey has not been
completely ignored by historians, her comments on American foreign policy
have received little scholarly attention. Thomas Paterson describes Kirchwey
as a "temperate Cold War critic," and he points out that she deserves more
attention. June Sochen also acknowledges Kirchwey's expertise in foreign
policy. In addition, Alonzo Hamby, Barton Bernstein, and Mary McAuliffe
have cited Kirchwey in their work on American liberalism. Sarah Alpern
has written a dissertation about Kirchwey and her relationship with *The
Nation.*[1]

Kirchwey was born and raised in New York. Her father, George W.
Kirchwey, was Dean of Columbia Law School. Shortly after graduating
from Barnard College in 1915, Kirchwey married Evans Clark. In 1918,
after working briefly for the New York *Morning Telegraph, Every Week,*
and the *New York Tribune,* Kirchwey joined *The Nation*. She advanced
rapidly. In 1919 she was head of the International Relations Section and an
associate editor. Three years later she became managing editor. By 1933 she
was executive editor, and in 1937 she assumed the additional responsibility
of publishing the journal. She continued to edit and publish *The Nation*
until her retirement in 1955.[2]

From 1944 through 1947 Kirchwey voiced a liberal perspective on the
Cold War. It was one that in retrospect seems somewhat wide of the mark.
Yet Kirchwey made important points about both the origin and the nature
of the Cold War.

During 1944 Kirchwey wrote numerous editorials and delivered one major speech on the subject of postwar relations between the United States and the Soviet Union. In almost every editorial and in her February 27 address to a New York audience, Kirchwey discussed what seemed to her the most important lesson of World War II, that fascism must not be tolerated in Europe after the war. Indeed, she believed it should be eliminated completely, and she anticipated it would be if Europeans were given opportunities to control their own destinies.

Kirchwey was as staunchly antifascist as many Americans were anticommunist. Her conviction was deeply rooted in the events of the 1930s. According to Sarah Alpern, fascism was dangerous in Kirchwey's opinion for three reasons. It was undemocratic, it was aggressive, and it was a threat, not only in Europe, but also in the United States and Latin America.[3]

Kirchwey spent much of her professional life opposing fascism. In the thirties her opposition caused her to fundamentally alter *The Nation*'s editorial position on America's proper role in international affairs. The journal had long advocated an independent American role in foreign affairs, but under Kirchwey's direction it supported internationalism and collective security. This involved considerable risk, for it meant a decisive break with Oswald Garrison Villard, the former editor and publisher whose family had founded *The Nation*.[4] It also meant the loss of thousands of readers who were loyal to Villard and his point of view. Eventually enough subscribers were attracted by *The Nation*'s new editorial stance to keep the publication afloat, but the change was costly.[5] Clearly Kirchwey was determined to speak her mind, and she did so with deep conviction.

About the time an Allied victory in Europe seemed only a matter of months away, Kirchwey began expressing her concerns about the remnants of fascism that would exist in Europe. Unlike many Americans she did not assume that the war represented a final defeat. Kirchwey never quite forgot the Spanish Civil War and the failure of the United States government to do more on behalf of the beleaguered Republicans. Spain remained a central cause and concern throughout her life. But her concerns about the dangers of fascism were not limited to Spain or confined to the Spanish experience. In fact, they were central to her analysis of the postwar world.

Typically Kirchwey expressed her opinion bluntly and succinctly. If fascism remained a political option in Europe after the war, something she argued that could only happen by design, Europe would eventually be divided into two blocs. The Soviet Union would be compelled to establish a sphere separate from the West to protect its own national interest. During the 1930s the Soviets had fought fascism. Kirchwey predicted they would do so again if necessary. Postwar unity, in Kirchwey's analysis, was directly related to the nature and structure of postwar European society.[6]

This analysis in turn was based in large measure upon Kirchwey's assessment of the dynamics of European society, torn apart by war and with revolutionary change almost inevitable. Kirchwey worried that the western democracies, including the United States, would once more attempt to salvage as much of the old order as they could in this revolutionary setting. In doing so, Kirchwey feared, they would place themselves in opposition to the legitimate claims of leftist elements. They would also be tempted to bolster conservatives who represented plausible alternatives. The results would be disastrous because the old order, which she held responsible for the tragedy of world war, would retain control. The mistakes of the past would be repeated. The wartime alliance of Russia, Great Britain, and the United States would collapse.[7]

Kirchwey saw conservative church, business, and government leaders in both the United States and Great Britain supporting conservatives, including fascists. And she was convinced that their influence was actually greater in 1944 than it had been in the prewar years. These people, she believed, would make strong efforts to prop up conservative, reactionary governments which they saw as stable, safe alternatives to revolutionary regimes. "The illusion that peace is secured by propping up reactionary governments threatens the success of a new world order," she wrote in 1944.[8]

Kirchwey fought this trend by constantly voicing her hopes for democratic alternatives, especially in editorials written in 1944 and 1945. She also expressed strong disapproval of any accommodation with fascism. For example, *The Nation* called for the resignation of James C. Dunn from the State Department on the grounds that he had been supportive of fascism. Kirchwey criticized Admiral William Leahy for an attitude toward Vichy France which she felt was too friendly. When Leahy became a member of President Harry Truman's staff, Kirchwey objected.[9]

Not many Americans shared Kirchwey's concerns about fascism in postwar Europe. And, as it turned out, not many agreed with her views of Russia, either. Kirchwey admitted that the Soviet Union was not the first choice of Britain or the United States as an ally against Hitler. But she clearly understood what many Americans found difficult to accept, that the war had elevated Russia to great power status.

Alpern provides a helpful interpretation of Kirchwey's pre-World War II views of Russia. She believes that Kirchwey saw Soviet communism as a matter of choice, a decision made by the Russian people and thus a legitimate system of government. This was the basis for her acceptance of Russia, an attitude which she did not modify later, even when under pressure to do so.[10]

Americans responded differently to Russian communism. Liberals were no exception. During the 1930s when some liberals felt compelled to take a public stand against the purges underway in Russia, others strongly opposed this action. Kirchwey refused to enter this fray.[11] Eventually she had to abandon the middle ground. When she did, she moved into what is

159

occasionally called the noncommunist group, as opposed to the anticommunist faction.

She condemned the Moscow-Berlin Axis, but predicted it would not last. She recognized the alliance had provoked hostility toward Russia among the American public. She warned against hysteria and urged caution.[12] Perhaps because of her acceptance of the authenticity of the Bolshevik regime, Kirchwey's attitude toward Russia remained basically favorable. In any case, in 1944 she clearly thought that Russia was a power that the United States could live with.

In 1944 Kirchwey predicted that the Soviet Union would dominate Eastern Europe. She believed that if fascism remained a viable option in Europe, Russia would try to control that region. But she saw other reasons the Russians might wish to create a *cordon sanitaire* around themselves. They might do so for protection from reactionary governments, or perhaps, as she put it, "in any case, just to be on the safe side."[13]

Even before the Russian army made its spectacular advances in the summer of 1944, Kirchwey noted that it was carving out new boundaries in Eastern Europe. She assumed military domination would be translated into political influence for the Russians as it had been earlier for the British and the Americans in Italy. The prospect did not alarm her. Russia was going to protect its interests and would, she predicted, reject anti-Soviet governments in Eastern Europe if only for the sake of security. The most the United States could achieve was "some modification of revolutionary control."[14]

Literature on the origins of the Cold War has reached substantial proportions, yet the question of Russian motivation remains controversial. Clearly Kirchwey rejected the view that the USSR was a militant expansionist as well as the corollary assumption that communist expansion represented a threat to American interests. Her point of view coincides more closely with that of the revisionists who see security and self-interest as fundamental reasons for Russian policy in Eastern Europe. Like the revisionists Kirchwey argued that Russian insecurity would result in a tighter grip on Eastern Europe. For her the best solution was cooperation, not confrontation.

In 1944 she briefly discussed possibilities for commercial agreement between the Soviet Union, the United States, and other Western nations. Not worried about an American depression, as many of those were who called for increased east-west trade, she did note that American labor would benefit from improved commercial relations with the Soviet Union. She wanted continued Allied unity and she saw such economic arrangements as one way of meeting a crucial Russian need, restoration of its shattered industrial structure.[15] Economic cooperation would also complement a system of collective security which would in turn produce the stability required for future peace.

The fragile nature of the alliance between the Big Three did not escape Kirchwey. Though she called for solutions to difficult problems such as eastern Poland, she was often better at defining the problems than suggesting ways of resolving them. Even as she spoke about the need for unity among the Big Three, Kirchwey understood how difficult it would be to maintain that unity once the war was over.

About 1960, in her prospectus for a history of *The Nation,* Kirchwey wrote that the journal had tried to head off the Cold War "which could be seen approaching close on the heels of the San Francisco conference."[16] The problems centered on Eastern Europe, especially Poland. Kirchwey had not only predicted that the Russians would establish a sphere of influence in that region, she had accepted it as a reality. She was critical, therefore, of American attempts to diminish Russian influence in Eastern Europe. In her opinion these efforts amounted to bickering and they obscured the major challenge, which was forging a cooperative spirit that would replace the wartime alliance.[17]

Probably Kirchwey never won many Americans to her point of view. Indeed, she acknowledged that the settlement in Poland was one that angered both liberals and conservatives. She pronounced the Yalta decision on Poland "a pretty decent compromise." Although historian Robert Messer suggests that she could not have known exactly what that compromise was, Kirchwey would have agreed with Roosevelt that he had done the best he could for Poland.[18] An anti-Russian government in that country was unacceptable to the Soviet Union. Kirchwey recognized that Roosevelt was in for a fight over Yalta, and presumably she was ready to support him. His March speech to Congress on the conference disappointed her. She wrote that, ". . . the substance of the address seemed thin and the total effect rather loose-jointed and inadequate." But she added that the storm the president was facing would not be dissipated by a speech, no matter how effective. Fear of Russia motivated many and, Kirchwey noted, Senator Burton Wheeler was already proclaiming the betrayal of Poland.[19]

Kirchwey had actively campaigned for Roosevelt in 1944. She thought his reelection would be an important factor in US-Russian relations. When Roosevelt died, she observed that the balance of political forces would probably shift to the right. She described the new president as a practical politician who had his "feet on the ground."[20]

Nevertheless, the Truman administration and Kirchwey were soon at odds on the question of Eastern Europe. Kirchwey maintained that Russia was acting no differently there than the British were in Greece or, for that matter, the Americans in Japan and the Philippines.[21] Though she approved of Harry Hopkins's mission to Moscow in late May 1945, she described it as "an emergency salvage operation." By June she observed that a cycle of fear and reprisal had set in. She also noted that "the problem of establishing a solid basis for peaceful, cooperative relations remains unsolved and, for the most part, unfaced."[22] This dangerous trend could be averted, she argued, not by pressuring Russia, but by allaying its fears and suspicion.

In May Kirchwey had flown to San Francisco to cover the United Nations conference. She observed that the United States was forcing the Russians to justify every move. Kirchwey thought this was counterproductive. She commented that the Russians could not be bullied. Ending lend lease and withholding loans would not make the Soviets more cooperative in Eastern Europe. More importantly, she argued, reduction of Russian power was not an alternative available to the United States.[23]

All this does not mean that Kirchwey placed the entire blame for the Cold War on the United States. She thought Russia sincerely wanted an international organization such as the United Nations to succeed, but she realized the Russians were also acting in their own self-interest in ways that undermined the UN's objectives. Nevertheless, Kirchwey was willing to give the Russians considerable latitude. She called for actions totally unacceptable to the Truman administration, which was moving toward a hard line on Soviet affairs. For example, Kirchwey would have allowed the Russians influence in the Mediterranean.[24] She also recommended that they be given full information about the atomic bomb. Neither of these recommendations was acceptable to the administration in 1945—or later, for that matter.

When the American bombs exploded over Hiroshima and Nagasaki, the United States had no atomic policy. Many Americans believed the widespread but mistaken notion that there was such a thing as an atomic secret and that it could be kept for the foreseeable future. The perceptive comments Kirchwey made about the atomic bomb in the fall of 1945 parallel those made by Gregg Herken in 1983. As early as August 1945 Kirchwey argued that it was an "absurdity" to try to limit knowledge of the bomb to the United States, Britain, and perhaps other friendly countries. Other nations, including Russia, would discover how to crack atoms. The secret was not a secret at all. "Atomic energy," she wrote, "should no more be controlled by a few sovereign nations than it should be by a few private companies." Furthermore, the secret might turn out to be a weapon aimed at Americans, she predicted, because if, as she assumed, the United States did not intend to use it first, Americans were creating suspicion "without any compensating benefit." President Truman and George Marshall might see the bomb as a sacred trust, but not everyone in the world was certain the United States would not violate that trust. An Anglo-American monopoly of the atomic bomb was not a solid foundation upon which to build international trust.[25]

Although the United Nations was the logical organization to control atomic weapons, in 1945 Kirchwey was reluctant to give such responsibility to the organization without changes in its structure and rules. Also, both the Western powers and Russia would have to accept genuine international control of atomic power and the requisite changes in the UN. In early December *The Nation* sponsored a public conference on the subject of the atomic bomb whose final recommendation supported civilian control of atomic power.[26]

Most astute was Kirchwey's comment that the bomb was not a bargaining counter to be used to extract concessions from Russia. She was right. At the September 1945 Foreign Ministers' Conference in London, possession of the bomb did not give the Americans dominance and indeed it contributed to a deadlock in the negotiations.[27]

By the year's end Kirchwey was disappointed. She had recognized that the wartime coalition might break down. She had warned about the consequences of such a collapse. Russia, she argued, needed peace even more than the United States did. But Russia was not as weak in 1945 as it had been in 1918. It was politically stable and it had acquired a sizable industrial plant, millions of workers, and "vast experience in planning." German material and perhaps labor would be available to Russia.[28] The Soviet Union could, if necessary, stand alone. Neither military nor economic pressure would force Russia into positions which compromised its security. Americans, she wrote, were "romantic egotists" who sometimes had "delusions of superiority."[29] When agreements on the Balkans were reached later that year in Moscow she commented that they came months too late and at the cost of ill will and defeat.[30]

Adding to Kirchwey's disappointment was the fact that remnants of fascism remained in Europe and the Western Hemisphere. Franco still controlled Spain. In the spring of 1946 the issue of fascism was receiving attention because of elections in Argentina and consideration being given Spain by the United Nations. Kirchwey still held the conviction that fascism threatened every democratic principle Americans have ever professed. President Truman and Secretary of State James Byrnes were, she maintained, repeating old mistakes by opposing both an open debate on Spain in the Security Council and a plan for multinational sanctions against fascism. Already the admission of Argentina to the United Nations and Peron's victory in February elections in that country alarmed Kirchwey. Although the United States was working behind the scenes on a Vatican proposal to replace Franco with a more moderate regime, Kirchwey intended to speak out against Franco as long as he remained in power. She personally visited members of the American delegation to the United Nations in the fall and wrote letters to President Truman and Secretary of State Byrnes.[31]

I. F. Stone, who was on *The Nation*'s staff in the 1940s, was equally critical of the United States' position on Spain. He saw it not as a repetition of past error but as a result of the Cold War. Because American policy makers viewed the world as split into two hostile blocs, they were unwilling to take risks in Spain. Stone write that American officials "would rather have some kind of reactionary regime in Spain other than Franco's, but they prefer Franco to a republic, in which the leftist parties might be in power."[32]

For the second time in her life Kirchwey traveled in Europe during the spring of 1946. Her trip included a stop in Paris during the third Foreign

Ministers' Conference and visits to the Middle Eastern nations of Palestine, Lebanon, and Egypt. Whether something happened on this trip is not clear, but by August 1946 Kirchwey had modified her position on Russia. She became more critical of Russian policies in Eastern Europe which she described for the first time as repressive. She may have been disappointed that Russia's heavy hand was causing the loss of popular support among Europeans who would otherwise affirm the Soviet Union's revolutionary aspirations. For the first time during the early Cold War she acknowledged that Russian actions were perceived as violating individual and political freedom.[33] It is not certain that she agreed with this view, but if she did it represented a reversal of her earlier position that Russian communism was not a threat to democracy. A clue to her thoughts may be found in a comment she made in the fall when she observed that Russian charges against the United States would sound self-serving "as long as large contingents of the Russian army graze on the poor lands of Eastern Europe and reparations draw a big portion of the area into Russian hands."[34] Interestingly, she did not renew her earlier suggestion that strengthened economic ties between the United States and the Soviet Union would benefit both. Perhaps she thought such arrangements were beyond the realm of possibility. Perhaps what she observed firsthand in Paris caused her to describe the Russians' attitude as one of "implacable hostility even where policy should have dictated conciliation."[35] This position, she observed, weakened the Russians' case and strengthened the hand of Byrnes and Senator Arthur Vandenberg.

During the spring and summer of 1946 Byrnes made proposals for Germany that won approval from many Americans, including Kirchwey, but not from the Russians. As a result Germany was eventually divided. Kirchwey held the United States partially responsible for this division because it was reluctant to endorse basic changes in German society. This point was related to another key element in Kirchwey's analysis of American foreign policy during the early Cold War era, her conviction that revolutionary changes in Europe were not only inevitable but absolutely necessary. Throughout 1946 she reiterated her belief often. Surely her message was not one the Truman administration wanted to hear. "The issue of revolutionary change," she wrote in October 1946, "is the one great overriding issue in all Europe." The war had shattered Europe's economy and there was "the glaring need of a planned, closely integrated system of production and exchange. . . ."[36] Free enterprise principles, no matter how excellent in theory, did not fit the situation. Moreover, to the degree Americans insisted upon these principles, they appeared self-serving.

Kirchwey also made a specific connection between democracy and socialism. "Many powerful democratic elements [in Western Europe] firmly believe their only chance of holding on to political freedom is by moving as fast as possible toward a Socialist economy." She added, "The heavy weight of America on the capitalist and reactionary side is losing us allies among these groups. . . ."[37] Kirchwey did make a distinction between democratic socialism and revolutionary socialism, but it was neither sharp nor clearly defined.

Kirchwey applied this analysis to Germany and later to Greece. She suggested that pre-World War II forms of capitalist organization should give way to new arrangements: ". . . the old system must be replaced with some form or degree of collectivist control, under democratic sanctions." Among the first to go would be the German cartels. Like James Warburg, an expert on German affairs and a fellow Cold War critic, Kirchwey opposed revitalization of German cartels, particularly because they had given Hitler important support.[38] She understood the preference of American industrialists and financiers with German ties for rebuilding old economic institutions and reviving former ways of doing business. Such inclinations had to be resisted, she argued, if Germany was to be truly reformed. "The prospect of restoring private enterprise in Germany will appeal only to the class which financed the Nazi movement." A thorough revolution in Germany meant "division of the big estates, the demolition of the ruling class, the smashing of its trusts, an end to the whole structure of power—industrial, agrarian, military—that degenerated during the bitter inter-war years into fascism."[39] This had to be done, Kirchwey argued, or Germany might be lost to the West, unless of course the economic and political influence of the United States checked the impetus toward socialism in Western Europe. As early as September 1946 Kirchwey was aware that this very well might happen.[40]

The Cold War contributed to an unusual political event in the fall of 1946. President Truman approved, then disavowed, a speech his Secretary of Commerce Henry Wallace delivered in Madison Square Garden in September. Wallace called for reconciliation between the two superpowers. Secretary of State Byrnes, then in Europe, felt the ground had been cut out from under him. Truman responded by firing Wallace.

Coincidentally the Nation Associates, an educational and fund-raising organization, was meeting in Los Angeles in September. Their topic was timely: "The Challenge of the Postwar World to the Liberal Movement." Kirchwey was a scheduled speaker and she titled her remarks, "The Challenge of Henry Wallace." She endorsed Wallace's proposal that the United States as the strongest power in the world should attempt "a statesmanlike effort to crack the circle of enmity by a direct effort to relieve Russia's fears and dissipate its suspicions." Kirchwey hoped Wallace's actions would rally liberal supporters for "a democratic foreign policy." These progressive forces would counter the right-wing coalition then dominating American foreign policy under the label of bipartisanship. This kind of political action was what she had implied was necessary in 1944.[41] Ultimately, of course, the movement Wallace began in 1946 floundered in the presidential campaign of 1948. Kirchwey did not endorse Wallace in that election.

By the spring of 1947 the British grip on Greece had slipped so far that they notified the United States of their imminent withdrawal. Without the British presence civil conflict, barely under control, was likely to escalate into war. The Truman administration decided it should intervene. The rationale for the American action came to be known as the Truman Doctrine and the policy as Containment.

Kirchwey was not the only commentator who responded negatively to the Truman Doctrine. The respected journalist Walter Lippmann agreed with Kirchwey's criticism of the unilateral nature of the American action which bypassed the United Nations, not only in Greece, but also in Turkey.[42]

The anticommunist nature of the Truman Doctrine bothered Kirchwey. The aim of the United States was to stop the Russians, she suggested, "because if we don't, Russia won't stop short of—well, where? Perhaps Iran, perhaps China, perhaps Rio or New York. Who knows?" American fears of Russian designs on the Mediterranean, Africa, the Far East had brought the United States to the point where it was issuing a declaration of "political and economic war on Russia."[43]

For Kirchwey the discouraging point of all this was the fact that the revolution in Greece was not made in Moscow. It was, Kirchwey believed, an indigenous revolution, symptomatic of a society in need of reform. The British had long thwarted change and now the Americans were going to pick up where the British left off. Even if the Americans succeeded where the British had failed, Kirchwey warned, victory might be temporary. ". . . stabilizing an economic system that needs to be rooted out and strengthening a government that needs to be . . . at least invited to resign—are not going to provide a lasting substitute for thoroughgoing social change." President Truman was declaring a war America might not be able to win.[44]

Kirchwey realized the cost would be high. Though the administration asked for a limited sum in March 1947 Kirchwey correctly perceived that Containment meant stopping communism "whatever the means or the cost." She argued that Americans could not assume their arms and money would prevail. She clearly understood that the Truman Doctrine represented a major expansion of the American economic and military commitment. The United States, she wrote on March 22, "is going to support its rapidly expanding interests in every continent." Consequently American arms went to Turkey, where Kirchwey argued the United Nations should respond to any Russian threat, and no American aid went to give or sell wheat to Yugoslavia. The discrimination was clearly political.[45]

As for the second half of the Containment policy, the Marshall Plan, Kirchwey was ambivalent. She recognized Europe needed help and that the

United States had the funds. She also perceived the plan as something different from Truman's policy in Greece and Turkey, a substitute for that policy. She applauded the Marshall Plan's multinational character and anticipated that this time the UN would not be bypassed. She hoped all European nations would be included, even socialist or revolutionary countries.[46]

Her reservations, and later her criticisms, involved the nature and motivation of the plan. She warned against an effort to build "an economic Maginot line" against socialism, and she cautioned against the expectation that the American system could be duplicated in Europe. She also noted the enormous economic benefits Americans would receive if the markets of Europe were revitalized. American prosperity was directly related to the economic health of Europe.[47]

By late fall Kirchwey's apprehensions became reality. The Russians left the Marshall Plan talks and the East European countries followed them. The hope of a general reconciliation based upon economic cooperation was dashed. The West would rebuild alone. Equally disappointing for Kirchwey was the exclusion of the UN from the reconstruction program.

By the end of 1947 Kirchwey had altered her views in a limited sense. She was less concerned about fascism and its implications for American foreign policy. She was more critical of the Soviet Union though her opinion that Russian communism was not a threat to the United States remained unchanged. She remained hopeful, but not optimistic, that relations between the United States and Russia could be improved.

Kirchwey was worried about the expanding American commitment to prevent the spread of communism wherever it might threaten. Many times she pointed out that the way to deal with communism was "to recognize the industrial and agrarian revolution that is sweeping Europe and Asia and to work with not against it." If this were done, she argued, Americans would be able to "take the revolution away from the Russians."[48]

She did not believe Americans were either naive or innocent, though they might act as if they were when it was to their advantage. Americans' sense of superiority led them to assume that other nations wanted to emulate them or to believe that they had a right to tell other nations how to conduct their affairs. She warned that the American system was not always appealing to others and could not always be duplicated elsewhere.

Although Kirchwey believed American policy stemmed from a determination to protect and advance American economic interests, she did not connect this directly to the swelling tide of anticommunist sentiment in the United States or to the policy of Containment. In addition she generally underestimated the enormous power of the American economic system. Yet by 1947 she had come to recognize the significant and overwhelming economic advantages Americans had in comparison to the rest of the world.

These advantages could not be translated into security, she warned, and she observed that security would remain an elusive goal as long as the Cold War was being waged.

The challenges and the dangers facing the United States in 1947 were as great as, if not greater than, they had been in 1945. The obvious reason for this was the onset of the Cold War, something Kirchwey had hoped could be avoided. She continued to warn Americans of the dangers of their foreign policy and to suggest alternatives. She made a significant contribution to the dialogue about American foreign policy in those crucial years.

The Atomic Temptation, 1945-1954

Lloyd C. Gardner

Appearing before a secret session of the Senate Foreign Relations Committee in early 1953, outgoing Army Chief of Staff General Omar N. Bradley told the senators use of the atomic bomb in the Korean War had been discussed "many times." The problem had always been to find a proper target, one that "we think is sufficiently remunerative" to warrant depleting the "stockpile." "However, get them out in the open, and I think we would have to consider it very seriously." Bradley's reluctance to promise instant results from the use of the nuclear option and his apparent willingness to accept that the risks of such a move outweighed the benefits left many committee members unsatisfied. Republican Senator Homer Ferguson expressed this frustration with a question others had been asking since the outbreak of the war nearly three years before: "Can't we wipe them out, so that they will have to quit?"

General Bradley's answer was not encouraging: "If you want to go to full mobilization and go to an all-out war with China, you will have a chance of doing that. I still would not swear that will end it."[1]

A few days later the new Secretary of State John Foster Dulles reported to this same committee that the Eisenhower administration had underway a review of the entire situation, and was considering the "possibility of a blockade" of the China coastline, along with measures to increase reliance on South Korean forces. But he, too, slid away from the sixty-four dollar question. "Our Allies," he said, were "particularly anxious for assurances that we will not use atomic weapons from British bases without British consent—as well as from other areas."[2] It was part of the basic dilemma, he added, that had made it extemely difficult to find the right course for

American foreign policy. Typically, Dulles put the blame on the nation's allies. They were "old, tired, worn out, and almost willing to buy peace in order to have a few years more of rest." But the "leadership of the world" had passed to the United States, "and the free world will only be saved if it gets out of us what is lacking in the rest of the world."[3]

From the dropping of the atomic bombs on Hiroshima, August 6, 1945, and on Nagasaki three days later, down to the stalemated Korean War, and beyond that to the first Indochina crisis in the spring of 1954, American policy makers wrestled with the considerations that General Bradley and Secretary Dulles laid before the Senate Foreign Relations Committee:

> First, How could the atomic bomb be used without destroying what it is one is trying to save, or without causing an all-out war with the Soviet Union?
> Second, How could the bomb be employed diplomatically, or, put another way, how could nuclear energy be reconverted to achieve political ends?

I

"The Greatest Scientific Gamble in History"

In Mark Twain's *A Connecticut Yankee in King Arthur's Court,* the Connecticut Yankee is matched against the wizard Merlin in a fateful test to see which of them can restore the waters of a holy fountain to which generations of pilgrims had come to refresh themselves and restore their faith. The theme is not unique to Twain. Henry James, for example, also dealt with variations, many times over, of the confrontation between new world "knowledge" and old world "mystery," political innocence and jaded sophistication. In Twain's version, the old abbot of the monastery where the fountain is located implores the Connecticut Yankee and Merlin to save them. "An we bring not the water back again, and soon, we are ruined, and the good work of two hundred years must end." Merlin tries all his magic—and fails. In despair, the abbot turns to the man who will be dubbed Sir Boss for the feat he is about to perform. The visitor from the future tells the abbot that Merlin is right about one thing: the well has been put under a spell by "that spirit with a Russian name."

The Connecticut Yankee, meanwhile, has discovered that no spell has caused the trouble, but rather an underground leak. He is rather sorry to have made this discovery, however, for it had occurred to him that many centuries later blocked oil wells could sometimes be blasted out with a dynamite torpedo. "If I should find this well dry and no explanation of it," he muses, "I could astonish these people most nobly by having a person of no especial value drop a dynamite bomb into it. . . . However, it was plain that there was no occasion for the bomb. One cannot have everything the way he would like it."

Yet, he continued musing, "that bomb will come good yet. And it did, too." Having repaired the leak in secret, Sir Boss places several hogsheads of rockets at strategic places in the surrounding courtyard. Uttering strange incantations, he signals aides to start the pump going, at the same time he touches off the rockets. "A vast fountain of dazzling lances of fire vomited itself toward the zenith with a hissing rush, and burst in mid-sky into a storm of flashing jewels!" Science had triumphed over magic, at least for the moment, in King Arthur's time. But the people had been deceived in the process. If the ultimate objective was to release the grip that magic had over reason in men's minds, here was perhaps a bad omen. Science had triumphed by *becoming,* in outward form at least, a kind of magic. Yet Sir Boss had no doubts or regrets. "It was a great night, an immense night. There was reputation in it. I could hardly get to sleep for glorying over it."

President Harry S. Truman's reaction to the dropping of the atom bomb on Japan reads like a line from *Connecticut Yankee.* "This is the greatest thing in history." The press release, first prepared months earlier, used the words "marvelous" and "amazing" to describe what had been achieved in the United States. "It is doubtful if such another combination could be got together in the world. What has been done is the greatest achievement of organized science in history."[4] Those who had watched the first test of an atomic bomb on the Day of Trinity, July 16, 1945, experienced both the awe and the satisfaction of Sir Boss and Harry Truman. Some who worked on the bomb had already come to fear, however, that using the new weapon to hasten Japan's defeat, however many American lives would be saved, might endanger the ultimate purpose of their work: to make war impossible.

On November 2, 1945, J. Robert Oppenheimer, scientific director of the Manhattan Project, delivered a farewell message to five hundred of his colleagues at Los Alamos. Oppenheimer reviewed the reasons why they had all worked so hard to make the bomb: originally there had been the fear that the enemy might achieve the weapon first and, when that concern abated, other reasons surfaced, among them curiosity and a sense of adventure. Then there had been the political arguments. In this last category some felt that the only way to make the world aware of the danger that was now only one war ahead was to build the bomb—and use it. Oppenheimer, although he did not mention it here, was among that number. "And there was finally," he concluded, "and I think rightly, the feeling that there was probably no place in the world where the development of atomic weapons would have a better chance of leading to a reasonable solution, and a smaller chance of leading to disaster, than within the United States."[5]

For the atomic scientists building the bomb had been an "organic necessity," an unstoppable drive to find out how the world works and then "to turn over to mankind at large the greatest possible power to control the world and to deal with it according to its lights and its values." As Oppenheimer's remarks demonstrated, he was already aware of the atomic temptation, and did not claim immunity for himself. Where the scientists took satisfaction in their understanding of science's "mission" in America, which ennobled even motives of curiosity and desire for adventure, the nation's political leaders were already proclaiming the bomb's achievement a uniquely American accomplishment, bestowing upon them an obligation— and now the ability—to reorder the affairs of a world that had come so near to ultimate disaster in World War II.

Sometimes regarded by others (and sometimes self-defined) as politically naive, Oppenheimer examined the subtle intricacies of the atomic temptation that scientists had placed before statesmen. Even a nation as fully democratic as America was, and as generously inclined, would have to take care to avoid the approach, "We know what is right and we would like to use the atomic bomb to persuade you to agree with us." For those willing to work on a new "Manhattan Project," then, the task was to educate politicians to the fullest recognition of the opportunities and limitations the new atomic age permitted and required. It would be a delicate undertaking. Oppenheimer had been reading, he said, about how Abraham Lincoln had by-passed the temptation to strike out at slavery at the outset of the Civil War, relying instead upon preservation of the Union—the community—to work the eradication of the evil that had caused the war. Scientists must learn from this example. The lesson seemed to be, although Oppenheimer was not exactly clear in his meaning, that neither political leaders nor scientists could run very far ahead of the community. Scientists must be willing to pace themselves as properly as Lincoln did to save the Union and, as a result, to eliminate slavery.[6]

Oppenheimer attempted to pace himself in this fashion on an individual basis, and found, to his dismay, that the opinions of the scientific community were not sought, except when they coincided with those of the political community. The relationship between the scientific and political cultures in the United States had been an exceedingly useful and important one from the nation's beginnings. But the established pattern, above all the superior role of political decision making, was not altered by the discovery of a weapon that promised what Americans had been looking for throughout their history. And when the immediate postwar confusions solidified into the Cold War bipolarity of the 1950s, the dissenting atomic physicists were replaced at court by a congeries of "strategic" thinkers drawn also from the ranks of mathematicians, social scientists, and, increasingly, a hybrid mix of academics professing expertise in the new field of deterrence calculations.[7]

II

From Forts to Fortress America

Most studies of the evolution of nuclear strategy begin the story in the post-World War I era when the ideas of the Italian air power enthusiast, Giulo Douhet, began to be circulated widely in military circles. In America, for example, Douhet's principal disciple was the romantic figure of movie legend, General Billy Mitchell. Douhet prophesied that aerial bombardment would cause a complete breakdown of the social structure in industrial society, thereby forestalling the mobilizations of mass armies. Mitchell went even further, predicting that "a few gas bombs" would paralyze a city, and the ability to paralyze several cities in like fashion would win the war.[8]

Whatever validity these theories would have in the atomic age, to begin the story in the post-World War I years is to start too late. Much had already happened that would shape strategic decisions not only in that decade or in World War II, but well into the future—indeed into our midst in the 1980s.

From the beginning of this nation's history, strategic decisions were influenced by both geographic and political considerations. Isolated from Europe by the Atlantic Ocean, Americans enjoyed not perfect security from potential enemies, but a wider range of options from which to choose a defense strategy. Fearful of large standing armies and strongly centralized governments, dedicated to the doctrine of economic liberalism, and characterized by a reliance upon their "native" penchant for inventiveness, Americans devised a strategic "mix" as early as 1794 that included a limited navy, a small regular army (capable of being expanded by a citizen militia), and extensive coastal fortifications. Just before the War of 1812, budget allocations for this purpose totaled up to 10 percent of the national budget. Construction of these forts continued for nearly a century and a half, as the United States became the first nation in the world to construct seacoast defenses on such a large scale. In peacetime, the forts would require only maintenance. Here was a solution that would avoid huge army budgets, and the inevitable expansion of federal power that would follow. "They could stand virtually empty awaiting, like the militia, the call to arms when war broke out." Reflecting the defensive emphasis on strategy, the forts "also reflected an American emphasis on technology as an alternative to the maintenance of substantial military forces."[9]

The outbreak of war in Europe in the summer of 1914 caused policy makers to rethink the strategic defense problem, but not to abandon their conviction that America could not "afford," either economically or ideologically, to imitate the "armed camps" that European nations had become. Intervention in the war was risky for the well-being of democracy, as no one understood better than the president, but the choice was either that or face a greater danger that defense budgets would grow and grow over the years, starving out vital social programs, and thus undermining democracy without a shot being fired. Woodrow Wilson's quest to make the world safe for democracy ultimately ended in frustration, a fact that has too long overshadowed a larger truth about the plan for the League of Nations. In Wilson's original scheme for an international army, all governments would be spared the necessity of yielding to pleas for ships and guns, instruments that, in the thought of the day, made men slaves to their scientific creations, and produced the fateful arms race and the secret diplomacy that all but made war inevitable. And that, even without war, destroyed liberal democracy from within.[10]

Wilson's idealistic internationalism, condemned by conservatives and liberals alike in the wake of the failed effort to secure the Senate's adherence to the peace treaty, was, nevertheless, a perfectly legitimate rendering of themes handed down from the Founding Fathers. Having authorized the building of the seacoast forts, they agreed with General George Washington who, as first president of the land, admonished his successors to avoid entangling alliances as the mainstay of national defense. "The thing that he longed for," Wilson declared upon returning from Paris in 1919, "was just what we are about to supply; an arrangement which will disentangle all the alliances in the world."[11]

Naturally, not everyone agreed with Wilson that he had been doing Washington's work in Paris. To many, on both the right and the left, the only result of American participation in "Mr. Wilson's War" had been to plunge the United States into the roiling waters of European politics. And there was at least a potential alternative available. Already apparent in World War I, air power suggested, as Douhet and Mitchell would proclaim, that a nation with enough technological skill and capacity could protect itself without compromising its political principles or exhausting itself with military spending. As Wilson foresaw, air power would have great appeal for isolationist thinkers, and for all those who rejected both the idea of a supranational authority as well as the projected costs of maintaining an armed force adequate to intervene abroad. Air power represented the antithesis of his program. "I desire no sort of participation," he said of nascent air strategies, "in a plan . . . which has as its object promiscuous bombing upon industry, commerce, or populations in enemy countries disassociated from obvious military needs to be served by such action."[12]

As an isolationist-minded Congress in the early New Deal years prepared to investigate the possibility that a conspiracy of munitions makers and bankers had pushed America into the maelstrom of war in 1917, the Army Air Corps was inviting contractors to submit bids for a multiengine bomber. The aircraft must have a range of 1,020 miles, be able to carry a 2,000-pound bomb load, and fly at speeds of at least 200 miles an hour. The Boeing Aircraft Corporation won the bid, and produced such a plane within a year. "In 1936 the Army agreed to buy thirteen such planes, which it designated the B-17 and called the Flying Fortress, in politically expedient but ironic suggestion that the purpose was thoroughly defensive."[13]

Franklin Roosevelt shared none of Wilson's fears about air power. A Navy man brought up on Admiral Mahan's geopolitical theories, as well as the vision pioneered by his cousin Theodore's building of the "Great White Fleet," FDR watched the world crisis deepen in the 1930s and tried to plan his options accordingly. In the dark period after the fall of France in the spring of 1940, Roosevelt issued a challenge. America would build 50,000 airplanes—a year![14]

The basic decision on air power planning and deterrence had been made earlier in White House meetings with military advisors at the time of the Munich Conference in September 1938. Up until that time, in fact, Air Corps theorists had been blocked by the General Staff whenever they brought forward their plans for a bomber force that would make the B-17s seem primitive. General Henry "Hap" Arnold called Roosevelt's decision in favor of heavy bombers the "Magna Carta" for the Air Corps. It is particularly noteworthy, in this regard, that while the Axis threat of a choice between war or peace by blackmail was the precipitating factor in the White House decisions, and while American military planners pointed to Hitler's air force as the dominant consideration in the Anglo-French appeasement policy, they did not think tht Germany understood strategic air strategy. Certainly, it was asserted, the German dictator did not display any great awareness of what it would take to defeat England. "If the Germans had 'understood' strategic bombing," it was asserted, "and had constructed appropriate weapons and tactics, they could have reduced Britain to a shambles in 1940."[15]

American air doctrine, then, did not take its clue from the experiences of other nations, but proceeded on its own momentum toward the strategy of deterrence and, when that failed, daylight precision bombing. Confident of Roosevelt's backing, the Air Board submitted a study on September 1, 1939, calling for the acquisition of an airplane that would have at least twice the range of the B-17. This study led ultimately to the building of the "Super-fortress," the B-29, that would come into its own in the latter stages of the Pacific War and which, when modified, became America's first atomic "delivery system." The rationale for the B-29 finally abandoned the emphasis upon defense, substituting for that concept the newly formulated politico-military strategy Roosevelt favored: deterrence.

In requesting Army Chief of Staff General George C. Marshall to approve research on still larger planes than the planned B-29, the Air Corps argued in June 1940 that the United States should have weapons to carry the strategic offensive into an enemy's homeland. The ultimate objective should be a bomber capable of reaching Berlin from the United States, in retaliation for any aggressive acts which the Germans might make against this continent. Possession of such weapons would do more to insure Western Hemisphere security than any other measure. Hitler feared attacks on his homeland, said Air Corps spokesmen, and unless the Germans could outbuild the United States, and develop bombers with a longer range, the outcome was certain. In fact, there would be no outcome at all, because there would be no war.[16]

For the time being, of course, America had no airplane capable of reaching Central Europe. To compensate for that gap in air power theory, Roosevelt moved in 1940 and 1941 to secure advanced bases for the air fleet he had ordered constructed. Invoking the Monroe Doctrine as justification, the United States in early 1941 declared that "defense facilities in Greenland should be constructed and protected by and be under the sole jurisdiction of the United States." An "agreement" had been negotiated with the Danish Minister in Washington, but everyone knew that America had made an offer that could not be refused. Greenland thus became an American protectorate, at least for the duration. The immediate stimulus for American action had been the appearance of German airplanes over Iceland, but behind that was concern over Canadian interest in building air bases on Greenland. Roosevelt, in fact, had recently become troubled about British moves in the North Atlantic, specifically London's decision to occupy Iceland with military forces. Publicly, he had welcomed the British decision; but in private he expressed concern that the same thing not be tried in Greenland. To prevent that from happening, and to preempt any German attempt to counter with plans of its own for air bases on those territories, Roosevelt acted.[17]

The military protectorate over Greenland has slipped out of historical memory, except for specialists in the World War II era. Used primarily as a ferrying point for the transfer of American bombers to England during the war, the Greenland air bases later became an essential outpost in the Cold War. The one built at Thule, for example, was constructed with runways 2 miles long, necessary for the "Super-fortress" B-29s, and their successors the B-36s. Thule was 800 miles from the North Pole, and 2,800 miles from Moscow. After a tour of the completed base in September 1951, the Army Chief of Engineers praised the feat as "the biggest job in Army engineering history."[18]

That was high praise, indeed, for a proud corps that had built the seacoast fortifications in the nation's first century and a half, the years of strategic defense. But a decade before the first bombers roared down Thule's runways, the era of deterrence had dawned; it awaited only "the weapon" to hasten the final transformation of theory into reality. Assistant Secretary of State Adolf Berle, a former "Brains Truster" in the early New Deal, immediately grasped the significance of what had happened:

> This of course is the first true "strategic point" (European style)—a case where we are forced to move primarily lest a military enemy should grab it

first and make trouble for us. I am glad that there is not very much territory in the Arctic, and so few people. . . But it is, I think, a distinct step in the American position. For the first time, the Monroe Doctrine has to be implemented on a frontier.[19]

III
S-1, The Redeemer

During a break in the Potsdam conference, General George C. Marshall paid a visit to two American military commanders—Generals Maxwell D. Taylor and George Patton—at Berchtesgaden. After lunch the three retreated to the local sports field to watch army athletes perform in a track meet. There, in the warm Bavarian sunshine, recalled Taylor, General Marshall casually imparted the news of the test of the atomic weapon at Alamogordo. "Gentlemen, on the first moonlight night in August, we will drop one of these bombs on the Japanese. I don't think we will need more than two."[20]

Like many others hearing the news for the first time, Taylor also recalled, his first thought was that the world would never again have to fear a Hitler or Mussolini. He soon changed his mind about what he would label the "Great Fallacy," deprecating reliance on the bomb and the "new strategic creed, eventually to be known as Massive Retaliation."[21]

Army officers had watched the growth of air power doctrine and strategy with mixed feelings. As it happened, however, General Marshall had been a strong supporter of Roosevelt's position favoring heavy bombers. The performance of the B-17s, as airplanes, had rewarded the faithful, yet the strategic results in Europe did not demonstrate the bomber to be a conclusive factor in warfare. The advent of long-range fighter craft had finally enabled the B-17s to carry out their mission—daylight precision bombing—but the length of time it had taken to get to this stage hardly warranted celebrations of Billy Mitchell as the prophet of a new era. Once advanced as a more humane form of warfare, the reality of strategic bombing now suggested that the *only* way it could achieve what enthusiasts promised was by being the most inhumane form of warfare known. Air Marshall Sir Arthur "Bomber" Harris, for instance, was enthusiastic about plans for leveling Berlin, believing that night air attacks might force the Germans to surrender without any invasion at all. The Germans retaliated with the V-1 and V-2 campaigns against London, which came too late to influence the outcome, but hinted at what one could look forward to in the next war, should there be one.[22] Americans professed to be repulsed by such terror tactics, and their moral objections were in line with American air doctrine, but in February 1945 American bombers participated in massive raids on several German cities, culminating in the famous attack on Dresden. These were to be preludes to the Pacific air campaign of 1945, which, General Curtis LeMay confidently predicted, would at last prove beyond doubt the arguments of strategic bombing theorists.

The Pacific air campaign had begun, of course, with the Japanese attack at Pearl Harbor on December 7, 1941. The effectiveness of that raid, ironically, had provided the most convincing demonstration prior to the last year of the war of air power's usefulness. The raids on German factories after the start of the war certainly did not prevent mobilization, and up until mid-1944 had barely made a dent in war production. Pearl Harbor, on the other hand, had forestalled an enemy's ability to mobilize large forces rapidly. But it had not knocked America out of the war. And it dulled moral sensitiveness to a revenge bombing campaign against the Japanese home islands. Neither result was what Douhet or Mitchell had promised.

General LeMay's argument for imitating RAF bombing methods in Asia stressed the difficulty of achieving precision results where an enemy's industrial capacity was indivisible from its cities. Whether Pearl Harbor memories or reports of Japanese atrocities made a difference or not, LeMay had clear sailing for his new style bombing campaign. Using stripped-down B-29s capable of carrying heavier loads of incendiaries and of flying at low levels, he initiated an area bombing campaign at the same time American officials in Europe were still criticizing the British bombing offensive. On March 9, 1945, LeMay sent 334 of these specially modified B-29s against Tokyo. In loss of life this was to be the most destructive air raid in history. A quarter of the city's buildings were destroyed, a million left homeless, and over 83,000 killed.[23]

Secretary of War Henry L. Stimson "thought it was appalling" that there was no public outcry in the United States against the fire raids, but he did not order them stopped. For a time LeMay's insistence that air power alone would force Japan to surrender was enough. "I don't think he can keep his cities from being burned down—wiped right off the map," LeMay said of the enemy. If this "works we will shorten this damned war out here." His best estimate of when the war would end was October, when his air command would run out of targets.[24]

LeMay was not the only military or political leader with a huge stake in strategic bombing, however. Roosevelt's commitment to the long-range bomber, at the expense of creating a more balanced military force, and his decision to place a ceiling on army manpower in order to avoid wartime political turmoil and to minimize postwar demobilization trauma, reflected past American attitudes and governed behavior into the future. A great deal was on the line. Personal reputations were at stake, but after Roosevelt's death the real issue was no longer what "Dr. Win-the-War" had prescribed, but the search for "Dr. Win-the-Peace." Every day that the second front had been delayed in Europe made that search more difficult. At first there had been the threat of a separate peace in the East, then, as the tide of battle turned on the Russian front, the ominous forward thrust of the Red Army into Eastern and Central Europe.

Denial of Russian requests for four-engine bombers under the Lend-Lease agreement appeared, in this context, a message about the postwar world. Whatever the Soviets knew about S-1, the atom bomb project, and whatever Americans *feared* they knew about it at this stage, no doubt added to anxieties about the success of strategic bombing. From a Russian point of view, what the Americans believed about their weapon was intelligence information as important as the details of the way they were going about building it. Similarly, from an American point of view, concern about German progress in developing an atom bomb soon ran behind a growing preoccupation with preventing the Russians from knowing how close the United States was to a successful test of the weapon.[25]

The Western Allies had denied the Soviets four-engine bombers for the same reason that FDR had sought to deny Greenland to the Nazis. But the "Flying Fortress" strategy had not been effective in the European theater until 1944, and it actually worsened the situation diplomatically by slowing production of airplanes for tactical use in troop support.[26] Yet, there remained a continuing desire to demonstrate the effectiveness of air power, both for historical reasons having to do with purely domestic concerns, and to boost leverage in the postwar world. Stalin always asked how many divisions a country seeking great power status could mobilize; Roosevelt and his successors were more concerned with how many squadrons of planes were available.

With evidence of Japan's continued "fanatical" resistance on Okinawa and Iwo Jima before them, however, General LeMay's assertions appeared less than fully convincing to military planners. The growing likelihood was that it would take an invasion of Japan to "win" the war in Asia, though a few—a very few—questioned the need for "unconditional surrender." Revenge was the primary motive for carrying the war to the home islands even after it was clear that Japan could not project its power abroad; but there was also the problem of the Japanese troops in Southeast Asia and Manchuria.[27] Based on the experience of the bloody island campaigns, General Marshall asserted on behalf of the Joint Chiefs of Staff that an invasion would have to be launched at the beginning of November—a month after LeMay predicted strategic bombing would have won the war—and that it would cost the United States up to a million casualties.[28] In private, moreover, Marshall was seriously considering whether it would be necessary to break the taboo on the use of poison gas to eliminate the nightmare of seeking out the "fanatical" Japanese resisters with the expected high casualties that would cost. The initiation of gas warfare, he suggested to Admiral Ernest King in a memorandum of June 14, 1945, at a "militarily sound time" would hold down expected American losses.[29]

Four days later, at a White House conference, General Marshall summarized the situation as the Joint Chiefs saw it. To force Japan into unconditional surrender would require air bombardment and a sea blockade as well as an invasion, "perhaps coupled with the entry or threat of entry of Russia into the war . . ." Russian entry into the war, or even the threat of Russian entry, he added, might well be "the decisive action levering them into capitulation. . . ."[30] The desire for Russian entry into the Far Eastern war had led Roosevelt to seek an overall arrangement with Stalin at the Yalta Conference, and in recent days the desire for Russian participation in order to save American lives had been reconfirmed, but national leaders had always been uneasy in their innermost thoughts about how Americans and Russians could cooperate in postwar Asia, especially in China, under conditions of a vastly enlarged Soviet military presence in the Far East. Added to the perennial Russian longing for warm water ports, warned a State Department memorandum in 1943, was a Soviet determination to control all revolutionary movements in areas that came under their influence. Because of the chaos the Japanese withdrawal would leave behind, local authorities might seek to counter Russian pressure with an appeal to the United States for aid. The results could be serious for hopes of avoiding a postwar confrontation.[31]

Pre-Cold War concern existed, then, and the changeover in viewpoint in 1945, it should be emphasized, was not a necessary condition to the search for an alternative to the possibility of an unwanted collision with the Russians. A Russian request for a share in the occupation of Japan would also clash with American determination to "reform" the feudal empire and bring it into line with modern liberal-capitalist societies, a guarantee, it was thought, of future peace in Asia. At most, then, early Cold War fears were an added stimulus. To these considerations should be added the concern the new president's close advisors felt about boosting his self-confidence. The great danger of the hiatus created by FDR's death on April 12, 1945, believed many policy makers, was the problem of slippage. If Truman was unable to grasp the reins quickly enough and firmly enough, the peace could be lost. At the same time, there was the problem that Stimson and others encountered whenever they attempted to talk seriously with Truman about any modifications in the unconditional surrender position toward Japan. The president clearly did not want to listen to such proposals. As far as he was concerned, Roosevelt's policy in that regard would remain unchanged.[32]

With military victory assured, the United States faced the future in a curious frame of mind. On the one hand, it was clear that the nation would emerge as the "superpower" of the postwar world. Yet in important areas serious self-doubts remained. Among the greatest of these in the political-military area was the still undemonstrated validity of strategic bombing. What hung on the outcome of strategic bombing—or appeared to—was not only military victory, but, as we have seen, a collection of related concerns that went to the heart of American*ism*. This included those long-held beliefs Americans cherished about themselves and their institutions: faith in technology, diplomatic "independence" from the "old world," and the tenets of "liberalism" as they applied especially to the limited role of military spending and controls on the central government. Yet not only had FDR's original faith in deterrence been undermined, but the failure of strategic bombing to bring about Japan's unconditional surrender had forced American military men to accept a previously repugnant area bombing offensive—and even to consider using poison gas—to attempt to do so.

Beyond victory also loomed a series of other problems, including not only relations with the Soviet Union in the immediate future, but the long-range problem of establishing a world order that would last. Woodrow Wilson had originally imagined an international army for his collective security organization. What power did FDR plan to give the United Nations? Decisions would have to be made almost immediately and Roosevelt was gone. "Over any such tangled weave of problems," wrote Secretary of War Stimson in his diary, "the S-1 secret would be dominant and yet we will not know until after that time [the proposed Big Three Conference] probably . . . whether this is a weapon in our hands or not. We think it will be shortly afterwards, but it seems a terrible thing to gamble with such big stakes in diplomacy without having your master card in your hand."[33]

Almost from the first full day of his presidency, April 13, 1945, when James F. Byrnes rushed back from South Carolina to consult with Truman, S-1 was held out to the president as his "master card." Whether it was the opportunity to end the Far Eastern war without an invasion and save thousands of lives or, as was now being suggested in the Interim Committee Roosevelt had appointed to discuss use of the bomb, ways to "manage" the Russians in postwar Europe or, finally, how to establish the foundations of a new world order, S-1 emerged at the top. This is not to say that the decision to use the bomb was an unorthodox military choice, or intended as a shot across Stalin's bow. Quite the opposite. But it would also be wrong to assume that S-1 and use of the bomb itself were one and the same thing: the latter was a particular application of the former.

In their anxiety to reassure President Truman (and themselves?) of America's vast military and political capabilities, and thereby to bestow upon him Roosevelt's cloak of leadership among the Big Three, Byrnes and Stimson exaggerated what scientists believed about the explosive power of the bomb into promises that he would be put into "a position to dictate . . . terms at the end of the war" (Byrnes), and that he must be concerned about "the role of the atomic bomb in the shaping of history as [much] as in its capacity to shorten this war" (Stimson).[34]

"I listened with absorbed interest," recalled Truman, who then approved the Interim Committee's decision not to stage a demonstration of the bomb before it was used on Japan, postponed the date of the Big Three meeting, hoping that the bomb would be tested first, and rejected the idea of asking Russia to join in an ultimatum calling upon Japan to surrender before or at the Potsdam Conference.[35] The bomb's potential had already erased distinctions in policy makers' minds between war and diplomacy, between unconditional surrender and future deterrence, between the problems of alliance politics and the transition to collective security in the United Nations. Whether one calls it "atomic diplomacy" or not, the reach of this new force now extended even to the selection—and in one case, to the rejection—of targets on which to deliver the bomb.

A prime consideration, recalled General Leslie Groves, military chief of the Manhattan Project , was to pick a target that would most adversely "affect the will of the Japanese people to continue the war." Such a target would have to be one not previously damaged by air raids, and of such size as to demonstrate the bomb's power. Strictly military considerations were of secondary importance. Among the targets Groves submitted to Stimson was Kyoto. Bombing Kyoto, Stimson then warned Truman, would be a "wanton act" against a nonmilitary objective (Groves disagreed with this point), a city of great religious and cultural significance to the Japanese, and it might make it impossible to achieve a Japanese-American reconciliation after the war. "It might thus, I pointed out, be the means of preventing what our policy demanded, namely a sympathetic Japan to the United States in case there should be any aggression by Russia in Manchuria."[36]

As details of the successful test of the bomb reached him at Potsdam, Truman was, according to Stimson and others, pepped up, "tremendously pleased," "confident of sustaining the Open Door policy" in China whatever now happened about Russian entry into the war, and "very greatly reinforced" about dealing with the Russians generally. "Believe Japs will fold up before Russia comes in," Truman wrote in a diary he kept at Potsdam. "I am sure they will when Manhattan appears over their homeland. I shall inform Stalin about it at an opportune time."[37]

IV
In Praise of the Bomb

In keeping with the advice given him by the Interim Committee, Truman gave Stalin only a bare hint about the "new weapon of unusual destructive force" America now possessed—only enough to avoid any later charges of bad faith. The Russians knew about the bomb anyway, and Truman thus deprived himself at the outset of one option in initiating atomic diplomacy: a direct approach to Moscow. There were several reasons why he had so chosen. A major factor was inertia. Roosevelt had withheld information about S-1 from the Soviets from the outset of the Manhattan Project, a time, of course, when the Soviet Union was allied to

Nazi Germany, down to his death. The efforts of some of the scientists working on the bomb to change that policy had gone nowhere.[38]

Writing to historian James L. Cate in the last days of his presidency, Truman reviewed the situation when America stood on the threshhold of the nuclear age: "Dropping the bombs ended the war, saved lives, and gave the free nations a chance to face the facts."[39] The last phrase in Truman's sequence is particularly tantalizing. How did he mean the bombs "gave the free nations a chance to face the facts"? Which nations? Which facts? Preparations to inform the world of the facts of the atomic bomb went back several months. A proposed statement for Roosevelt's use when the bomb was dropped asserted that the bomb "changed the very nature of warfare" and held out possibilities "of the most vital importance for the future peace of the world." "The matter has been surrounded with the greatest secrecy and this secrecy must and will be maintained as to methods of production for some time to come." It closed with a description of steps to be taken to investigate methods of control in domestic and foreign policy.[40]

After the test at Alamogordo, the proposed press release was drastically revised to reflect heightened confidence in the new weapon's power to work miracles. The bomb, it said, "was a harnessing of the basic power of the universe. The force from which the sun draws its power had been loosed against those who brought war to the Far East." Also added to this statement was the assertion that there had been a race to get the bomb before the Germans found a way "to add atomic energy to the other engines of war with which they hoped to enslave the world. But they failed. We may be grateful to Providence that the Germans got the V-1s and V-2s late and in limited quantities and even more grateful that they did not get the bomb at all. . . . We have spent two billion dollars on the greatest scientific gamble in history—and won." It had required not only the greatest scientific minds, but the marvelous capacity of American industry to build the bomb. "It is doubtful if such another combination could be got together in the world." This statement threatened the Japanese that if "they do not now accept our terms they may expect a rain of ruin from the air, the like of which has never been seen on this earth." And it closed with a more precise warning that the secrets of production and military application would not be revealed until the government had fully examined "methods of protecting us and the rest of the world from the danger of sudden destruction."[41]

These were the "facts" that Truman's press secretary read out after the bomb was dropped on Hiroshima. At the very moment he was doing so, General Groves still awaited word from the Pacific that the bomb had lived up to expectations.[42] The first results of this public diplomacy, on the other hand, were not entirely what Truman had expected. He found himself, in fact, defending the decision to drop the bomb to church leaders—"When you have to deal with a beast you have to treat him as a beast"—and explaining to an Oregon Democratic leader that his "jubilation" reported in the press "was over the fact Russia had entered into the war with Japan and not because we had invented a new engine of destruction."⁴³ The press release on the bomb had made the president vulnerable on both counts. And that was only the beginning of Truman's difficulties reconciling possession of the "absolute weapon" with public fears of atomic war, on the one hand, and the attempt to squeeze the bomb down to fit into a diplomatic attache case, on the other.

Upon his return from Potsdam, Truman had promised the nation that the Eastern European states under Russian military occupation would not become "spheres of influence of any one power."⁴⁴ Surely with the bomb in American possession the Russians would have to see that, as the president wrote his wife from Potsdam, "I mean business."⁴⁵ But just as surely, readers of the press releases would be justified in concluding, with the bomb in American possession, that the nation could demobilize as rapidly as possible. By its exaggerated praise of the bomb, the administration had sprung a trap on itself: the public would expect Truman to use the new weapon to secure the release of Russia's hostages in Eastern Europe. Anything less would be appeasement. But it would also expect American boys would come marching home—at once.

The only serious threat Truman made, however, was against French leader Charles de Gaulle, who came to Washington in August 1945 to discuss a number of complaints about Anglo-Saxon arrogance in denying France an equal place at the conference table. When de Gaulle pointed out that Moscow had seen fit to negotiate a security treaty with him, Truman brushed it aside as unimportant. "The United States possessed a new weapon," the president said, "the atomic bomb, which would defeat any aggressor." France should get in line, literally, for economic aid, and figuratively, by removing communists from its government and welcoming American businessmen who had thus far found their way blocked in resuming operations.⁴⁶

The assumption that the bomb could defeat any aggressor was highly questionable. The press releases had been designed to suggest, or at least implied strongly, that A-bombs were rolling off the assembly line like Model-T Fords. The truth was that after a third bomb had been made ready for delivery, there would have been an embarrassing period of atomic silence. The press releases did not mention, on the other hand, that the chances of a single B-29 getting through against an aggressor with fighter planes were considerably less than fifty-fifty. The number of bombs needed to defeat Russia—if they were all successfully detonated—would be estimated at over six hundred. To deliver that number would require, then, a safety margin of fifty percent—or more.⁴⁷

In effect, Truman was a prisoner of his own weapon. A direct approach to Stalin after the bomb had been used, finally, and to complete this circle, would be looked upon by the political opposition and the public (as well as members of his own cabinet) as appeasement bordering on lunacy. Yet he had promised the nation he would investigate measures of international control of the atom. At a key cabinet meeting on September 21, 1945, retiring Secretary of War Stimson offered arguments in favor of a direct approach to the Soviets. The object should be to involve Russia from the outset. In a memorandum prepared some days before, the secretary explained that he had changed his mind in the weeks since the Potsdam Conference. He had long believed that sharing "the atomic bomb with Russia while she was still a police state" was too dangerous. But he had come to fear more the dangers of attempting to use the bomb "as a direct lever to produce the change" desired. He also thought that Truman's only hope of getting the Russians out of Eastern Europe was to settle the atomic question first.[48]

The Cabinet divided over the Stimson plan. The president listened sympathetically, and called for additional written statements on the problem. How could he now go to Stalin to "give away" this awesome weapon? Explanations that he was "negotiating from strength," in a phrase Dean Acheson later made popular, probably would not do much good, for, if it came to that, most Americans would rather leave the Russians in Eastern Europe than yield the "secret" of the bomb. That would be true in 1945, and it would also be true in 1985. An unsigned memorandum in Truman's files dated October 19, 1945, provided an example of what Stimson took as his starting points—the deteriorating international situation, the military pressure for heavy armaments expenditure, and the hysterical public discussion that was developing in the absence of accurate information about policy—and offered a specific plan for overcoming them. It proposed that Truman ask for a Big Three conference at which terms for an international agreement "leading to renunciation of the making of bombs together with development of a scheme of cooperation through mutual inspection" could be explored.[49]

The time for such a direct approach and "negotiations from strength" had already passed. But there was a loophole. Stimson's seeming ambiguity about what Truman should share was cleared up by Acting Secretary of War Robert Patterson, who wrote the president that the elder statesman had not meant to include "secret ordnance" in the information that should be put on the table. That eased the pinch somewhat, and permitted Truman and his advisors to unite in good conscience. And so, having used the bomb, Americans succumbed to an understandable temptation: to believe that they had been appointed—indeed charged—with trusteeship of the bomb for humankind. Stimson feared that even with the best intentions this approach would produce precisely the wrong impression on the Russians, and all but insure an atomic arms race.[50]

V

Sending Russia to Coventry

Against a background now littered with broken hopes and made garish by sensational events—the Cold War-like confrontation in Iran, the exposure of Russian atomic espionage in Canada, and the well-publicized atomic tests at Bikini Atoll—the United States presented its plan for the international control of atomic energy to a special commission of the United Nations. The Baruch Plan, as it was now called, consisted of two main elements: a stage-by-stage process of internationalization, at the end of which the American monopoly would be surrendered, and elimination of the veto from the projected international atomic authority. "Unless we get a better working UNO," Bernard Baruch wrote to Byrnes in his original letter of acceptance as American negotiator, "which is the only hope of the world, we will be unable to discuss the elimination of the atomic bomb from armaments because we will be the only ones who will have them."[51]

Baruch was not alone in thinking "that the bomb could override not only the unfortunate decision to include the veto in the original United Nations plan—a mistake actually made by the Western powers—but also undo the post-Yalta solidification of Europe into spheres of influence. The Director of the Office of Scientific Research and Development, Vannevar Bush, had already warned that "our program toward international understanding should involve no premature 'outlawing of the bomb. . . .'" And the United States should not get discouraged. "We hope genuinely to open up Russia, and it will take time."[52]

From the outset the Russian counterproposals were to be based on what Bush deplored, an agreement to outlaw the bomb and dispose of all stockpiles. And the Russian political counterpart of the Baruch Plan would have "reengaged" the United States in Big Three diplomacy, if only to work out arrangements for completing such an agreement and enforcing it. Nevertheless, the Baruch Plan put the Soviets at a considerable disadvantage in terms of world opinion. As early as September 1, 1945, Russian commentators had insisted that the bomb did not revolutionize warfare; yet to dramatize the need for outlawing the weapon, they were forced to admit its power, and the determination of "reactionaries" to dominate the world with the bomb as their major contrivance to achieve this position. Official Stalinist dogma until the time of his death in 1953 was that the bomb could not win wars, that the outcome would always be determined by which society was the strongest, not only in arms but in total organization. Hence socialist states could not lose. But at the same time, in private, Stalin was imploring his chief nuclear scientist, Igor Kurchatov, "Provide us with atomic weapons in the shortest possible time. You know that Hiroshima has shaken the world. The balance has been destroyed. Provide the bomb—it will remove a great danger from us."[53]

The American presumption, then, that the Baruch Plan would force the Soviets into an awkward corner, was not ill founded. What the Russians could accomplish in their corner was another matter. For one thing they could build a bomb. The possibility of an early break in the American monopoly had been considered, but there was disagreement about how long it would take, and where the United States would be when that happened, that is, how far ahead in possessing bombs and their means of delivery. Even during the war the United States and Great Britain had worked closely together on an aspect of "atomic diplomacy," securing virtual control of all uranium sources outside the Soviet Union itself. This campaign was pushed right up to Russia's doorstep when efforts were made to obtain rights to Swedish ore. These failed, but it would have been difficult for the Soviets not to notice what was going on.[54]

One member of Baruch's negotiating team, engineer Fred Searls, thought that the monopoly on raw materials might be enough, in itself, to achieve the aim of opening up Russia. If the United States could prevent the Russians from getting outside sources of uranium, it would slow down work on a bomb considerably. "Ten years may well mean everything in relations with the Russians since, surely, it is only a question of time before internal opinions will force a change in their government's behavior to its own people and to foreign nations."[55] One did not have to agree with Searls about the impact of a raw materials boycott in producing a liberal Russia to accept the related idea that by isolating Russia in the United Nations politically, one could force movement within the Soviet Union toward an accommodation with the West, or, what was soon to become policy, produce a movement in the West toward a unified defense system.[56]

The determination to force the Baruch Plan to an early vote in the UN commission would have the dual benefit of isolating Russia and providing a moral basis for Western unity under the protection of the United States.[57] David E. Lilienthal, head of the Atomic Energy Commission, who had drafted many of the original ideas on which the Baruch Plan was based, felt troubled by Baruch's delight in pushing each phase of the plan to a vote in the commission. "We have made great progress," the negotiator had reported to Truman. "The Commission is with us by a majority of 10 to 2." Lilienthal regarded this as a "joke," but a serious one. "[S]ince it is Russia's agreement that everyone knows must be secured, this baseball score way of judging progress is rather funny if it were not actually pretty tragic."[58]

Cold War crises multiplied in 1947, and the Baruch Plan, in an unusual twist of fate, became a symbol of appeasement to Republican foreign policy critics and an object of derision to "realists," who sometimes blamed it for an extension of the "Yalta" mindset of American policy makers. Isolating Russia, on the other hand, which is what the Baruch Plan helped to accomplish, was a primary goal of the "containment" policy, that, under one name or another, continues to be Washington's approach to Soviet affairs to the present day.[59]

VI

War Gaming: The Early Years

American policy makers found it difficult to go beyond the Baruch Plan in their thinking about atomic issues. This was hardly surprising, because the plan was so typically "American." It had not left room for compromises, just as America's historic geographic isolation had not made them necessary, It assumed a continuation of the monopoly or, at least, the lead. But that was also a long-time pattern. The Truman administration had encouraged the notion that the bomb held the Russians at bay, permitting demobilization and the Fair Deal program to be enacted without undue sacrifice or strain upon the taxpayer. For their part, the Republicans, who won a majority in the 1946 congressional elections, promised economy in all things. Reliance on the bomb's ability to spread largesse, while encouraging thrift, solved age-old dilemmas for both parties.

Few troubled themselves about how "deterrence" really worked, or, indeed, if the United States actually possessed enough deliverable bombs to defeat the Soviets in the event of war. The number of bombs in the American arsenal was a closely held secret. President Truman assured those who asked that the United States had enough to win, but he, himself, had proved curiously reluctant to involve the White House in details of the stockpile. It remains unclear, observes historian David Rosenberg, whether or not the president and the National Security Council were consciously bluffing when they sent two bomber groups to England in 1948 at the height of the Berlin crisis, presumably to demonstrate America's nuclear muscle, for no bombs left American soil, and the bombers sent to England were not even the specially modified Silverplate B-29s capable of carrying the weapon.[60]

If they were bluffing, who was the target? Presumably, Soviet intelligence agents knew how to identify the Silverplate B-29s. In mid-summer 1948, the United States had approximately fifty deliverable weapons at the disposal of the Air Force. The reasons why this was so are easier to list than to explain: sluggish production, the lack of an integrated atomic war plan, overconfidence about the American monopoly, and the assumption that Russia would not put at risk its key industrial and political centers to add to its new empire. By 1950 that situation had been more than remedied, as the United States now possessed nearly three hundred weapons. Clearly, then, 1948 marked a turning point, but the administration's decisions taken in the wake of the Berlin crisis were as much economic and political as military. Building up the nuclear force was cheaper than trying to construct a balanced military force. In other words, Truman acted as Roosevelt had done in the World War II crisis.[61]

Both before 1948, when the bomb was viewed as backing for the Marshall Plan, and after, when the bomb was seen as a parsimonious response to an ongoing crisis instead of a stopgap, there were doubts about how useful it could be. Suppose the United States had had the six hundred bombs it would have taken to insure a "victory." How could that have been accomplished without destroying what one was trying to save? Bombing the Soviet Union would not drive out the invading Red Army; it might deter attack in the first place, but if that failed where would you lay down the bombs? "What would we do with them?" Dean Acheson asked about the bomb late in life, long after leaving office. "Bomb Moscow? Destroy Moscow? Then the Russian army would have moved West. This would have risked Western Europe. The atomic bomb is a very dubious weapon. We couldn't destroy Russia with it. We wouldn't have fought a land war in Europe."[62]

It is probably well to remember that the military decisions of 1948 were not made in a political vacuum. In that election year, Truman faced challenges on the left and the right, Henry A. Wallace and the Dixiecrat Strom Thurmond. Any sign of military weakness would alienate conservative voters, while building more bombs and airplanes substituted for highly visible military policies, such as Universal Military Training, that had gotten the president into difficulties with liberal voters. Granted this political dimension, the temptation to go for atomic "overkill" originated in both military and ideological concern that "containment" would not, as its author George F. Kennan had predicted, bring about a breakdown of Soviet society. Possession of the bomb had proven the tenets of strategic air warfare, provided one had enough weapons and reliable delivery systems. Possession of the bomb, on the other hand, had not achieved the same political end in the Cold War—the unconditional surrender of communism —as it had in making possible the reconstruction of Japan.

Worry about Soviet acquisition of the atomic bomb, the tension of waiting for the other shoe to drop, added to the pressure for "overkill" by making it necessary to have enough weapons on hand, said the Joint Chiefs of Staff, to "strike the first blow if necessary . . . when it becomes evident that the forces of aggression are being arrayed against us." When that might be, and what form it might take, was left unstated. The demand for expanding the stockpile was also explained as a need for obtaining enough weapons to "bring about capitulation, destroy the roots of communism, . . . [and] critically weaken the power of Soviet leadership to dominate the people." The effort to lever change in Russia had not changed since Stimson's warning, only now it had become a mystical numerical equation.[63]

Criticism of Air Force dedication to "destruction and annihilation" arose within the ranks of high Navy officials, but the administration had a good start down the path to "overkill" even before intelligence information revealed in September 1949 that the Soviets had exploded their own atomic weapon. According to some reports, the president at first refused to believe the evidence brought to him. He simply could not bring himself to believe, he was reported to have told a friend, that "those asiatics" could build something as complicated as an atomic bomb. A special committee was named to study the evidence, and to put their signatures on a statement that they really believed the Russians had done it.[64]

The Russian bomb implied stalemate in the Cold War. A more unpalatable end to the "American century" could not be imagined—or explained to the nation. A search for scapegoats began. Quiet deliberation about nuclear strategy and diplomacy could not be expected in an atmosphere where even normally sensible politicians demanded to know who betrayed America's secrets—or, even less rationally, "Who lost China?" Faced with the threat of "defeat" in the Cold War, the response was, as Senator Brian McMahon, Chairman of the Joint Congressional Committee on Atomic Energy, wrote Defense Secretary Louis Johnson, to deny "that we may reach a point when we have 'enough bombs.' To my mind, this doctrine is false." Piling the stockpile higher and higher became a reaffirmation of faith, as well as a requirement for an emerging "counterforce" strategy that would be aimed at Russia's submarine pens and airbases. An increment of bombs above the number (how many more McMahon did not say) needed to destroy industrial targets, "would mean the difference between victory and defeat."[65]

Discussing whether or not to proceed with the hydrogen bomb thus became little more than an academic exercise. Nevertheless, the Russian bomb did prompt a full review of nuclear strategy from a political viewpoint inside the Department of State. Chaired by the head of the Policy Planning Staff, George Kennan, the discussion centered on the bomb's overweening influence in all aspects of foreign policy. What had once been seen as a useful servant, a support system for the Marshall Plan, now revealed itself to be, in Kennan's view, a primordial force let loose to rampage against civilization. Its demands were insatiable. The goal of American defense policy, he said, should be to maintain a strong military machine so as to prevent a world war "where we would have to use it." Kennan called it a "dialectical connection." Others saw paradox. But it amounted to deterrence against one's own bombs:

> We are so behind the Russians in conventional armaments, and the attraction of the atomic bomb to strategic planners has been such, that we are in danger of finding our whole policy tied to the atom bomb. The question, then, in his mind is what we accomplish if we go in for the development of the super-bomb without showing the Russians any ray of light as far as their own policy is concerned; or, putting it another way, wouldn't we be pushing the Russians against a closed door and demanding that they go through it?[66]

Secretary of State Acheson listened to the discussion, and mused aloud at its conclusion about a possible 18 to 24 month moratorium on developing the super—"bilateral if possible, unilateral if necessary—during which time you do your best to ease the international situation . . ." But when he met with the committee Truman appointed to consider the super, David Lilienthal and Louis Johnson, the secretary of state finally came down against such a proposal and in favor of going ahead at once with the hydrogen bomb. Lilienthal had been arguing that "The act of going ahead would tend to provide a false and dangerous assurance to the American people that when we get this new gadget 'the balance will be ours' as against the Russians." Acheson argued in reply that pressure for a decision was too great, that Congressional feeling was so strong that he could not recommend that the president defer any longer. "We must protect the president," he said.[67]

The idea for appointing this subcommittee of the National Security Council apparently originated with a memorandum to Truman from his chief naval aide, Admiral Robert Dennison. Dennison had not talked about political pressure, however. Instead, he had emphasized the role "such an absolute weapon" could play in establishing "world order." His words have an eerie echo today: "It seems apparent that whatever the decision may be regarding the construction of a 'super' bomb we now have a most potent and perhaps critical tool to assist in our negotiations for world peace."[68] The decision for building the super in 1950, like the response in 1945 to Stimson's proposals, emerged out of an American tradition reconfirmed once more by a new discovery, and out of a fear that if the United States turned away from this technological imperative, disaster would follow. As Kennan had foreseen, however, no one felt the same sense of assurance that men controlled their destiny anymore. The world of the Baruch Plan already seemed a long time ago, replaced now by the world of NSC-68.

VII
Limits to Massive Retaliation

In approving the recommendation in favor of building the super, President Truman also accepted recommendations for a general reexamination of "this country's strategic plans and its objectives in peace and war." The result of this study was NSC-68, a basic blueprint that succeeded the much simpler formulations of the original "containment" doctrine of 1947. Its principal author was Paul Nitze. A member of the Policy Planning Staff, Nitze had been present when Kennan voiced his doubts about the danger of attempting to push the Soviets through a closed door. Nitze also believed that building the hydrogen bomb was potentially destabilizing, but unlike Kennan he did not see any alternative, any valid opportunity for attempting negotiations. Before the Russians had the bomb, he reasoned, they had no option for a preemptive strike; but that situation had changed. They might, he feared, reason that their bomb would stimulate American production to a point where the United States would feel itself safe in striking first, and indeed compelled to do so. Before that point was reached, however, there was a possible moment of least danger to themselves in striking first. "Put another way," suggests historian Joseph M. Siracusa, "Nitze had come to fear Soviet fear." And that was the rationale for NSC-68.[69]

The authors of this document predicted that if such a moment came it would most likely occur in 1954, when Russia had sufficient nuclear capacity to launch a strategic strike. America could best prepare against this eventuality by increasing its defense spending, as Kennan had suggested, rather than adopting a doctrine of preventive war. So NSC-68 did not, for all of its bellicosity (including for the first time a charter for clandestine operations by the CIA against Russian satellites), challenge Kennan's implicit paradoxical conclusion that the nation must now arm itself against the atomic temptation, its own as much as the Russian's.

Truman hesitated to put NSC-68 into operation. In the months before the Korean War he was still demanding a defense budget of less than $15 billion. Though it was about to be shattered, the taboo against large-scale military spending in peacetime—the very core of America's special variation on the "liberal" theme—was still strong. And again the bomb, and now the super hydrogen bomb, which had been seen as the way to sustain that core, proved its undoing. Just as the atomic bomb was needed to trigger the fusion explosion of the hydrogen bomb, so did it trigger the most expensive arms race of all. Economy was what the bomb had promised. But all that changed on June 25, 1950. The North Korean attack on Syngman Rhee's Republic of Korea, President Truman told the nation, demonstrated that the Russians had gone beyond subversion to open warfare in their quest for world dominance. Immediate consideration was given to using the atomic bomb to halt the attack. But, as in the European situation, where was the proper target? For one thing, the bomb would not be especially effective on the field of battle. It could not be used close to the front lines. Should an attack be made, then, on Pyongyang? Peking? Moscow?

If not militarily effective in Korea itself, would such an escalation serve American purposes? And what about world reactions to the danger of being plunged into atomic war to secure an area long contested by a myriad of factions and nations, not only Russia and America, but before them China and Japan? Korea was, as General Bradley would put it later, the wrong war, at the wrong time, in the wrong place—at least for atomic weapons. The only situation the military felt would demand the use of atomic weapons, Nitze advised Secretary Acheson, was if an overt Russian or Chinese intervention occurred, threatening an American humiliation.[70]

When the Chinese intervened in November 1950, Truman told a press conference that he had always had the bomb under consideration, and implied that the decision might be up to General MacArthur, the UN commander. That afternoon a hurried correction was issued from the White House. There had been no change. Only the president could authorize use of the weapon. If that authorization were given, however, "the military commander in the field would have charge of the tactical delivery of the weapon." Even this correction was not enough to calm the uproar in Europe, because it again raised the spectre of atomic war. Soon British Prime Minister Clement Attlee appeared in Washington seeking to satisfy himself that Truman did not have an itchy trigger finger, or a faulty communications system with MacArthur's headquarters in Tokyo.[71]

If anything, the Atlee-Truman talks persuaded the president that the United States must stand firm in Asia, must draw the line at the 38th parallel or somewhere close by, lest the rumors that the United States was influenced by appeasement talk make the situation worse. In a way, then, staying in Korea had become a demonstration of America's will to use its atomic weapons in a big war. Here was the most subtle aspect of the atomic temptation. Over and over again from Korea to the present, proof that America was—in the end—willing to use the bomb had to be established by not using it. This paradox forced the nation into a series of "limited wars," fought to preserve "credibility." No enemy should doubt America's intentions, it was argued, for if the United States faltered on any battle-ground anywhere, attempted to shirk even the nastiest or most dubious "communist-inspired" conflicts, it would have no alternative but to "go nuclear" when the Russians, emboldened by a string of successes, went "too far." The Korean situation thus became the model for later involvements. When Attlee asked the president to agree to put in writing a consultation arrangement, Truman refused. "[I]f a man's word wasn't any good it wasn't made any better by writing it down." In brief, America's allies must trust the United States to decide when to consult on atomic warfare.[72]

Yet there was a declining inclination in American policy-making circles to consider the bomb even as a means of last resort to halt a potential rout, should the Chinese hordes prove too much for the UN force. On occasion, policy makers would liken the situation to Dunkirk, an honorable withdrawal at the outset of World War II. Ironically, this position became more acceptable by reversing the logic that had led to an American commitment in Korea. Truman had justified sending American forces on the grounds that resisting aggression in Korea would demonstrate to the Russians that pressing on other hot spots would bring on a war neither side wanted. Now it was argued that the Soviets might well choose to open a campaign for world conquest in Asia, hoping that the United States would fight the Chinese first. Only Russia would benefit from a war between the United States and China. Whether or not a global war was planned, read a memorandum to Acheson, the Russians would gain by a "diversion of effective US and allied forces to operations in an indecisive theater and their attrition and containment there." In other words, the Russians were now not only capable of playing the nuclear game, but of attempting a "containment" policy of their own![73]

Superiority in nuclear weapons, George Kennan opined in one of the crisis discussions in December 1950, actually made it more difficult for the United States to use diplomatic avenues out of Korea. It was desirable to maintain some sort of position in Korea, but a request for a cease-fire would look to the USSR like a suit for peace. Moscow would use it to extract every possible political and propaganda advantage. A threat to use the bomb would, on the other hand, put the Russians in an impossible position. Negotiation from strength turned out to be unworkable in its first test.[74]

On December 22, 1950, President Truman responded to a letter from a Republican leader in the Senate, Henry Cabot Lodge, in which the latter had asked him to cut off Soviet access to American ports out of concern that the Russians might sneak in atomic bombs to destroy the nation's harbors. Truman replied that such a step had been under consideration since the Korean War began, but it had not been possible to find a practical way of doing it. "[Y]ou would be surprised at what a complicated network we get into and finally wind up with very little protection. Eventually we will get it worked out, I am sure."[75]

*   *   *

When the Republicans came to power in 1953 the stalemate in Korea forced President Eisenhower to choose again whether to use atomic weapons. A detailed examination of those discussions is not possible here. Historians still disagree about whether Ike actually ended the war on satisfactory terms by employing a direct nuclear threat. Eisenhower would soon have at his disposal large numbers of tactical weapons, and the means to deliver them. That choice was offered again in 1954 during the first Indochinese crisis. Eisenhower rejected it. But he was deeply troubled over the outlook for the future. American planning under NSC-68, or under containment in general, appeared to him to have put the nation into a situation of long-term disaster. "[I]f the contest to maintain this relative position should have to continue indefinitely, the cost would either drive us to war—or into some form of dictatorial government. In such circumstances, we would be forced to consider whether or not our duty to future generations did not require us to *initiate* war at the most propitious moment that we could designate."[75] On the threshhold of a major new departure in nuclear weaponry, it is well to ponder these words.

"Every System Needs a Center Sometimes"
An Essay on Hegemony
and Modern American Foreign Policy

Thomas McCormick

"Each time decentering occurs, a recentering takes place."
Fernand Braudel[1]

William Appleman Williams once observed that Americans made of their own Civil War "an event so strange, so mystic, so unique that it could have happened only to the chosen people."[2] As he has also suggested, much the same could be said of American perceptions of their international role in this century. Witness the strain of exceptionalism and American uniqueness that informs the queries of historians analyzing twentieth century American foreign policy and the Cold War that capped it. Did an exceptional society fulfill its divine mission to defend civilization against the forces of barbarism and destruction? Or, smitten by the arrogance of power, tragically betray its unique ideals and its special opportunities and launch a global expansion that inhibited democracy, development, and peace? Or merely get trapped in the destructive consequences of its own innocence and ill-conceived good intentions—like Graham Greene's *The Quiet American* in Vietnam? These are proper and pressing questions for everyone who still sustains the Enlightenment belief that issues of political economy and moral philosophy are inseparable. But the failure to go much beyond constitutes a kind of myopia that tends to blind one to the central feature of twentieth century world affairs and America's role in it: that is, the largely *un*exceptional nature of both. Viewed through the longer lens of history, modern American foreign policy (and its climactic Cold War) becomes less a moral fable for our time than yet another (albeit dramatic) chapter in the continuing, five century saga of capitalism's struggle to sustain itself as a viable world-system—a saga marked both by the "imagination of its profiteers and the counter-assertiveness of the oppressed."[3]

*   *   *

Capitalism has *always* been *international* in nature. The key to capital accumulation and profit maximization has always been the mobility of capitalists—especially large capitalists with political connections and economic reserves—to shift their activity from one place to another in order to secure greater returns, even if that other place be both distant and foreign. That was true of a Hanseatic grain merchant in the sixteenth century who rerouted his ships from the Baltic to the Adriatic to take advantage of local famine and exorbitant prices; it is true today of a multinational automobile corporation that relocates its engine production from Detroit to Sao Paulo to take advantage of lower factors of production. Moreover, that same fluidity of capital across international borders was not only key to initiating success but key to renewing capitalism's success after long slumps like those of 1650-1730 and 1870-1900. Such periodic slumps flowed from two antithetical tendencies: the tendency of individual capitalists both to maximize production to protect and enlarge market shares; and to minimize wage bills to reduce competitive costs of production. The social consequence of such cumulative individual decisions was a real or potential overproduction/underconsumption and a decline in the rate of profit. And historically, the major countervailing force to falling profits was international fluidity of capital and goods that optimized opportunities and options to enhance profits and capital accumulation.

In the last decade, a number of academic observers have suggested that this international fluidity had produced, by 1650, a configuration that could properly be described as a world system or a world economy. Rooted in the dense empiricism of Fernand Braudel and the sociological imagination of Immanuel Wallerstein, this analysis posits three central characteristics for that world system—as true in 1950 as in 1650.

1) At any given point in time, the system occupies a "given geographic space"—"one portion of our planet, to the degree that it forms an economic whole."[4] Moreover, that "geographic space" has tended to expand historically to integrate more and more of the earth and its inhabitants into a world market economy; that is, to enlarge the arena of capital mobility and profit maximization.

2) At any given point in time, the system requires a pole or center—a dominant city to act as the coordinator and clearing house of international capital: Venice in 1450, Antwerp in 1550, Amsterdam in 1650, London in 1850, and New York City in 1950.

3) At any given point in time, the system consists of successive zones, each performing a specialized function in a complex international division of labor. The center, or core countries, monopolize high-tech, high-value added, high-profit enterprises and their auxiliaries of finance and insurance; the hinterlands, or peripheral areas, are the "hewers of wood and the carriers of water," specializing in production of primary commodities both agricultural and extractive; and in between, the semiperiphery performs intermediate functions of semifinishing products, mobilizing local capital, and sharing in transport.

What is striking about this world system is that it is *always* changing and *never* changing. The geographic boundary of the world system is always expanding or (on occasion) contracting; but a discernible boundary is always there between the capitalist world economy and its external world— the minisystem of subsistence or the maxi-empires of the Ottomans, the Russians, the Chinese. The center is forever shifting, from the Mediterranean to Northern Europe to North America; but there is always some center. There is always mobility between zones, both upward as in the United States' case or downward as in Spain's; but the zones and their division of labor are always there. What constitutes high technology and low technology is forever changing; wheat, shipbuilding, textiles, or steel may have been high value in earlier epochs but are intermediate or low value in this age of electrical equipment. What remains constant is the monopolization of high tech (and high profits), at any given moment, by core countries. Hence, in 1685, a world system where northwestern Europe constituted the core (with Amsterdam its center) and specialized in diversified agriculture, textiles, shipbuilding, and metal wares; Eastern Europe, Scandinavia, Scotland, Ireland, and the Americas, as its periphery, produced grain, bullion, wool, sugar, and cotton; and the Mediterranean, as its semiperiphery, specialized in silk and in credit and specie transactions.[5] Hence, in 1985, a world system where North America, Japan, and Europe constitute the core (with New York City as its center) and specialize in electronics, capital goods, durable consumer goods, diversified agriculture, and finance; the Less Developed Countries (LDCs) of Africa, Southeast Asia, and the Caribbean basin, as the periphery, specialize in nonpetroleum raw materials; and the Newly Industrializing Countries (NICs) of Mexico, Brazil, South Africa, Israel, Iran, India, China, Eastern Europe, and the Asian rimlands, as the semiperiphery, specialize in consumer goods, shipping, petroleum, and credit transactions.

In its *real* life, the system's norm has been a state of tension between "haves" and "have-nots"; between tendencies toward concentration and toward redistribution; between cooperation and competition; between the general utility of peace and prosperity and the cyclical necessity for war and depression to weed out the inefficient, revive profits, and restore vitality. In its *ideal* life, the circumstances are rather different; and, on rare occasions, the real has come close to approximating the ideal—principally in the three golden ages of capitalism that followed the end of the Thirty Years War in 1648, the Napoleonic Wars in 1815, and the two World Wars in 1945. And the key to each of those epochs of peace and prosperity has been the same: the ability and will of a single power to arrogate to itself the role of hegemonic power in the world system.[6]

Hegemony rests upon the indispensable underpinning of economic supremacy. Any hegemonic power must simultaneously contain the dominant financial urban center; possess clear comparative advantage in a wide range of product lines, usually based on technological and managerial superiority (e.g., Fordism and Taylorism in 1920s America); and dominate world trade both quantitatively and qualitatively. But beyond mere economic power, a hegemonic nation must possess clear military superiority; it must be able to exert its political will over allies and enemies alike; and it must obtain ideological hegemony over the rest of the system—that is, have its basic ideas and principles command deference. In other words, it must be both feared and respected.

Why the utility of single power hegemony to the capitalist system? What makes it preferable to general competition or a balance of power? Simply put, hegemony historically has been the surest way to overcome the essential contradiction of a system that is economically internationalist but politically nationalist. On the one hand, as has been noted, the ability to accumulate capital and maximize profits depends on the fluidity and mobility of factors of production; there is an economic imperative that drives the system toward internationalization, integration, and interdependence. On the other hand, the system is compartmentalized into political units called nation states; and those units are wedded to specific territory and preoccupied with specific functions of sustenance and military defense. Those concerns for territory, sustenance, and defense create a bias on the part of state apparatus to interfere with the fluidity and mobility of factors of production through farm subsidies, military spending, protective tariffs, capital controls, currency convertibility regulation, and the like. That bias is immensely intensified in nation states using various forms of mercantilism as catch-up strategies to overtake more advanced, perhaps even hegemonic core countries—like the effort of British mercantilism to overtake the Dutch in the seventeenth century; or of Napoleon's Continental System to pass the British in the early nineteenth century; or of Germany's New Plan to supplant the British and withstand the Americans in the early twentieth century; or of Russia's "we will bury capitalism" program in the 1960s. Given such biases, the overwhelming inclination of nation states, in periods of competition or balance of power, is to pursue policies of economic autarky—of capitalism in one country or in one self-contained trading bloc. But such approaches are transparently inefficient; they tend to create a series of fragmented national economies that are redundant, not optimally sized, and uneconomical. And, in the long run, such inefficiency compounds the tendency of the rate of profit to fall.[7]

Single power hegemony acts to counter the tendency to national capital and self-sufficiency. It gives to one power an unequivocal interest to opt for an international capital approach rather than a national. As the dominant industrial, commercial, and financial center, it has the most to gain from a world of free trade, free capital movements, and free convertibility—a *free world;* and the most to lose from a world of mercantilist state interventions that seriously limit those freedoms. So it possesses built-in incentives to use its position as *workshop* and *banker* of the world system to create institutions and ground rules that foster the internationalization of capital; and to use its position as *theologian* of the system to preach the universality of freedom of the seas (the Dutch), and free trade (the British), and the open door (the Americans), and comparative advantage and specialized division of labor (all of the above); and to use its position as *umpire* and *cop* of the system to protect it against external antagonists, internal rebellions, and internecine differences; and to generally see that the ground rules are not impeded by friend or foe.

There are two consequences. First, hegemonic periods have tended to be the most prosperous, since the hegemonic country uses its power to sustain an economic order that both expands and integrates simultaneously; economic internationalism is more efficient and more profitable for the system as a whole than competitive economic nationalism. Second, hegemonic periods tend to be the most peaceful (at least within the core). The economic expansiveness of the system (the antithesis of a zero-sum game) often means that the material rewards (how the economic pie is sliced) are satisfactory enough to dampen the temptation of nonhegemonic core powers to use force (war) as a strategy of income/power redistribution. And even if the temptation persists, the military capacity of the hegemonic country to chastise, or to withhold protection against external enemies, tends to act as a deterrent to independent, autarkic action.

*   *   *

Hegemony is always impermanent. There are ultimately tendencies at work to transform hegemonic countries into *rentier* nations and into warfare states; and the transformations, in turn, undermine hegemony itself. On the one hand, there is a cumulative tendency to neglect investment in the hegemonic country's own industrial plant in favor of investment and lending abroad. Higher wage bills at home for both production and managerial workers combined with greater accessibility to the world system (the major price and the major perk of hegemony) make the export of capital more profitable than the export of goods. The resulting deterioration in domestic capital spending is then compounded by the hegemonic state's overspending on military power. Essential to the system as its military shield and its penetrating sword, that military spending always is a mixed blessing for the hegemonic country. On the one hand, it counteracts the tendency to a falling rate of profit by state subsidization of high profits. On the other hand, this forced consumption (by taxpayers) at artificially high prices (and profits) tends to divert capital from civilian production into military production—which again leads to the neglect of modernizing needs of the domestic industrial plant. Over time, both these *rentier* and military tendencies diminish the very comparative advantage, the very industrial supremacy, upon which hegemony originally rested. And, further, that decline in industrial supremacy may tempt the hegemonic power to overstress other major components of its dominance—chiefly its monopolization of the military protection racket and its continued financial might—to exact concessions from other powers to halt its decline. But such "imperial preference" (if you will) is itself uneconomical and inefficient for the system as a whole; and, to the degree that it rests on yet greater military spending, only further contributes to the deterioration in comparative advantage possessed by the declining hegemonic power.[8]

This impermanent character of hegemony helped produce the crisis of capitalism between 1870 and 1950, encompassing a thirty year slump (1870-1900) and a thirty year war (World Wars I and II, sandwiched around an even more serious depression). The key to this crisis in the capitalist world system was the decline in British hegemony, manifested by lower productivity and the loss of advantage in more and more product lines; by the increasing use of military force to create, perpetuate, and protect a formal, colonial empire in the periphery; and by its partial emasculation of free trade and multilateralism in favor of trading privileges for its own sterling bloc.

That decline in both British power and the deference accorded it made it possible for four other countries to pursue catch-up strategies of their own: the United States, Germany, Japan, and (more belatedly) Russia. Each built upon domestic catharsis and renewal—the American Civil War, German reunification, the Meiji restoration, and the Russian Revolution. Each initially used state intervention in the economy (national capital) to counteract British dominance in the world system (international capital): American import substitution and tariff protectionism, German central banking and trading quotas, Japanese oversight of investment strategies and capital flows, and Russian state ownership. Each participated in the new imperialism movement in Asia, Africa, or Latin America at the turn of the century, but with mixed results: a greater strategic presence astride world trading routes but little tangible and direct economic rewards. Each initially opted for a strategy of regional autarky—that is, partially removing a geographic area from the British-dominated international economy and integrating it into their own national economies: the Pan-Americanism of the United States; the *Mittel-Europe* of Germany; the Pan-Asianism of Japan; and socialism in one country (i.e., state capitalism in the Eurasian continent) by Russia.

World War I was a watershed in this destabilizing scramble for suzerainty. It began with Germany's first bid for hegemony: the effort to establish a German continental system, coerce the British empire into more agreeable coexistence, and initiate German penetration of America's new world sphere. It coincided with Japan's venture in regional hegemony with its absorption of the German sphere in China, the 21 Demands, and ultimately the intervention in Russian Siberia. It climaxed in the Russian Revolution with that country's withdrawal from the war, its consolidation of state power, its brief experiment with socialism as an alternative to market capitalism, and ultimately its transformation to state capitalism as a challenge to that world system. And it ended with the United States seemingly poised to assume the mantle of hegemony, or at least to share it for a time with the British as the latter's descent intersected with the American ascent. America was already the dominant workshop economy, and its technology and managerial efficiency was the source of envy and awe in both Europe and Japan. Now, as well, New York seemed ready to join London as banking center of the system. Now, as well, the American Navy seemed ready to join the Royal Navy as co-policers of the world's trade routes and exhibitor of military muscle to unruly parts of the periphery. Now, as well, an American president— Woodrow Wilson—seemed to grasp the ideological leadership of the system and preach the universal virtues of free trade, comparative advantage, decolonization, collective security, interdependence, and nonrevolutionary change. The end of empires: the dawn of hegemony.

Or so it seemed. This sun, however, took another twenty years to break clear of the eastern horizon. On the one hand, America did make efforts to modify the Versailles system through the Dawes-Young economic diplomacy, and to effect some reintegration of Germany into some concert of core powers. It did attempt similar integration of Japan through the architecture of the Washington Treaty System and the second China Consortium. And it did attempt to implement the principle of equal access to oil, rubber, and markets in the colonies and mandates of the periphery. Yet these fledgling American ventures in international leadership were counterbalanced by continued tariff protectionism, inappropriate lending policies and inflexible approaches to the war debt issue; and by the failure to embrace the League and Article X, to concern itself with European security, or to police the periphery outside the Western Hemisphere. So, in the end, the Versailles system was not substantively revised, the Washington treaty system crumbled, and much of the Third World was organized on closed door rather than open door principles. The reasons were several: the continued importance of traditional consumer manufacturers oriented toward the protection of home markets rather than foreign markets (national capital); the continued attachment of disadvantaged core countries to mercantilist strategies of preserving their home markets and colonies against American competitive superiority and Open Door tactics ("What's yours is mine; and what's mine is mine," as one wag described that American approach[9]); and, finally, the reluctance of American elites and public alike to take on the role of military police in the system—to limit, instead, the American role to economic muscle and "moral suasion," but not the "force of arms."[10] Many elite leaders, to be sure, did not object to the role in principle. But internationalists objected to a police role that enforced Versailles at the expense of German integration; and nationalists objected to a police role that enforced Article X in defense of European empires that more properly belonged now in an American sphere; and left-progressives objected to a police role that enforced the *status quo* in the periphery. Moreover, even had elite factions not possessed their own reservations, the inalterable fact remained that much of the American public still had not been socialized to the propriety and legitimacy of America's playing cop on the world beat. Indeed, a strong tradition of democratic dissent (sometimes called isolationism) and even anti-imperialism still persisted among city labor councils, various ethnic groups, and some petit-bourgeois elements.[11]

Whatever the reasons, the world system of the 1920s was neither wholly open nor wholly integrated. Redundant national economies limited trade between core countries while the great revolutions in Russia, China, and Mexico constricted core penetration of vast parts of the semiperiphery. The resulting tendency toward reduced consumption and depressed profits, in turn, led to a decline in capital expenditures and a dramatic increase in stock market speculation and unsafe lending. The consequence was a system-wide contraction in economic activity that came to be called the Great Depression. And it, in turn, unleashed centrifugal forces in the world system, as each nation attempted to save itself through autarkic measures of planned production at home and managed trade abroad. But all such efforts—from liberal versions like Roosevelt's New Deal to statist versions like Hitler's New Plan—floundered on the elemental fact that they tended to further contract world trade and forced individual states to make frightful choices about how to divide the shrunken economic pie. Policies that favored capital at the expense of workers' wages and welfare risked the wrath of social rebellion, while policies that favored labor at the expense of business profits risked the flight of capital elsewhere in search of better returns. Eventually, each state could resolve that contradiction in the only way that capitalism had ever resolved it: by an external expansion that would revive the rate of profit sufficiently to reward both capital and labor. In the cases of Germany and Japan, that expansion could only come through military force; through the use of war as a redistributive strategy. As "have-not" nations, desperately deficient in food and raw materials and dependent on industrial sales abroad to pay for their impact, they had to "export or die." But their early ventures in creating regional trading blocs—Germany in Central Europe and Japan in Northeast Asia—proved inadequate to their needs. So each turned to military force: Germany to create an integrated European common market under its aegis and Japan to create an integrated Asian crescent under its control; Europe's New Order and the Greater Asian Co-Prosperity sphere to meet and link in the Persian Gulf. *Lebensraum!* Living space!

But living space for Germany and Japan was dying space for American private enterprise and for capitalism as a world system. If the two Axis powers succeeded, the world system would devolve into four classic empires organized around the industrial cores of Western Europe, North America, Russia, and Japan. Even American control in Latin America would have to abandon the Good Neighbor tactic and embrace more structured means of preventing South American gravitation toward its natural, historic European markets. Four empires, each rationalizing and protecting its own space and resources, and pushing and probing that of its rivals. The whole arrangement would obstruct capital's inherent urge to maximize its universe of profit-making options; it would necessitate garrison measures and sustained, intensive military spending that would distort and weaken industrial economies; and it would up the rate of exploitation of the periphery by the core, and thus heighten the likelihood of social insurgency. Called by some Americans "the quarter-sphere" policy, and by others a "Fortress America," it was rejected by elite leaders on two grounds: *1)* it could only work with extensive government planning (state capitalism) that might destroy the prerogatives of private enterprise, reduce the rate of profit, and socialize institutions that might be usurped in the future by leftist governments and used against the interests of capital; and *2)* it abandoned three-quarters of the world system at the very historic moment when all the conditions for American hegemony were present; when the real possibility existed that America could be master of all it surveyed, and need not be satisfied with merely its own backyard.

Yet these same hankerers after hegemony declined to play that role until 1940, limiting themselves to an economic appeasement designed to persuade Germany and Japan that multilateralism, world markets, and disarmament could give rewards as great as bilateralism, regional markets, and militarism—and without the unacceptable risks of Armageddon. This self-limiting reflected numerous factors: the loss of international credibility occasioned by its earlier ineptness in handling the Manchurian crisis, its sabotaging of the London Economic Conference, and its own experiment with the Neutrality Laws; a military unpreparedness that made big stick diplomacy untenable and the carrot necessary; the fond hope that other core powers would do the dirty work on their own; and the awareness that external coercion would as likely lead Germans and Japanese to rally round their regimes as lead to their unseating. But, most importantly, this self-limited role reflected the continued tension between foreign policy elites and pluralist groups in American society. The former bought the notion that prosperity was indivisible, and that American private enterprise capitalism could only flourish in a free world; and, in the last analysis, gaining and keeping that free world was worth pursuing a risk-taking diplomacy or even fighting a global war. But the latter—composed of home market businessmen, labor councils, ethnic organizations, church groups and campus pacifists— either did not buy the notion that economic internationalism was indispensable for their well-being, or, if they did, did not believe it worth a global war. And these so-called isolationists constituted an antiwar, anti-intervention, neutrality movement—powerfully represented in Congress—that continued to set serious constraints on the hegemonic, police role that policy makers might wish to play. Still no consensus, no bipartisanship—the popular base of support so critical for a globalistic foreign policy.

1940 changed it all. France, the Low Countries, and Norway fell to German onslaught. Japan moved south into Indochina. And Germany and Japan (with Italy) signed the fateful Tripartite Pact. The "nightmare of a closed world" (to borrow from Patrick Hearden) had transcended bad dream and been made real. But in reality lay also hope. Britain and the British Empire held. British bases, British raw materials, the British Navy, and Britain itself as an island aircraft carrier and staging ground: all held. The horror film could be run in reverse, the nightmare yet transformed to dreams of free world, of open doors, of sugar plums dancing in one's head. Historical conjuncture was not lost, the opportunity for hegemony not dead. And American leaders seized the opportunity with a vengeance and a vigor that belied all past reservations. America would go to war. Germany would be crushed; and Japan too, if it proved necessary. Peace would be made on American terms. (Indeed, more than a year before America formally entered World War II, some American leaders had already begun the process of planning the peace that would follow inevitable victory.) And if antiwar, anti-internationalist sentiment still influenced public opinion, then that opinion would have to be brought around by political socialization where possible, or circumvented by deceit where not.[12]

World War II, then, was the means by which the United States asserted and assumed hegemony in the world system. Became the system's workshop and banker; its umpire and its cop; its preacher and its teacher. The potential for such arrogation of power had existed since 1919, but now war provided last ingredients: the will to power by elite leaders and the popular acceptance of the legitimacy and propriety of that will. Now the process begun in the first phase of this new Thirty Years War ended in the second. British hegemony was dead and so too any German pretense to hegemony. The twentieth century would yet be the American Century. Novelist Gore Vidal caught the full sense of it well in his *Washington, D.C.* when he described the last days of a fictionalized Franklin Roosevelt and the first days of his successor. [13]

> The elegant, ravaged old President . . . continued to pursue, even as he was dying, the high business of reassembling the fragments of broken empires into a new pattern with himself at center, proud creator of the new imperium. Now, though he was gone, the work remained. The United States was master of the earth. No England, no France, no Germany, no Japan . . . left to dispute the Republic's will. Only the mysterious Soviet would survive to act as other balance in the scale of power.

* * *

By 1945, it had become axiomatic to American leaders that two prerequisites were necessary for the world system to function in an economically efficient and political stable way. First, there had to be a constantly expanding world economic pie. Second, there had to be a hegemonic power capable of enforcing rules of behavior necessary to ensure that expansion, and punishing or isolating those who refused to accede to those rules. Neither prerequisite had obtained during the 1930s, and the lack of each had produced World War II. The economic pie had contracted and kicked off a scramble for scarce resources and profits; and the lack of a clearly dominant capitalist power removed any restraints on the more aggressive scramblers. Those American leaders emerged from World War II determined to rectify those glaring deficiencies, and to put the global "humpty dumpty" back together again after ten years of history's worst depression and six years of one of history's worst wars, to assume the burden of power themselves (as well as the profits and prestige), and to wield it in ways that would breathe life back into a nearly moribund system. [14]

In the five years that followed World War II (what some have called the First Cold War), American efforts concerned themselves primarily with reconstruction of the European and Japanese industrial cores—especially the revival of industrial productivity. For the first two years, the effort was *ad hoc* and piecemeal, parceled out on a country-by-country basis through UN agencies, the American Export-Import Bank, German and Japanese occupation funding, and the $3.75 billion loan to Great Britain. Those interim efforts failed. The goals of multilateral trade and free currency convertibility were as remote as ever; and the institutions designed to promote them—the World Bank, the International Monetary Fund, the International Trade Organization—were either nonfunctional or nonexistent. The shorthand symbol of that failure was the Dollar Gap that reached critical proportions by 1947. Europe and Japan had an almost insatiable

205

need for American capital goods, raw materials, and food to effect their recovery, but they lacked the dollars to pay for them. The consequent trade deficit forced them to cut back on purchases from the United States—both hurting their recovery and threatening American prosperity—and led them to experiment with autarkic measures to protect their currencies and minimize the deficit. In effect, it led Europe to consider nationalist rather than internationalist roads to reconstruction. This was especially true in governments where organized labor wielded some clout and pushed for economic policies geared to full employment and income redistribution (redividing the pie) rather than increased productivity for world markets (expanding the pie).[15]

These experiments in taking the national capital road led in a direction wholly opposite from the American-sponsored road of international capital— the latter clearly more profitable for the United States and its superior economy, but also (so American leaders believed) more efficient for world capitalism as a whole. The American view rested on two related concepts: *comparative advantage* and *economies of scale*. Each nation ought to produce only those things that could be created at comparable quality but lower prices than by other nations, and each nation ought to sell its specialized products in as wide a market as possible. That would permit optimum size and optimum production runs essential for maximum efficiency and thus maximum profits. (As always, the rate of profit was the bottom-line determinant.) Dividing the European industrial cores into a multitude of national economies, each producing a full range of products for their small, constricted, national markets, would only lead to redundancy, underscaled production runs, inefficiency and, ultimately, reduced rates of profit that were a drag on the entire world economy. It was the road taken in the 1930s; the road that led to war; the road that American leaders vowed to bulldoze when they entered that war. To American elites, it was a county trunk road in a world that required interstate highways.[16]

American efforts between 1947 and 1950 were bold, imaginative, sophisticated endeavors to end those autarkic experiments and commit Europe and Japan irrevocably to the course of multilateralism and interdependence. Of these, the Marshall Plan (European Economic Recovery program) was clearly the most stunning; indeed, the most revolutionary. Not only was its scale, duration, and governmental involvement unprecedented. More important (more important than the dollars themselves) was the use of leverage to force Europe to take the American road. Marshall Plan aid was used to move Europe in the direction of a common market and an industrial economy organized around the principles of comparative advantage and the economies of scale; and its veto over counterpart funds was used to force Europe to soft-pedal welfare programs, limit wages, control inflation, and create an environment conducive for capital investment— part of it financed out of labor's pocket. This was hegemony with a vengeance: American control over Europe's internal social and economic policies, in return for aid in making Europe more competitive with American capital. At the same time, in Japan, the infusion of capital through military subcontracting and the reduction of costs through austerity wages (the Dodge Plan) sought to make Japan independent of American occupation support and capable of competing again in world markets. In effect, the United States made some shortrun sacrifices to restore European and Japanese competition, on the assumption that, in the long run, the new economic equilibrium would revive world trade to pre-1929 levels (at least) and make America's own prosperity both better and more enduring.[17]

There were two potential enemies to this exercise in American hegemony —one within, one without. The external adversary was the Soviet Union, which re-entered the world system in World War II after twenty years of semi-isolation. After World War I, the failure of Central Europe to follow Russia's revolutionary example led that nation to partially withdraw from the world system and attempt to create a socialist enclave—an external world, if you will. But foreign intervention and capitalist encirclement, the decimation of the working class by civil war, and the opposition of the peasantry all produced a grand distortion in the Russian economy that some have dubbed "war socialism": that is, an economy where inordinate amounts of scarce resources went into a modern, military industry and all too little went into agriculture and civilian industry. A society at once modern and fearsome, backward and ineffectual. Under the influence of Stalin and the weight of bureaucratic momentum, that war socialism devolved into simply another variant of state capitalism—with the state simply replacing the private corporation in accumulating capital, appropriating workers' surplus, and making investments; and this state capitalism, in turn, coexisted in shifting tension and tolerance with "black capitalism" (the black market) in consumer goods and services. In effect, Russia experimented with its own varieties of mercantilism; again, as a catch-up strategy to overtake western capital, preparatory to re-entering and competing in the world system.

That re-entry began tentatively in the mid-1930s with Russia's popular front diplomacy, advanced on a different front with the Russo-German pact of 1939 and the Russian occupation of Finland, the Baltic states, and eastern Poland; and became a *fait accompli* after the victory at Stalingrad and the push of the Red Army into Eastern Europe and Germany. Next to the emergence of American hegemony, this re-entry of Russia into the world system was the most significant consequence of World War II; and that re-entry constituted a serious potential threat to the exercise of that hegemony. Save for a fleeting moment in late 1943 and early 1944, the threat was not military. The success of the "second front" in 1944 and the acquisition of the atomic bomb monopoly in 1945 put an end to that. But the threat came in other forms. Russian success at autarkic development might spur on Europeans inclined to take the national capital road; Russian

207

connections to European communist parties and labor organizations might undermine American efforts at social and economic engineering; Russian control of Eastern Europe, historic source of food, markets, and raw materials for Western Europe, might make the latter's recovery more difficult; Russian share of German occupation might limit American options on the crucial question of German recovery; and, over the long haul, Russian military power might tempt some Europeans to opt for neutralism as a means of diffusing any Russian threat.

These threats left American policy makers with two choices. Either accept Russian re-entry into the system in return for Russian acquiescence in the American-imposed rules of the game; or revert back to the interwar policy of attempting to isolate ("contain") Russia and minimize her participation in world affairs. Roosevelt first attempted to seduce Russian cooperation through the Yalta system; and Truman sought to coerce it in alternating fits of economic diplomacy and atomic diplomacy. In the end, none of the efforts worked—largely because one postwar issue proved a nonnegotiable obstacle. And that issue was not Eastern Europe, where there was in fact some give in the American position; nor the Middle East, where there was considerable give in the Russian position. That issue was Germany, which from the Berlin blockade to the Berlin wall was to dominate a good deal of Soviet-American conflict; and which remains at the heart of "missile diplomacy" even now in the 1980s. The United States ultimately could not conceive of a way of making European capitalism once more viable without German reindustrialization acting as engine to pull the train; and Russia, burned twice and horribly by German military-industrial might within the space of twenty-five years, could not conceive of a way of making itself really and psychically secure if it permitted that reindustrialization to occur. At loggerheads, then, the American government gratefully accepted the rationale provided by George Frost Kennan in his "Mr. X" article, and committed itself by 1947 to the famous "containment" policy, made global and sacrosant by the so-called Truman Doctrine early in that year.

If Russia was the external devil, there was also an "enemy within" that threatened America's hegemonic internationalism. The major component of that internal opposition was the residue of the 1930s antiwar, anti-intervention movement, augmented by a much smaller component of radical labor leaders and popular front politicians. The former was clearly the greater enemy that forever bedeviled New Dealers and business internationalists with the penultimate fear: a revival of isolation. Made politically potent by the Republican election victory in 1946, apparent representatives of such sentiments made abundantly clear their wariness about foreign aid, downward revision of the tariff, or participation in international banking and monetary agencies. They simply did not buy the logic or accept the imperatives of economic internationalism—either for the interests of their constituents or for the nation as a whole. Ultimately, the threat of such nationalists was blunted in several ways: symbolic politics were invoked, such as the notion of bipartisanship: that peace like war had its perils, and required that politics stop at the water's edge. Home market businessmen were persuaded that subcontracts from foreign market multinationals were crucial to their own prosperity. Center-right labor leaders were persuaded that popular front politics and redistributive strategies were dead in the postwar Republican revival, and that only global economic expansion offered any real hope for full employment.[18]

But the major method was to invoke the communist menace. Not the very real Russian menace that elites themselves feared, but a simpler, more stark, more militarized, more (secularly) evangelical menace. A button that, once pushed, would evoke the deepest fears about threats to the bedrock values of American life and to the very physical security of the American nation. And that button was pushed: first in the overblown Greek crisis of 1947; and finally even in the Marshall Plan debates when economic and humanitarian arguments seemed insufficient to carry the day. The same button, pushed to disarm nationalist critics of American hegemonic policies, could be used to disgrace and discredit more radical critics. Indeed it was: in 1947, to denounce leftist opposition to the Truman Doctrine; in 1948, to condemn Henry Wallace and the Progressive Party as tools or dupes of international communism; and in 1949, to purge the American labor movement of radical influences. (A liberal version of McCarthyism before the real thing ironically turned to devour liberals themselves.)[19]

*   *   *

The contours of the Cold War have paralleled those of the international business cycle. What some have called the Second Cold War coincided with the Long Boom that made the period between 1950 and 1973 the most sustained and profitable period of economic growth in the history of world capitalism. Over that quarter of a century, the Gross *World* Product grew to be 2.25 times larger, and global industrial output averaged an increase of 5.5 percent per year. That compared favorably with the world economy's best previous record: the 4.5 percent annual average during the 1899-1914 period. Capital became more fluid and free to maneuver in the world system than ever before, and the extent of world economic integration and interdependence was unprecedented, perhaps even sufficient to realize the American goal of rendering autarkic options simply unfeasible.[20] And, of course, hegemonic America reaped its share of this growth and integration. By 1967 22 percent of American profits were being earned in overseas economic activity, and the annual gross product of American multinational corporations, estimated at $120 billion, was larger than the GNP of any other capitalist country, including Germany or Japan.[21]

Both the Long Boom and the Second Cold War grew out of American responses to a network of crises in 1949. One part of the crisis was the seeming deterioration in postwar recovery witnessed in the American recession of 1949 to early 1950; the British currency crisis; bottlenecks in the European Economic Recovery program that impeded integration; the fiasco of the Dodge Plan in Japan and the near-bankruptcy of that nation's economy; and the political certainty that even invocation of the communist menace was unlikely to move Congress to extend foreign aid beyond the Marshall Plan cut-off in 1952. The measure and the metaphor for this crisis continued to be the Dollar Gap. Even with an increase in the percentage of American exports financed through aid rather than trade, European nations continued to run a horrendous deficit. (For example, Great Britain's trade deficit with the United States was twice the amount it received in Marshall Plan aid.) While the causes of this multifaceted crisis were complex, one was most basic. While European and Japanese production did begin to revive, viable markets for that production remained stagnant. As George Frost Kennan put it in August 1949, "It is one thing to produce; it is another thing to sell."[22] Domestic consumption in Europe and Japan suffered from austerity-imposed low wages and the foreign markets necessary to take up the slack did not materialize. The largest capitalist market (the United States) was partially restricted by Congressional protectionism; the socialist market (the Soviet bloc) was obstructed by the developing Cold War; and the Third World periphery (including Southeast Asia) had not been sufficiently revived and reintegrated as suppliers of food and raw materials and as consumers of finished products. Clearly, unless Europe and Japan could find viable markets, as well as cheap raw materials to reduce their own manufacturing costs, they could not continue indefinitely to sustain their then enormous trade deficit with the United States. They might be forced to defy American hegemonic rules and resort to the protectionism, currency restrictions, and capital controls that had characterized foreign economic policies in the Great Depression.

Two other key factors exacerbated this circle in postwar capitalism, and both involved the Soviet Union. The first was the Russian explosion of a nuclear test device in late 1949 that unexpectedly ended America's monopoly of the atomic bomb. While most American leaders, interestingly, did not fear the military implications of this event, they did fear its political and psychological implications. They were concerned that Europe and Japan might question the credibility of America's military shield; might wonder whether the United States would risk atomic attack on its homeland in order to defend them against possible Russian intimidation. In other words, American leaders feared the atomic bomb less than they feared atomic diplomacy; feared that Europe and Japan might waver in their deference to American hegemony and be tempted to play the Russian card—to work out some economic and political accommodation with the Soviets that might isolate the American rules of economic internationalism and collective security. The second exacerbating factor was the final triumph of Mao Zedong and the communist party in the Chinese civil war, and the signing of a Sino-Soviet pact in February 1950. The development seemed to signal China's partial withdrawal from the capitalist world system and raised further concern that the Asian rimlands of Korea, Taiwan, and Southwest Asia would soon emulate that withdrawal. Given Japan's near-bankruptcy and its historic economic dependence on northeast and southeast Asia; given Britain's economic stake in Hong Kong, Singapore, Malaya and, beyond, to India—there was real fear that the Japanese and/or the British might be tempted to play the China card—to work out an economic and political accommodation with the Sino-Soviet bloc that again would undermine the free world rules of economic internationalism.

Consider what all this meant! For five years, American elites had attempted to use their hegemonic power and position to effect the recovery of the European and Japanese industrial machines and to restore world trade to predepression levels and, at the same time, to isolate ("contain") the Soviet bloc that declined to defer to American hegemony and accept its rules of the game. Now all that seemed terribly jeopardized. Japan's economic recovery was in shambles and Europe's was disappointing. Most of Eurasia, from the Elbe to the Amur, had partially withdrawn from the world economy. The Asian rimlands seemed destined soon to follow and, who knew, could much of the Third World be far behind? In addition, America's atomic diplomacy and the credibility of its military shield appeared much in doubt. In short, 1950 seemed frighteningly like 1930, with strong centrifugal tendencies pushing nation states to revert to their inherent nationalist tendencies; to protect their own economies through state regulation of trade and investment; and to play their Russian cards and China cards to ease their own deficit/debtor dilemmas. In other words, American hegemony was facing its first and severest postwar test and, if the hegemony could not be maintained, there were serious questions in the minds of American elites as to whether the capitalist world economy and the American free enterprise system could survive and prosper.

The American response to this midcentury crisis established the central tendencies of American paramouncy for more than two decades thereafter. First, American leaders chose to militarize the Cold War. They built the H-bomb, quadrupled the military budget, replaced foreign aid with military aid, transformed NATO from a political alliance to a military pact, rearmed Germany, and held open the option of rearming Japan. All this would maintain the credibility of the American military shield for its allies and would be easier to sell than tariff revision and foreign aid at home. Second, they attempted to speed the integration of European economies and the creation of a common market, hoping to create a larger internal market for European trade. This European integrationism and the

Cold War's militarization were intimately connected, for German rearmament was a powerful incentive to European economic cooperation, the major means of subsuming German freedom of action—including the freedom to do military mischief—within a matrix of economic interdependence. Third, they determined upon a concerted effort to develop Third World extractive economies and integrate them into the industrial cores of Europe and Japan; to provide the markets and raw materials essential for full recovery. This object too was tied to militarization, for parts of the periphery— especially the Asian rimlands—were so immersed in revolution and civil war that military pacification seemed necessary as a prelude to stable economic growth. Militarization, European integration, and Third World orientation—these were the dominant characteristics of American foreign policy from 1950 to 1973.

All of these facets contributed to the Long Boom. The American military shield did become a major means for commanding deference to American hegemony and its rules of international capital; military alliances did provide the glue that sealed the economic parts of the system; and American military spending did provide shortrun stimulus to capital expenditure and profits within America, while its shouldering of that burden did release European and more especially Japanese capital to develop further their civilian technology and production. Indeed, in some ways, American military spending fueled the entire world economy, for in raising American demand for strategic raw materials from LDCs, it made them better customers for finished products from Europe and Japan. In effect, a crucial triangular trade developed in which Europe and Japan exported manufactured products to the Third World; it, in turn, exported raw materials to the United States; and the United States exported capital goods and food to Europe and Japan.[23]

Likewise, European integrationism did lead to the European Economic Community (EEC) and to greater specialization geared to an enlarged common market. And for all the remnants of bottlenecks and interest-group nationalism, it was an integrated Europe largely committed to the original American ideals of capital fluidity, currency convertibility, and multilateral trade. In 1950, such notions had been an American pipedream; by 1960, they were a reality—symbolized in 1958 by worldwide acceptance of currencies freely convertible in dollars, and the end of the Dollar Gap that had plagued the world system for more than a decade. Moreover, any anxiety that the EEC might work to restrict American economic access (and become another nightmare of a closed world) was largely allayed by the success of American capital in leapfrogging tariff barriers to build branch plants and establish multinational corporations directly in Europe itself.[24]

Finally, the new focus on the Third World did pay off—especially for Japan. Both in Northeast Asia and, more importantly, Southeast Asia, Japan secured imported raw materials and foodstuffs from the periphery countries of Malaya, Thailand, the Philippines, and Indonesia; upped its rate of profits by transferring much of its consumer, light industry to the semiperiphery of South Korea, Taiwan, Hong Kong, and Singapore (one-third of its overseas investment went to those export platform economies); and upped the market potential of the whole area for Japanese durable goods. As a consequence, Japan's ephemeral recovery, induced by the Korean War, now became permanent; the Asian rimlands became show-cases of capitalist development; Japan's temptation to play the China card was lessened; and, instead, China found itself pulled down the capitalist road by the early 1970s. Similar if less spectacular developments occurred in parts of Latin America, the Mediterranean world, and southern Africa; and with considerable rewards for the system's dominant power. For while two-thirds of American investment went to Europe and Canada, the one-third invested in the Third World generated more profits. Indeed, three-quarters of America's investment profits overseas came from Latin America and the Middle East, especially in oil. Interestingly, if one excludes oil, core country investment in peripheral raw materials slowed down after the 1950s, and increasing amounts went into manufacturing in countries like Mexico, Brazil, and the Asian semiperiphery.[25] This fascinating development represented the start of a geographic shift in the manufacturing zones in the world system, as the German Ruhr, the British north country, and the American northeast quadrant began to decay and their runaway shops started their overseas trek. As a consequence, manufacturing in the core increased only 1.2 percent annually between 1960 and 1973, while it grew 4.2 percent annually in the NICs of the semiperiphery. Begun as a defensive response to the economic nationalism and import-substitution tactics of the Third World, this redivision of international labor was ultimately embraced by multinationals for the more positive reason that it lowered their corporate costs and increased their corporate profits.[26]

*   *   *

The militarism and economic intergrationism of the Second Cold War helped create an interdependent and fluid world economy, but they also laid the groundwork for a crisis in American hegemony. Militarization ultimately distorted the American economy grotesquely, creating a kind of "war capitalism" as mirror image to Russia's "war socialism." Cost-overrun contracts and skewed bidding made military spending a state subsidy for guaranteed exorbitant profits; and, as such, magnetically lured capital and credit that otherwise would have gone into civilian research, modernization, and production. As a consequence, American industry sharply declined in its productivity and lost its comparative advantage to Japan and Germany in a whole range of product lines long dominated by the United States. By 1973, America's only significant comparative advantage was in "guns and butter": military hardware, commercial aircraft, and agriculture.

Relatedly, the success in integrating Germany into the common market, Japan into the Asian rimlands, and both into the mainstream of world triangular patterns only reinforced their competitiveness relative to the United States. Once more, the measure and the metaphor was the dollar—only a dollar drain rather than a dollar gap; an American trade deficit. The first inkling had come at the start of the Long Boom when the export of American consumer goods began to decline after 1951; but that was more than counterbalanced by an enormous increase in the export of American capital goods. But beginning as early as 1965, privately financed American exports began to decline relative to imports, and by 1968, those private commercial transactions were running an absolute deficit. Only government-financed trade made the overall trade balance marginally positive for another five years; and from 1973 onward, America confronted its first negative balance of trade in almost a century. Short-term fixes in dollar devaluation in 1971 and 1973 were wholly inadequate, and the only long-term hope was that American investment overseas would prove sufficiently large and profitable that multiplying returns—ten, twenty, or thirty years down the line—would compensate for the deficit in commodities. Clearly, by 1973, the economic base of hegemony—its veritable underpinning—was seriously stressed.[27]

So too, ironically, was its credibility base. The American pretense of hegemony rested on its claim that its leadership could give maximum economic efficiency and peace to the world system. And the Long Boom and the nonappearance of World War III endowed that claim with some legitimacy. But efficiency is not necessarily equity (indeed, it may come at the expense of equity); and the absence of global wars between core powers did not mean the end of neocolonial wars waged on alienated parts of the periphery. So it came to pass that America presided over an international division of labor that was predicated upon core exploitation of the periphery—in which prices of periphery commodities declined and the terms of trade worsened; in which the profits of fledgling industrialization in the semiperiphery were repatriated to corporate headquarters in New York, Frankfurt, Antwerp, London, and Tokyo; in which dependency became a palpable reality and not simply an economic theory. "Rich lands and poor," as Gunnar Myrdal described it—and the rich indeed got richer, and the poor got poorer.[28] And so too it came to pass that America, as hegemonic power, had to confront the revolt of parts of the periphery, spurred on by mixtures of economic radicalism, political nationalism, cultural pride, and racial backlash—Vietnam and Cuba, Indonesia and Chile, Egypt and India, Algeria and Guatemala, the Congo and Bolivia. Hegemony required the confrontation, but the manner of its resolution often weakened the very credibility upon which hegemony rested.

Vietnam was the quintessential example during the Long Boom. The American commitment began in 1950 as part of a concerted policy of preventing the Asian rimlands (Korea, Taiwan, Southeast Asia) from drifting into the Sino-Soviet Asian trading bloc, and tempting a depressed Japan to follow suit; or, more positively, to integrate Japan and the rimlands into the world system and ultimately tempt China to junk its Russian connection and follow the path marked international capital. From its inception in 1950 to its fateful conclusion in 1973 (the same temporal frame as the Boom), the American policy was a conscious act of hegemony. America itself had little direct interest of its own in Southeast Asia, either materially or strategically. But Japan did—with its pressing need for markets, food, and raw materials, and its dependence on Persian Gulf oil that had to traverse the narrow straits of the Southeast Asian archipelagos. In effect, the United States acted as surrogate for Japan, acted in its police role to militarily stabilize Southeast Asia in order to effect political stability and to render economic development and integration into Japan's "workshop" economy finally possible. But the commitment once made had to be kept; for, given the web of American commitments (political-military pacts with some forty-two nations, as Dean Rusk often noted), the failure to keep one jeopardized all. Or, once begun, the effort to demonstrate that revolution was an unacceptable way to restructure the world division of labor had to be successful—especially in light of the radical Cuban revolution in America's most immediate sphere. So what began as an exercise in hegemony—acting for the whole system rather than immediate American interests—had to be continued and successfully completed if the credibility necessary for hegemony was to be sustained. On the other hand, hegemony also rests on presumptions of legitimacy and rationality. Thus, when the antiwar movement threatened to produce an alienated generation that would not accept the legitimacy of the police function (or play their predestined role as engineers, managers, and lawyers); or when Europe and Japan began to question, not American power, but the rationality of its application (the reasonable relationship of means to ends); only then did American leaders determine that sustaining the Vietnam commitment was more damaging to American suzerainty than gradually liquidating it through so-called Vietnamization. But the damage was already done. Not only was American economic supremacy in question by 1973, but so was the efficacy of its military shield and its political preachments.[29]

*   *   *

Cold War and business cycle have continued to follow their symbiotic course since 1973. Just as Russo-American detente gave way first to ambivalence and then to a Third Cold War, so too did stage one of an extended economic contraction (the Long Slump) give way first to uneven recovery and then to a second, harsher stage of tough times. Moreover, the changes in both the Cold War and the international economy facilitated the emergence of new power centers in American society, and the unfolding of an ongoing debate over the status of American hegemony and the best means, if any, of revitalizing it.

In the early to mid-1970s, a number of factors pushed both the United States and Russia toward detente. In the United States, the self-doubts generated by the failure in Vietnam (the post-Vietnam syndrome) raised questions about the power and will and ethics of America's international police role, or even the practicality of imposing military solutions on complex problems that defied military solutions. Relatedly, the decline of the Imperial Presidency after Vietnam (and Watergate) made it easier for a more pluralist Congress to impose limits on that police function. This dimunition of the American military role led in two directions: to sub-imperialism—the use of regional surrogates to help perform that role (the Shah's Iran in the Persian Gulf, Brazil in the South Atlantic, Somoza in Central America, and perhaps Japan in Asia); and to detente and a stabilization of the arms race, thus minimizing Russia's exploitation of America's half-step backward. But another powerful factor reinforced that detente tendency, and that was American reaction to stage one of the Long Slump.

Like the Great Depression, the lengthy decade-long contraction grew out of the decreasing ability of the American locomotive to pull the international train behind it. That decreasing ability was rooted in declining productivity and profitability—reflections of depreciated older machinery, uneven capital investment prompted partly by military distortions, high and uncompetitive wage bills (especially for a bloated and inefficient managerial workforce), and an overextended tax base that dampened middleclass consumption. The OPEC "oil shock," the American trade deficit, the decline of the dollar, and the dismantling of the Bretton Woods international monetary system—all made solutions to the American problem more difficult. But they were not the cause of the crisis in productivity and profits. They were more largely its consequences.[30]

There are always several possible responses to a crisis in the rate of profit. One can up the rate of labor exploitation in order to cut costs; and indirectly that was done through elevated unemployment and inflation ("stagflation," as it was called). One can weed out inefficient business competition and further integrate and rationalize the practices of those that remain; and indeed, both stages of the Long Slump saw an increase in bankruptcies, mergers, and vertical integration. One can use war to destroy antiquated, existing capital stock and update its replacements, and indirectly that too was done through planned obsolescence in military hardware and the incremental export of ever-newer weaponry to rivals in the periphery and semiperiphery. And finally, one can do what capitalism has always done; attempt to integrate more and more of the hinterlands, more and more effectively, into a commercial nexus and a global market. More than anything, that too was done, as unprecedented amounts of investment capital, bank loans, and engineering and capital goods flowed from the United States and other core countries into the semiperiphery. That semiperiphery, and the multinationals embedded in it, took on an increasing share of manufacturing the world's consumer goods, steel, vehicles, and durable goods. Overall, the rate of profit was twice as high for capital invested in the semiperiphery (especially the Asian rimlands) as in core economies. Nowhere was that more true than for large international banks; Citibank Corporation, for example, earned 82 percent of its profits abroad by 1977.[31] Like the new world redressing the balance of the old, the semiperiphery had come to redress the profits of the core.

All this is germane to detente. One of the major components of the semiperiphery was Eastern Europe and the COMECON trading bloc.[32] Russia had long sought ways to put Eastern Europe on a self-sustaining basis to ease the economic burdens of a Red Army socialism in Eastern Europe whose costs were borne by the Russian people, and whose deferred material rewards those people would not long do without. In the late 1960s, Russia had experimented with economic decentralization. But this had threatened entrenched bureaucracies, lapsed over into political liberalization, and raised questions about the loyalty of the Eastern bloc; and Czechoslovakia in 1968 put an end to the experiment. The problem, however, still remained, and one tempting though risky solution was to open COMECON to western trade financed by western banks. The import of engineering and capital goods would upgrade Eastern bloc industry, while the necessity of exporting to pay for the imports would force greater efficiency on state managers and workers. In theory, Russia would retain the political-military whiphand, while using western economies to ease their own burden. In effect, detente marked a partial return of the Soviet bloc to the capitalist world system, a return marked by a proliferation of joint banks, joint manufacturing ventures, and subcontracting arrangements with foreign firms. By 1976, one-third of COMECON's trade was determined by world market prices. As one Hungarian put it: "We are a socialist planned economy under the control of the market."[33]

The economic recovery of 1976-78 diminished some of the economic incentive for detente by the United States. Moreover, it did so at a time when the unhappy denouement in Vietnam in 1975 renewed sentiment that America demonstrate concretely that it was no "paper tiger"; and at a time when "human rights" diplomacy had become a handy way to win back the moral legitimacy tarnished in Vietnam by participation in what many saw as a racist, colonial war. Looking to recoup some measure of hegemony—a little fear, a little respect—detente became a nonword by 1976. The effort to link human rights and Russian trade ended by damaging both; Poland was declared "independent" by an American president (a "Fordism" more insightful than his critics imagined); and Salt II became more a confirmation of Russian military parity than an effort to reduce the arms race. Yet, for all that, there was a dominant tendency in the early Carter administration to soft-pedal Russo-American conflict; to see events in the Third World, even revolutions, as indigenous rather than Russian-inspired; to talk about a new world order bargain that would ratify the economic gains won by the semiperiphery during the earlier slump; and to downplay the efficacy of military solutions. In short, it was a period of confusion and countervailing tendencies and, in part, they mirrored the mixed picture of the world economy: the semiperiphery doing seemingly better; the periphery still mired in economic despair, quite unrecovered from the collapse of world commodity prices in 1974; and the core in an uneven shape, with Japan and Germany showing more growth and profit than others.

The second economic collapse from 1979 to 1983 ended that confusion. The underlying problems remained much the same as they had in 1973, essentially continued stagnant investment. But this time there was no salvation from the Third World. In the urgency of NICs to industrialize and the eagerness of western banks to profit, the semiperiphery—from Mexico to Poland—borrowed heavily to finance their western imports. The result was a ''debt trap'' that grew by leaps and bounds, from $9 billion annually in 1970 to $100 billion annually in 1978.[34] That debt trap, in turn, forced austerity deflation and high interest rates in the semiperiphery in order to service the debts; but it also led to a sharp decline in imports from core countries. Ultimately, only a second round of borrowing from western banks could sustain those imports, but that in turn produced a yet more grinding debt load. In the case of the Polish example, western debts reached $27 billion by 1981. The government attempted to force cuts in domestic consumption and increases in domestic production (against the opposition of Solidarity); its failure led Polish exports to the West to decrease by half in 1981. That meant in turn forced cuts in western imports, with most of the imports coming in food and seed, but few capital goods and spare parts for industry, so that finally, by 1982, Poland gave up on its program of diversified industrialization and determined to specialize only in select exports to pay off its foreign debt. As one observer put it: ''The world market began to choose those items in the [Eastern bloc] that it needed and to bankrupt those it did not. It was forcing [them] into a particular role, into a specialized function in the world division of labor.''[35] Stage two of the Long Slump had hit every part of the world system hard, and it was this pervasive quality that made the latest contraction more threatening than the first.

This economic contraction coincided with the failure of America's regional surrogate policy, witnessed by the revolutionary overthrow of the Shah in Iran and Somoza in Nicaragua. The interaction of both forced a great debate in policy-making circles, one that would partly end the confusion and ambivalence of the short recovery period. In some ways, it was a replay of the 1950 debate over NSC-68 and the recommendation to militarize the Cold War.

There were still those, like Cyrus Vance, who argued against remilitarization. More representative of old wealth and old power, they were more inclined to be sanguine and accept the loss of hegemony and make do in a more multipolar world; to consign limits to America's police role; to stress moral leadership and human rights instead; to put their faith in reindustrialization to restore America's capacity to compete and prosper in the world system; to explore the possibilities of renewed detente and arms agreements; and to coexist with and profit from Third World revolutions—knowing that whatever they were and whatever they called themselves (Marxist-Leninists, African socialists, Sandinistas) they could not deliver on their material promises to their subjects without coming to the West, hat in hand, for trade, capital, and technology.

Two factors damned this group and gave victory to their opponents. First, changes within American society produced new challengers to old wealth. Partly, this was the product of demographic changes that shifted the regional locus of power south and west. Partly, it grew out of the Long Slump itself, which produced an economic shakedown that, in purging the inefficient and rewarding vitality, tended to diminish the ranks of the old and enhance the power of the new. And finally, it reflected the regional distortions created by military spending and its disproportionate outlays in the west and the south. This new power group, dubbed by some the "Prussians," was not disposed to be sanguine about the loss of hegemony; as newcomers, recently arrived at the economic trough, they were not inclined to accept limits at the very moment of their greatest opportunity. Nor were they inclined to relinquish America's military function, integrated as they were into the war capitalism sector.

At the same time, events in the world system shifted the framework of the debate in their favor. The collapse of the world economy and the decline of American hegemony sparked a rash of revolutionary crises throughout the Third World: from Poland to Portugal, from Afghanistan to El Salvador, from Iran to Nicaragua, from Lebanon to Grenada, from Angola to Argentina, from South Africa to the Philippines. Almost all spilled over into the Third Cold War and exacerbated Russo-American conflict. Sometimes the initiative was American; sometimes Russian; and often as not, it was the tail wagging the dog—Third World client states soliciting aid that their patrons could not refuse without risking (in America's case) hegemonic credentials or (in Russia's case) revolutionary legitimacy.

The "Prussians" won the debate in 1979 during the late Carter administration, and ratified it with Reagan's victories in 1980 and 1984. Like Dean Acheson and Paul Nitze in 1950, they determined to rebuild and solidify American hegemony on the basis of an enlarged and modernized military shield. Their assumptions were that American dominance of the world "protection racket" would merit special rewards and preferences not due other core powers; that human rights diplomacy was ineffectual—that deference based on fear was more real than deference based on sentimentality; that an open door for Third World revolutions may be profitable, but negated the major *raison d'etre* for remilitarization, and was not so profitable as a wholly capitalist road; and that restoring American economic supremacy—the basis of hegemony—could not be done by reindustrializing weak and archaic industries, but only by a massive state sponsorship of a technological revolution that would make America the first truly postindustrial society. Star Wars: the defense system that probably won't; the economic system that might.

There is compelling logic to the "stand-tall-in-the-saddle" position. The system does seem to need a center in order to survive. Certainly it has not done well in past periods of competing power centers and autarkic policies. So the revival of world protectionist sentiment and the drift toward competition and new coalitions (the EEC, Russia, Japan-China, and North America) are not reassuring. The New Imperialism was tried a century ago and found wanting as a guarantor of global peace and a provider of profits. On the other hand, hegemony too has been tried and likewise found wanting; found to rest on an hierarchical and often cruel division of labor, and upon harsh repression, when need be, to sustain that hierarchy. Such a choice: where efficiency exploits and peace kills. Somehow an old political catchphrase comes to mind: "The system isn't the solution. The system is the problem."

Writings of
William Appleman Williams

A Bibliography

I do not remember whether I wrote you about your article at the time; I should have. Better than almost anything since Becker it combines grace, humor, and insight.

Henry Steele Commager
Amherst, Massachusetts, 1984

I hope that I have not—in these few lines—expressed values or sentiments that contradict the intentions behind The Tragedy of American Diplomacy. *As I write, it seems to me that there is a sort of secrecy involved in one's relationship to some very few books—a kind of secrecy that should perhaps not be offended. My purpose, after all, is just to express gratitude for one of the reading experiences that makes one wonder and look around with different eyes.*

Niels Thorsen
Copenhagen, 1985

Memoir
"A Good Life and a Good Death: A Memoir of an Independent Lady. By Her Son . . . for Her Grandchildren." Waldport, Oregon, 1984.

Books
The International Impact of National Economic Planning. Leeds, England: University of Leeds (1948).

American-Russian Relations, 1781-1947. New York: Rinehart (1952).

The Tragedy of American Diplomacy. Cleveland: World Publishing Company (1959). Revised 1962, 1972. Also published in Spanish and Japanese translations.

The Contours of American History. Cleveland: World Publishing Company (1961). Also published in British edition; Italian translation.

The United States, Cuba, and Castro. New York: Monthly Review Press (1962). Also published in Spanish translation.

The Great Evasion. An Essay on the Contemporary Relevance of Karl Marx and on the Wisdom of Admitting the Heretic into the Dialogue about America's Future. Chicago: Quadrangle Books (1964).

The Roots of the Modern American Empire. A Study of the Growth and Shaping of Social Consciousness in a Marketplace Society. New York: Random House (1969). Also published in British edition.

Some Presidents: Wilson to Nixon. New York: A New York Review Book distributed by Vintage Books (1972).

History as a Way of Learning. New York: New Viewpoints (1974). Also published in Spanish translation.

America Confronts a Revolutionary World: 1776-1976. New York: Morrow (1976).

Americans in a Changing World: A History of the United States in the Twentieth Century. New York: Harper and Row (1978).

Empire as a Way of Life: An Essay on the Causes and Character of America's Present Predicament Along with a Few Thoughts about an Alternative. New York: Oxford University Press (1980). Also published in British edition; Spanish, German, and Japanese translations.

Edited Works With Commentaries

The Shaping of American Diplomacy 1750-1955. Chicago: Rand McNally (1956). Revised 1972.

America and the Middle East: Open Door Imperialism or Enlightened Leadership? New York: Rinehart (1958).

From Colony to Empire: Essays in the History of American Foreign Relations. New York: John Wiley and Sons (1972). Also published in Italian translation.

America in Vietnam: A Documentary History (with Walter F. LaFeber, Thomas J. McCormick and Lloyd C. Gardner). Garden City, New York: Anchor Press/Doubleday (1985).

Selected Articles

"A Frontier Federalist and the War of 1812," *The Pennsylvania Magazine of History and Biography*, LXXVI (January 1952): 81-85.

"Brooks Adams and American Expansion," *New England Quarterly*, XXV (June 1952): 217-232.

"A Second Look at Mr. X," *Monthly Review*, 4 (August 1952): 123-128.

"Moscow Peace Drive: Victory for Containment?" *The Nation*, 177 (July 11, 1953): 28-30.

"A Note on the Isolationism of Senator William E. Borah," *Pacific Historical Review*, XXII (November 1953): 391-392.

"The Legend of Isolationism in the 1920s," *Science and Society,* XVIII (Winter 1954): 1-20.

"Raymond Robins, Crusader—The Outdoor Mind," *The Nation,* 179 (October 30, 1954): 384-385.

"Cold War Perspectives—A Historical Fable," *The Nation,* 180 (May 28, 1955): 458-461.

"The Historical Romance of Senator Neuberger's Election," *Oregon Historical Quarterly,* LVI (June 1955): 101-105. Reprinted as "Neuberger Ducked the Basic Issues," *Frontier,* 6 (October 1955): 5-6.

"The Frontier Thesis and American Foreign Policy," *Pacific Historical Review,* XXIV (November 1955): 379-395.

"Babbitt's New Fables," *The Nation,* 182 (January 7, 1956): 3-6.

"Great Boomerang: The Irony of Containment," *The Nation,* 182 (May 5, 1956): 376-379.

"Challenge to American Radicalism," *Frontier,* 7 (June 1956): 5-6.

"On the Restoration of Brooks Adams," *Science and Society,* XX (Summer 1956): 247-253.

"Reflections on the Historiography of American Entry into World War II," *Oregon Historical Quarterly,* LVII (September 1956): 274-279.

"A Note on Charles Austin Beard's Search for a General Theory of Causation," *The American Historical Review,* LXII (October 1956): 59-80.

"Taxing for Peace," *The Nation,* 184 (January 19, 1957): 53.

"Latin America: Laboratory of American Foreign Policy in the 1920s," *Inter-American Economic Affairs,* 11 (Autumn 1957): 3-30.

"China and Japan: A Challenge and a Choice of the Nineteen Twenties," *Pacific Historical Review,* XXVI (August 1957): 259-279.

"The American Century, 1941-1957," *The Nation,* 185 (November 2, 1957): 297-301.

"A Note on American Foreign Policy in Europe in the 1920s," *Science and Society,* XXII (Winter 1958): 1-20.

"The Age of Mercantilism: An Interpretation of the American Political Economy, 1763-1828," *The William and Mary Quarterly,* XV (October 1958): 419-437.

"Needed: Production for Peace," *The Nation,* 188 (February 21, 1959): 149-153.

"Take New Look at Russia," *Foreign Policy Bulletin,* 38 (April 15, 1959): 118-119.

"Samuel Adams: Calvinist, Mercantilist, Revolutionary," *Studies on the Left,* 1 (Winter 1960): 47-57.

"On the Origins of the Cold War," in "The Origins of the Cold War—An Exchange," *Commentary,* 31 (February 1961): 152-153.

"Protecting Overseas Investors," *The Nation,* 193 (August 26, 1961): 100-101.

"The Irony of the Bomb," *Centennial Review,* V (Fall 1961): 373-384.

"Foreign Policy and the American Mind: An Alternate View," *Commentary,* 33 (February 1962): 155-159.

Contributor to "American Socialism and Thermonuclear War: A Symposium," *New Politics,* 1 (Spring 1962): 40-45.

"Cuba: The President and His Critics," *The Nation,* 196 (March 16, 1963): 226 ff.

"Historiography and Revolution: The Case of Cuba," *Studies on the Left,* 3 (Summer 1963): 78-102.

"American Intervention in Russia: 1917-1920," *Studies on the Left,* 3 (Fall 1963): 24-48; 4 (Winter 1964): 39-57.

"Cuba: Issues and Alternatives," *Annals of the American Academy of Political and Social Sciences,* 351 (January 1964): 72-80.

"The Vicious Circle of American Imperialism," *New Politics,* IV (Fall 1965): 48-55.

"The Cold War Revisionists," *The Nation,* 205 (November 13, 1967): 492-495.

"How Can the Left Be Relevant?" *Current,* 109 (August 1969): 20-24.

"Notes for a Dialogue with Messrs. Harrington, Schlesinger, and Zinn," *Partisan Review,* XXXVIII (January 1971): 67-78.

"A Historian's Perspective," *Prologue: The Journal of the National Archives,* 6 (Fall 1974): 200-203. Excerpt from an address to the 1973 Annual Meeting of the American Historical Association.

"Is the Idea and Reality of America Possible Without Empire?" (an adaptation of the forthcoming *Empire as a Way of Life), The Nation,* 231 (August 2, 1980): 104-119.

"Notes on the Death of a Ship and the End of a World: The Grounding of the British Bark *Glenesslin* at Mount Neahkahnie on 1 October, 1913," *The American Neptune,* XLI (1981): 122-138.

"Thoughts on Rereading Henry Adams" (presidential address to the Organization of American Historians), *The Journal of American History,* 68 (June 1981): 7-15.

"Radicals and Regionalism," *democracy,* 1 (October 1981): 87-98.

"History as Redemption: Henry Adams and the Education of America," *The Nation,* 234 (March 6, 1982): 266-269.

"Procedure Becomes Substance," *democracy,* 2 (April 1982): 100-102.

"Thoughts on the Fun and Purpose of Being an American Historian," *OAH Newsletter,* 13 (February 1985): 2-3.

Selected Book Reviews

"Collapse of the Grand Coalition," *The Nation,* 179 (November 6, 1954): 408-409. Review of *America, Britain and Russia: Their Cooperation and Conflict, 1941-46* by William Hardy McNeill.

"The Age of Re-forming History," *The Nation,* 182 (June 30, 1956): 552-554. Review of *The Age of Reform* by Richard Hofstadter.

"The Convenience of History," *The Nation,* 183 (September 15, 1956): 222-224. Review of *Russia Leaves the War* by George F. Kennan.

"Schlesinger: Right Crisis—Wrong Order," *The Nation,* 184 (March 23, 1957): 257-260. Review of *The Crisis of the Old Order: 1919-1933* by Arthur M. Schlesinger.

"Loss of Debate," *The Nation,* 186 (May 17, 1958): 452-453. Review of *The Ordeal of Woodrow Wilson* by Herbert Hoover.

"Fire in the Ashes of Scientific History," *The William and Mary Quarterly,* XIX (April 1962): 274-287. Review of several books on historiography.

"The Acquitting Judge," *Studies on the Left,* 3 (Winter 1963): 94-99. Review of *Imperial Democracy: The Emergence of America as a Great Power* by Ernest R. May.

"Officers and Gentlemen," *The New York Review of Books,* XVI (May 6, 1971): 3-8. Review of nine books "From MacArthur to Mylai."

Some Contributions to Compiled Works

"Introduction," (with Harvey Goldberg) and "Charles Austin Beard: The Intellectual as Tory-Radical," in *American Radicals: Some Problems and Personalities,* edited by Harvey Goldberg. New York: Monthly Review Press (1957).

"The Age of Mercantilism: An Interpretation of American Political Economy, 1763-1828," and "The Legend of Isolationism in the 1920s," in *Essays in American Diplomacy,* edited by Armin Rappaport. New York: The Macmillan Company (1967).

"Raymond Robins," in *Dictionary of American Biography,* Supplement 5, 1951-55, 578-580. New York: Charles Scribner's Sons (1977).

"Amerikas 'idealistischer' Imperialismus, 1900-1917," in *Imperialismus,* edited by Hans-Ulrich Wehler. Konigstein: Athenaum/Dusseldorf: Droste (1979).

"The City on a Hill on an Errand into the Wilderness," in *Vietnam Reconsidered: Lessons from a War,* edited by Harrison E. Salisbury, New York: Harper & Row (1984).

Commentaries

Clifford Solway, "Turning History Upside Down," *Saturday Review* (June 20, 1970): 13ff.

Carl N. Degler, review of *The Roots of the Modern American Empire,* in *The American Historical Review,* LXXV (October 1970): 1780-1782.

Robert James Maddox, *The New Left and the Origins of the Cold War.* Princeton: Princeton University Press (1973).

Christopher Lasch, "William Appleman Williams on American History," *Marxist Perspectives,* 3 (Fall 1978): 118-126.

John Lukacs, review of *Empire as a Way of Life,* in *The New Republic,* 183 (October 11, 1980): 31-33.

Edward S. Shapiro, "Revisionism R.I.P.," *The Intercollegiate Review,* 17 (Fall/Winter 1981): 55-60.

William Marina, "William Appleman Williams," *Dictionary of Literary Biography,* 17, *Twentieth Century Historians.* Detroit: Gale Research Company (1983).

Bradford Perkins, "The Tragedy of American Diplomacy: Twenty-Five Years After," *Reviews in American History,* 12 (March 1984): 1-18. (Reprinted in this volume.)

Foster Church, "A Troublesome Character," *Northwest: The Sunday Oregonian Magazine* (October 28, 1984): 4-9.

David W. Noble, *The End of American History.* Minneapolis: University of Minnesota Press (1985).

Interviews

Michael Horowitz, "William Appleman Williams: A Name to Remember," *Northwest: The Sunday Oregonian Magazine* (February 21, 1971): 4-7.

John Strawn and Tom Bates, "William Appleman Williams: In the Eye of the Revolution," *Oregon Times,* V (June 1975): 10-14.

Mike Wallace, "William Appleman Williams," in *Visions of History,* edited by Henry Abelove, Betsy Blackmar, Peter Dimock, and Jonathan Schneer. New York: Pantheon Books (1984).

Notes

William Appleman Williams:
"Doing History is Best of All. No Regrets."

William G. Robbins

1. Corvallis (Oregon) *Gazette-Times,* December 30, 1984.

2. William Appleman Williams, "A Good Life and a Good Death: A Memoir of an Independent Lady," unpublished manuscript in possession of the author, I, 1-2.

3. *Ibid.,* III, 3-7; IV, 1-4; V, 2-3.

4. Salem (Oregon) *Statesman-Journal,* December 17, 1978; Williams, "A Good Life and a Good Death," II, 18-20.

5. Mike Wallace, "William Appleman Williams," in *Visions of History,* edited by Henry Abelove, Betsy Blackmar, Peter Dimock, and Jonathan Schneer (New York, 1984), 126-127.

6. *Gazette-Times,* February 27, 1978; William Marina, "William Appleman Williams," in *Dictionary of Literary Biography,* vol. 17, *Twentieth Century Historians* (Detroit, 1983), 450.

7. *Gazette-Times,* February 27, 1978; Fred Harvey Harrington to the author, February 22, 1985.

8. Harrington to the author.

9. Harrington to the author; William Appleman Williams, "A Historian's Perspective," *Prologue: The Journal of the National Archives,* 6 (1974): 201.

10. Harrington to the author; William Appleman Williams, *History as a Way of Learning* (New York, 1974), xiv.

11. *Visions of History,* 129; Walter LaFeber, "The Impact of Fred Harvey Harrington," paper delivered at the annual meeting of the Organization of American Historians, Minneapolis, April 19, 1985, 5.

12. Walter LaFeber to the author, February 9, 1985; LaFeber, "The Impact of Fred Harvey Harrington," 5.

13. LaFeber, "The Impact of Fred Harvey Harrington," 8; *Statesman-Journal,* April 26, 1976; LaFeber to the author.

14. William Appleman Williams to the author, March 19, 1985.

15. Wallace, "William Appleman Williams," 130.

16. Marina, "William Appleman Williams," 451; Wallace, "William Appleman Williams," 130-131.

17. Wallace, "William Appleman Williams," 130-131.

18. Easum is quoted in Harrington to the author.

19. Williams to the author, March 17, 1985.

20. *Ibid.*

21. Wallace, "William Appleman Williams," 132; Williams to the author, March 17, 1985.

22. Williams to the author, March 17, 1985.

23. Marina, "William Appleman Williams," 452; *The Shaping of American Diplomacy,* vol. 1, Second Edition (Chicago, 1970), xvi, xviii.

24. Williams to the author, March 17, 1985.

25. *Ibid.*

26. Harrington to the author; Williams to the author, March 17, 1985.

27. Harrington to the author; Williams to the author, March 17, 1985.

28. Bradford Perkins, *"The Tragedy of American Diplomacy:* Twenty-Five Years After," *Reviews in American History,* 12 (1984): 1 (reprinted in this volume).

29. Lloyd Gardner to the author, March 19, 1985.

30. LaFeber to the author.

31. Gardner to the author.

32. LaFeber to the author.

33. Gardner to the author.

34. Wallace, "William Appleman Williams," 134; *Gazette-Times,* February 27, 1978.

35. Williams to the author, March 17, 1985; *Gazette-Times,* February 27, 1978.

36. Wallace, "William Appleman Williams," 133-134.

37. *Ibid.,* 134.

38. *Ibid.*

39. Foster Rhea Dulles, in *American Historical Review,* 64 (1959): 1922-1923; John Braeman, in *American Political Science Review,* 66 (1962): 1005-1006; Oscar Handlin, in *Mississippi Valley Historical Review,* 48 (1962): 743-745; Williams, *The Contours of American History* (New York, 1966), 4.

40. Williams to the author, March 17, 1985.

41. *Ibid.;* LaFeber to the author; Perkins, "Twenty-Five Years After," 1.

42. "Eugene Genovese: The Uncommon Marxist," an interview by J. Robert Moskin in *Intellectual Digest* (October 1970): 79; *Wall Street Journal,* October 20, 1971.

43. Williams, "Thoughts on the Fun and Purpose of Being an American Historian," *OAH Newsletter,* 13 (February 1985): 2; Harrington to the author.

44. Gardner to the author.

45. LaFeber to the author; Gardner to the author.

46. Williams to the author, March 17, 1985.

47. *Ibid.*

48. Hugh Wubben, conversation with the author, March 27, 1985; Williams to the author, March 17, 1985.

49. Williams to the author, March 17, 1985.

50. *Ibid.*

51. *Ibid.*

52. *Ibid.*

53. *Ibid.,* March 18, 1980.

54. *Ibid.,* no date, and August 16, 1979.

55. *Ibid.,* March 17, 1985; William G. Robbins, "William Appleman Williams: A Profile," *Prism: The OSU Magazine* (Spring 1976): 7.

56. Robert MacVicar to the author, April 5, 1985.

57. Williams to the author, March 17, 1985.

58. Quoted in Foster Church, "A Troublesome Character," Portland *Oregonian,* October 28, 1984.

59. Perkins, "Twenty-Five Years After," 10.

60. John Lukacs, in *New Republic* (October 11, 1980): 31-33; Edward S. Shapiro, "Revisionism R. I. P.," *The Intercollegiate Review* (Fall/Winter 1981): 60.

61. John H. McMillan to the author, March 15, 1985.

62. *Oregonian,* February 10, 1985.

63. *Ibid.*

64. John V. Byrne to the author, March 19, 1985; Williams, "A Historian's Perspective," 203; Williams to the author, March 19, 1985.

"The Tragedy of American Diplomacy": Twenty-Five Years After

Bradford Perkins

1. Charles A. McClelland, review, *American Political Science Review,* 53 (1959): 1196.

2. William Appleman Williams, *The Tragedy of American Diplomacy,* rev. ed. (1962), 11. (Hereafter cited as *Tragedy 1962.*). The phrasing, although not the idea, is new in the 1962 edition.

3. William Appleman Williams, *The Tragedy of American Diplomacy* (1959), 39-40. (Hereafter cited as *Tragedy.*)

4. *Ibid.,* 64.

5. Williams did not so much disagree with as ignore classical economic theory, which denied that trade was "a zero-sum game in which American export sales corresponded to foreign losses. . . . [G]lobal trade was a positive-sum game in which all participants gained—[though] not necessarily equally . . ." (Alfred E. Eckes, Jr., "Open Door Expansionism Reconsidered: the World War II Experience," *Journal of American History,* 59 [1972-73]: 914). On the other hand, even in revisions, Williams did not incorporate "dependency theory," although its thrust would have reinforced his arguments. (See especially André Gunder Frank, *Capitalism and Underdevelopment in Latin America* [1967].)

6. *Tragedy,* 150.

7. But see William Appleman Williams, "The Age of Mercantilism: An Interpretation of the American Political Economy, 1763-1828." *The William and Mary Quarterly,* 3rd Series, 15 (1958): 419-437.

8. Contrast *Tragedy,* 25, with William Appleman Williams, *The Tragedy of American Diplomacy,* 2nd rev. ed. (1972), 25. (Hereafter cited as *Tragedy 1972.*) In *Tragedy 1972* Williams inserted a long passage (23-27) incorporating arguments from his *The Roots of the Modern American Empire* (1969) that agriculturists contributed first and perhaps most to expansionism of the later nineteenth century.

9. *Tragedy 1972,* 55. How far the expansionist theme can be carried has recently been demonstrated by Emily S. Rosenberg, *Spreading the American Dream: American Economic and Cultural Expansion, 1890-1945* (1982). Rosenberg describes overseas economic activities of the American government and business, but she also includes missionary activity, philanthropy, the Office of War Information, and a wide variety of overseas activity. The result is a diffuse eclecticism.

10. *Tragedy,* 35; *Tragedy 1972,* 45.

11. *Tragedy,* 63; *Tragedy 1972,* 93.

12. *Tragedy 1972,* 173, 185. Williams thanks Lloyd C. Gardner for exchanging notes and ideas on the Roosevelt period (177n), but his account is even less nuanced than Gardner's *Economic Aspects of New Deal Diplomacy* (1964).

13. Jerald A. Combs, *American Diplomatic History* (1983), 257.

14. *Tragedy 1972,* 1, 307. For the same thought, see also Williams, *Roots,* 451-453, where the noncapitalist but non-Marxist prescription is endorsed. Initially, *Tragedy* concentrated on the drive to increase manufactured exports, but now agricultural interests are seen as equally involved. Reform, as opposed to fundamental change, is thus a less likely answer.

15. Combs, *American Diplomatic History,* 256.

16. Williams also cited unpublished student papers, conversations and exchanges of research notes with colleagues. The exchange of notes, frequently mentioned by Williams's students, offers obvious problems, since the donor has already screened the sources.

17. William Appleman Williams, "Open Door Interpretation," in *Encyclopedia of American Foreign Policy,* edited by Alexander Deconde (1978), 708.

18. David F. Healy, *The United States and Cuba, 1898-1902* (1963); Robert Freeman Smith, *The United States and Cuba: Business and Diplomacy, 1917-1960* (1962). Healy minimized the influence of businessmen on Cuban policy, and in a

later work, *U.S. Expansionism: The Imperialist Urge of the 1890s* (1970), he down-played economic considerations. Smith viewed policy toward Mexico in much the same spirit in *The United States and Revolutionary Nationalism in Mexico, 1916-1932* (1972). Both Healy and Smith, like Fred Harvey Harrington, in *God, Mammon and the Japanese* (1944), a study of relations with Korea, devoted much attention to developments in the target country. An unfortunate legacy of *Tragedy*, not consid-ered in this essay, is the emphasis on the sources of American policy at the expense of diplomatic history as a study of interaction.

19. J. A. Thompson, "William Appleman Williams and the 'American Empire,'" *American Studies, 7* (1975): 1n.

20. Walter LaFeber, *The New Empire* (1963). Just as LaFeber buttressed Williams's argument after it appeared, so Ernest A. Paolino, in *The Foundations of the American Empire* (1973), a study of William H. Seward's expansionism, docu-mented on the basis of manuscript research, what LaFeber argued on the basis of limited published materials.

21. Howard Schonberger, *Transportation to the Seaboard* (1971); Tom E. Terrill, *The Tariff, Politics, and American Foreign Policy* (1973); Edward P. Crapol, *America for Americans* (1973).

22. Gardner, *Economic Aspects of New Deal Diplomacy,* paperback ed. (1971), xi-xiii; Dick Steward, *Trade and Hemisphere* (1975); David Green, *The Contain-ment of Latin America* (1971); Frederick C. Adams, *Economic Diplomacy: the Export-Import Bank and American Foreign Policy* (1976).

23. Thomas J. McCormick, *China Market: America's Quest for Informal Empire, 1893-1901* (1967), 9; Marilyn Blatt Young, *The Rhetoric of Empire, 1895-1901* (1968); Carl P. Parrini, *Heir to Empire* (1969); Michael J. Hogan, *Informal Entente* (1977). McCormick's study began as a dissertation under Harrington.

24. Norman A. Graebner, *Empire on the Pacific* (1955). Two textbooks apply-ing *Tragedy's* approach do cover the entire chronology: Lloyd C. Gardner, Walter F. LaFeber, and Thomas J. McCormick, *Creation of the American Empire* (1973), and William Appleman Williams, ed., *From Colony to Empire* (1972). In the latter, however, chapters on the transcontinental sweep are by Richard W. VanAlstyne, whose criticisms of American aggressiveness long precede *Tragedy*. See also Thomas G. Paterson, J. Garry Clifford, and Kenneth J. Hagan, *American Foreign Policy* (1977), which much less rigorously follows the Williams model.

25. Howard Schonberger, "William H. Becker and the New Left Revisionists: A Rebuttal," *Pacific Historical Review,* 44 (1975): 249. Thomas J. McCormick, himself an early revisionist, estimates that between 25 and 30 percent of works published in the 1970s and 10 to 15 percent of those appearing in the early 1980s might be categorized as revisionist ("Drift or Mastery? A Corporatist Synthesis for American Diplomatic History," *Reviews in American History,* 10 [1982]: 318).

26. William H. Becker, "American Manufacturers and Foreign Markets, 1870-1900," *Business History Review,* 47 (1975): 466-481; "Foreign Markets for Iron and Steel, 1893-1913," *Pacific Historical Review,* 44 (1975): 233-248; *The Dynamics of Business-Government Relations* (1982), xiv; Eckes, "Open Door Expansionism"; Alfred A. Eckes, Jr., *A Search for Solvency* (1975), 275.

27. Robert W. Tucker, *The Radical Left and American Foreign Policy* (1971), 56, 14.

28. *Ibid.,* 70.

29. *Ibid.,* 111.

30. *Ibid.,* 81.

31. *Ibid.,* 148.

32. Thompson, "Williams and the 'American Empire,'" 103. For a recent restatement, see Richard A. Melanson, "The Social and Political Thought of William Appleman Williams," *Western Political Quarterly,* 31 (1978): 392-409.

33. *Tragedy 1972,* 207.

34. For a lucid Marxist critique of Williams's *Contours of American History,* see Herbert Aptheker," American Development and Ruling-Class Ideology," *Studies on the Left,* 3, 1 (1963): 97-105.

35. McCormick, "Drift or Mastery?," 319.

36. Melvyn P. Leffler, "The Origins of Republican War Debt Policy, 1921-1923," *Journal of American History,* 59 (1972-73): 601; Melvyn P. Leffler, *Elusive Quest* (1979); Hogan, *Informal Entente.* See also Burton I. Kaufmann, *Efficiency and Expansion* (1974), and, though centering on Europe, Stephen A. Schuker, *The End of French Predominance in Europe* (1976).

37. N. Gordon Levin, Jr., *Woodrow Wilson and World Politics* (1968), vii.

38. See, e.g., Michael Leigh, "Is There a Revisionist Thesis on the Origins of the Cold War?," *Political Science Quarterly,* 89 (1974): 101-116.

39. For example, Denna Frank Fleming began work on his revisionist study, *The Cold War and Its Origins,* 2 vols. (1961) in 1947, did not include Williams in a long list of acknowledgments, and only briefly mentioned the open door thesis, yet is identified as a disciple by Richard A. Melanson ("Social and Political Thought of Williams," 392).

40. Gabriel Kolko, *The Politics of War* (1968), vii. (Kolko also thanked N. Gordon Levin.) Joyce and Gabriel Kolko's *The Limits of Power* (1972) includes an extended discussion of the Marshall Plan. For Kolko's earlier views, see especially *The Triumph of Conservatism* (1963).

41. However, for an argument similar to Williams's, see William O. McCagg, Jr., *Stalin Embattled, 1943-1948* (1978).

42. Robert James Maddox, *The New Left and the Origins of the Cold War* (1973); Richard A. Melanson, "Revisionism Subdued? Robert James Maddox and the Origins of the Cold War," *Political Science Reviewer,* 7 (1977): 270, 266.

43. *Tragedy,* 180, 150, 163-164, 151. Williams later denied that he had claimed that "the United States started or caused the Cold War." He merely maintained, he said, that American policy "hardened the natural tensions . . . into bitter antagonisms and inflexible positions" (*Tragedy 1972,* 206-207). This rather fine distinction is a rare softening of the 1959 version. For a similar statement, see Lloyd C. Gardner, *Architects of Illusion* (1970), x.

44. Gerald K. Haines and J. Samuel Walker, eds., *American Foreign Relations: A Historiographical Review* (1981), 198.

45. Thomas G. Paterson, *Soviet-American Confrontation* (1973), 260. Economic goals are similarly minimized in Thomas G. Paterson, *On Every Front: The Making of the Cold War* (1979), especially in ch. 4.

46. Bruce Kuklick, *American Policy and the Division of Germany* (1972), 237, 239, 4.

47. Melanson, "Revisionism Subdued?," 23; Maddox, *New Left and the Cold War,* 13.

48. *Tragedy 1972,* 288.

49. For the latter, see Richard Dean Burns, ed., *Guide to American Foreign Relations since 1700* (1983), 709-712. All but five of the listed items appeared before 1975.

50. Sir John Wheeler-Bennett and Anthony Nicholls, *The Semblance of Peace* (London, 1972); John W. Spanier, *American Foreign Policy Since World War II* (1960; 7th ed., 1977).

51. John Lewis Gaddis, "The Emerging Post-Revisionist Synthesis on the Origins of the Cold War," *Diplomatic History, 7* (1983): 171-190; Warren F. Kimball, "Comment," *ibid.,* 199; John Lewis Gaddis, *The United States and the Origins of the Cold War, 1941-1947* (1972); Daniel Yergin, *Shattered Peace: The Origins of the Cold War and the National Security State* (1977); Combs, *American Diplomatic History,* 331.

52. Gaddis, "Post-Revisionist Synthesis," 180-181, makes the most of these points, although the bulk of this article is devoted to a criticism of revisionism for errors of omission and commission.

53. George F. Kennan, *American Diplomacy, 1900-1950* (1951); Norman A. Graebner, *Cold War Diplomacy* (1962); Ronald Steel, *Pax Americana* (1967).

54. Tucker, *Radical Left and American Foreign Policy,* 146-147.

William Appleman Williams and the Crisis of Public History

David W. Noble

1. Thomas Bender, "The New History—Then and Now," *Reviews in American History,* 12 (December 1984): 613, 614, 618, 619, 622.

2. Gene Wise, *American Historical Explanations* (Homewood, 1973).

3. Charles Beard, *The Industrial Revolution* (London, 1901). Williams, *American-Russian Relations* (New York, 1952).

4. Williams, "Radicals and Regionalism," *democracy,* 1 (October 1981): 88.

5. For an analysis of Beard's belief in the exceptionalism of American history, see David W. Noble, *The End of American History: Democracy, Capitalism, and the Metaphor of Two Worlds in Anglo-American Historical Writing, 1880-1980* (Minneapolis, 1985).

6. These patterns in Niebuhr's thinking also are discussed in *Ibid.*

7. Williams, *The Tragedy of American Diplomacy* (New York: 1959). Williams's relationship to the Progressive and counter-Progressive paradigms is a major theme in Noble, *End of American History.*

8. Williams, *American-Russian Relations,* 3, 4.

9. *Ibid.,* 23, 157, 192.

10. Reinhold Niebuhr, *The Irony of American History* (New York, 1952). Williams, *American-Russian Relations,* 283.

11. Williams, "The Frontier Thesis and American Foreign Policy," *Pacific Historical Review,* XXIV (November 1955): 379, 380, 383, 389.

12. *Ibid.,* 389, 391.

13. Niebuhr, *Irony of American History,* vii, viii.

14. Williams, *Tragedy of American Diplomacy,* 1, 2.

15. *Ibid.,* 9, 22, 50.

16. *Ibid.,* 49, 50.

17. *Ibid.,* 83.

18. *Ibid.,* 158, 159.

19. *Ibid.,* 206.

20. Williams, *The Contours of American History* (Cleveland, 1961), 56, 57.

21. Williams, *The Great Evasion* (Chicago, 1964), 19.

22. *Ibid.,* 114, 164.

23. *Ibid.,* 173, 175, 176.

24. Williams, *Some Presidents from Wilson to Nixon* (New York, 1972), 12.

25. Williams, *America Confronts a Revolutionary World* (New York, 1976).

26. Williams, *Americans in a Changing World* (New York, 1978), 81.

27. Williams, *Empire as a Way of Life* (New York, 1980), 58, 213.

28. Williams, "Radicals and Regionalism," 91, 95.

29. *Ibid.,* 96. Williams discusses the development of his understanding of history in *Visions of History* (New York, 1984), edited by Henry Abelove, Betsy Blackmar, Peter Dimock, and Jonathan Scheer.

Theories of Imperialism

Carl Parri

1. A subtle rejection of the significance of economic imperialism began with the publication of William L. Langer's "A Critique of Imperialism," *Foreign Affairs,* 14 (1935-36): 102-119, in which Langer stressed the weaknesses in Hobson's analysis. Subsequently the differences between socialist and nonsocialist interpretations became more pronounced. Hans Morgenthau in his *Politics among Nations: The Struggle for Power and Peace* (New York, 1948): 52-53, 65, took Langer's work to its ultimate absurdity by asserting that imperialism involved illegitimate, that is forceful, changes in the balance of power. This clearly eurocentric construct had the ludicrous result of making British efforts to maintain their power in India against Indian nationalists (and their Japanese allies) "anti-imperialist." In later editions (1964 for instance) Morgenthau modified this, but the basic approach continued to pivot around the needs of the European victors of World War I. D. K. Fieldhouse continued the Langer pattern in his "Imperialism: An Historiographical Revision,"

The Economic History Review, XIV (December 1961): 187-209. But a nonsocialist scholar, the late Eric Stokes, in his "Nineteenth Century Colonial Expansion and the Attack on the Theory of Economic Imperialism: A Case of Mistaken Identity?," *The Historical Journal,* XII (No. 2, 1969): 285-301, dealt rather effectively with Fieldhouse's confusion of Hobson and Lenin, hence with Langer's earlier conflation of Hobson and Lenin.

2. A good sampling of the nonsocialist writers on imperialism would include the following. Henry Noel Brailsford, *The War of Steel and Gold, a Study of the Armed Peace* (London, 1917). Charles A. Conant, "The Economic Basis of Imperialism," *North American Review,* 167 (September 1898). Herbert Feis, *The Diplomacy of the Dollar 1919-1932* (Baltimore, 1950). Fredrick C. Howe, "Dollar Diplomacy and Financial Imperialism under the Wilson Administration," *Annals of the American Academy of Political and Social Sciences* (No. 1916): 68. J. A. Hobson, *Imperialism: A Study* (Ann Arbor, 1971). Leland H. Jenks, *The Migration of British Capital to 1875* (New York, 1923). Walter Lippmann, *The Stakes of Diplomacy* (New York, 1915). Paul Leroy Beaulieu, *De la colonisation chez les peuples modernes* (Paris, 1886). Socialist writings on imperialism dealing with matters leading up to World War I include the following. Nicolai Bukharin, *Imperialism and the World Economy* (New York, 1929). Rudolph Hilferding, *Finance Capital: A Study of the Latest Phase of Capitalist Development* (London, 1981). Karl Kautsky, "Ultra-imperialism," *New Left Review,* 59 (January/February 1970). V. I. Lenin, *Imperialism, The Highest State of Capitalism: A Popular Outline* (New York, 1939). Rosa Luxemburg, *The Accumulation of Capital* (New York, 1968).

3. Most of this debate has been among socialist theorists. Perhaps the most significant issue was whether or not imperialism was an inevitable stage of the normal development of industrial capitalist political economy. Lenin argued that it was; see *Imperialism,* 85-94. Kautsky argued that it was a conscious choice which statesmen made just as free trade was a chronologically prior conscious choice; see "Ultra-imperialism," 45-46.

4. According to Say's law of markets—now called Say's identity—production creates its own demand at relatively full employment of labor and resources.

5. Harry Magdoff, *The Age of Imperialism* (New York, 1969). Bill Warren, *Imperialism, Pioneer of Capitalism* (London, 1980). A mixture of socialist and nonsocialist works agree that "surplus capital" as the term was employed by Hobson and Lenin did not exist or was of little significance. John Maynard Keynes accepted the existence of surplus capital, which Keynes labeled "redundant capital at home." See *The Collected Writings of John Maynard Keyres,* edited by Elizabeth Johnson and Donald Moggridge (London, 1979), 29. J. M. Keynes, *The General Theory of Employment Interest and Money* (New York, 1936). A. K. Cairncross, *Home and Foreign Investment 1870-1913* (Cambridge, 1953).

6. Langer, "Critique of Imperialism," 102-114.

7. *Ibid.,* 102-118.

8. Hobson, *Imperialism,* 65-67, 82-90.

9. Lenin, *Imperialism,* 62-63, 92-93; Conant, "Economic Basis," 330, 337-338.

10. Luxemburg, *Accumulation,* 352-353; Lenin, *Imperialism,* 85-87; Stokes, "Late Nineteenth Century Colonial Expansion," 285-301.

11. Carroll D. Wright, *Industrial Depressions.* First Annual Report of the United States Commissioner of Labor (Washington, 1886), 256-257.

12. Conant, "Economic Basis," 328-331, 333, 337-340.

13. *Ibid.* See also the following works by Conant. *A History of Modern Banks of Issue* (New York, 1896), 453-553. "Crises and Their Management," *Yale Review,* 9 (February 1901): 374-398. "The Struggle for Commercial Empire," *Forum,* 27 (July 1899): 427-440. "The United States as a World Power. II. Her Advantages in the Competition for Commercial Empire," *Forum,* 29 (August 1900): 673-687. "The Growth of Public Expenditures," *Atlantic Monthly* (January 1901): 45-47. "The Law of the Value of Money," *Annals of the American Academy of Political and Social Sciences,* XVI, (July-December 1900): 169-210. "Is an Ideal Money Attainable?," *The Journal of Political Economy,* 11 (1902-1903): 399-415. "The Function of the Stock Produce Exchanges," *Atlantic Monthly,* XCI (April 1903): 433-442. "The Function of the Banker," *Quarterly Journal of Economics,* 17 (1903): 476-491. "The World's Wealth in Negotiable Securities," *Atlantic Monthly* (January 1908): 98-104. "Putting China on the Gold Standard," *The North American Review,* 177 (1903): 691-704. "Can New Openings be Found for Capital?," *Atlantic Monthly,* 92 (November 1899): 600-608. *The United States in the Orient* (Boston, 1900). Also see Carl P. Parrini and Martin J. Sklar, "New Thinking About the Market, 1896-1904: Some American Economists on Investment and the Theory of Surplus Capital," *The Journal of Economic History,* XLIII, 3 (September 1983): 564-571.

14. Conant, "Economic Basis," 337-339. *Latin America and the United States: Addresses by Elihu Root,* edited by Robert Bacon and James Brown Scott (Harvard, 1917), 246.

15. Parrini and Sklar, "New Thinking," text and note 29.

16. William Howard Taft to US Senate in *US Senate 57th Congress, 1st US Senate Committee on the Philippine Islands, January 1902 Hearings on Affairs in the Philippine Islands,* 408-409. "A Special Report on Coinage and Banking in the Philippine Islands, Made to the Secretary of War by Charles A. Conant of Boston, November 25, 1901," Appendix G in *Annual Report of the Secretary of War,* 1901. Conant to Secretary of the Treasury Lyman Gage, October 16, 1900; Gage to Root, November 8, 1900; Conant to C. R. Edwards (Chief, Division of Insular Affairs, War Department), July 9, 1901; Root to Taft, July 23, 1901, all in War Department *Record Group 350,* National Archives. Taft to Root, October 14, 1901, *Root Ms.,* Library of Congress. Henry C. Lodge to William Howard Taft, November 22, 1900, *Taft Ms.* Series 3, Box 64, Library of Congress.

17. Paul Leroy Beaulieu, *Essai sur la repartition des richesses et sur la tendance à une moindre inegalité des conditions* (Paris, 1879) and *Le collectivisme examen critique de nouveau socialisme* (Paris, 1902). Root in Bacon and Scott, *Latin America,* 246. Henry C. Morris asserted the existence of surplus capital in a paper entitled "Some Effects of Outlying Dependencies upon the People of the United States," *Proceedings* of the American Political Science Association, Third Annual Meeting, 194-210. Paul Reinsch, "The New Conquest of the World," *World's*

Work, I (February 1901): 425-431. Hobson, *Imperialism.* Kautsky, "Ultra-imperialism." Lenin, *Imperialism.*

18. Lenin, *Imperialism,* 88-90.

19. Lenin, *Collected Works: Notebooks on Imperialism* 39 (Moscow, 1968), 420; *Imperialism,* 99-108, 83-94.

20. Lenin, *Imperialism.* Kautsky, "Ultra-imperialism," 39-46.

21. Kautsky, "Ultra-imperialism."

22. Lenin, *Imperialism,* 99-108; *Notebooks on Imperialism,* 420. Warren, *Imperialism,* 11-47. Warren attacks Lenin for departing from Marx's view that imperialism was developmental and brings strong evidence to support development after World War II. See *Marx and Engels on Colonialism* (Moscow, 1974), 40-41. The argument that capitalism is nondevelopmental is developed in many sources; typical of these is A. G. Frank, *Latin America: Underdevelopment or Revolutions. Essays on the Development of Underdevelopment and the Immediate Enemy* (New York, 1969).

23. Lenin, *Imperialism,* 83-94. Also see Bill Warren, "Imperialism and Capitalist Industrialization," *New Left Review,* 81 (September/October 1973): 3-53. Carl P. Parrini, *Heir to Empire. United States Economic Diplomacy 1916-1923* (Pittsburgh, 1969). Parrini and Sklar, "New Thinking," 559-578. Richard C. Gardner, "Sterling Dollar Diplomacy," in *Current Perspective. The Origins and Prospects of our International Economic Order* (New York, 1980).

24. Luxemburg, *Accumulation,* 348-385. Lenin, *Imperialism,* 91. Lenin argues against Kautsky that "the characteristic feature of imperialism is precisely that it strives to annex not only agricultural regions but even highly industrialized regions," implying that uneven development allows for "realization" and even necessitates realization by developed nations in the "imperialized" territories of other developed nations.

25. *Marx and Engels on Colonialism,* 40-41.

26. Warren, "Imperialism and Capitalist Industrialization," 12-39, 42. Warren acknowledges that Britain used its political control to avoid authentic development of India, but he argues that this has changed since World War II. For a different opinion, see Harry Magdoff, "Imperialism Without Colonies," in *Studies in the Theory of Imperialism,* edited by Roger Owen and Bob Sutcliffe (London, 1972), 144-170.

27. Warren, "Imperialism and Capitalist Industrialization," 15, 17. D. C. M. Platt, "Economic Imperialism and the Businessmen," in Owen and Sutcliffe, *Studies,* 305-309. Alvey Adee to W. W. Rockhill, undated memorandum attached to Charles Denby, SR. to Secretary of State Richard Olney, January 14, 1897, Despatch No. 2670, Diplomatic Despatches, *Record Group 59,* US National Archives. Adee calls direct investment by American capital in manufacturing in China "simply a local cheap labor dodge," which would interfere with potential direct exports from the United States. But the failure of the reciprocity movement, which began under President McKinley in 1897, led to a reevaluation of opposition to direct investment in manufacturing. The failure of the effort to obtain reciprocity with Canada led to massive investment in foreign manufacturing, later spreading from Canada to other areas.

28. Warren, "Imperialism and Capitalist Industrialization," 42. David Healy, *The United States in Cuba, 1898-1902* (Madison, 1963).

29. Lenin, *Lenin on the United States: Selected Writings by V. I. Lenin,* (anonymously edited) (New York, 1970), 488-499. In an address titled "From the Report on Concessions Delivered to the R. C. P. (B) Group at the Eighth Congress of Soviets," December 21, 1920, Lenin strongly endorsed concessions by the Soviet government to American capitalists through the National City Bank (Rockefeller) complex despite leftist opposition from both within the communist party and noncommunist elements within the Congress of Soviets. Also see Carl P. Parrini, *Heir to Empire,* 138-171. Samir Amin, *Accumulation on a World Scale* (New York, 1974) developed an analysis very similar to that of Soviet leftists. Most Leninists, neo-Leninists, and theorists of underdevelopment and dependency would argue that a large nation—such as Soviet Russia, China, India, perhaps Brazil—could accept foreign capital and determine its uses; small nations would be overwhelmed by foreign influence and political power accompanying the foreign investment. This is a serious weakness in Warren's position, especially as it regards small underdeveloped nations neighboring a large power such as the Central American and Caribbean area republics strategically close to the United States. But for the overwhelming number of medium-sized nations, such as Argentina and Nigeria, I do not think that foreign capital poses any insurmountable barriers to development. Yet it is clear that this problem needs much study.

30. Parrini and Sklar, "New Thinking," 566-571, including footnotes 17 to 27.

31. Surplus capital is still a reality in the present. Jay Forrester, developer of the computer models used in the book *The Limits of Growth,* argued in 1978 that the United States economic system was unbalanced because it was stocked with "too much capital" (see *Fortune* [January 16, 1978]: 145-148). Indeed, the concept of plethora of capital was a common way for business investment services to explain investment "busts" even before the Great Depression in the midst of the high prosperity of the 1920s. For example, see *Moody's Investors Service,* (January 7, 1926, No. 1): 1-6.

The Foreign Policy of Antislavery 1833-1846

Edward P. Crapol

1. Eric Foner, *Politics and Ideology in the Age of the Civil War* (New York, 1980), 50. See also Foner's *Free Soil, Free Labor, Free Men, The Ideology of the Republican Party before the Civil War* (New York, 1970), and David Brion Davis, *The Slave Power Conspiracy and the Paranoid Style* (Baton Rouge, 1969).

2. The exception would be Thomas P. Martin. See for example his "The Upper Mississippi Valley in Anglo-American Anti-Slavery and Free Trade Relations: 1837-1842," *Mississippi Valley Historical Review,* 15 (1928): 204-220.

3. Lydia Maria Child, *An Appeal in Favor of That Class of Americans Called Africans* (Boston, 1833).

4. Committee on Manufactures, Minority Report by J. Q. Adams, February 27, 1833, House of Representatives, 22nd Cong., 2nd Sess., Register of Debates, Vol. 9, 54.

5. Timothy Pitkin, *Statistical View of the Commerce of the United States of America* (New Haven, 1835), 219.

6. Child, *Appeal,* 121.

7. *Ibid.*

8. Benjamin Lundy, *The Origins and True Causes of the Texas Insurrection, Commenced in the Year 1835* (Philadelphia, 1836), 31; see also his *The War in Texas: Instigated by Slaveholders, Land Speculators, etc, For the Reestablishment of Slavery and the Slave Trade in the Republic of Mexico* (Philadelphia, 1836).

9. John Quincy Adams to Benjamin Lundy, May 20, 1836, Adams Papers, microfilm edition, Reel 152.

10. John Quincy Adams to Charles F. Adams, May 24, 1836, Adams Papers, microfilm edition, Reel 503.

11. William Jay, "A View of the Action of the Federal Government in Behalf of Slavery," in *Miscellaneous Writings on Slavery* (Boston, 1853), 218-219.

12. *Ibid.,* 323-332.

13. *Ibid.,* 337.

14. Gordon S. Wood, "Heroics," *New York Review of Books* (April 2, 1981): 16.

15. American Anti-Slavery Society, *Sixth Annual Report,* 14-15. The Garrisonians rejected the idea of creating a separate political party, although many of them accepted the basic tenets of the abolitionist ideology.

16. *Emancipator,* May 1, 1840.

17. James G. Birney to Myron Holley, Joshua Leavitt, and Elizur Wright, Jr., May 11, 1840 in *Letters of James G. Birney 1831-1857,* edited by Dwight L. Dumond (Gloucester, Mass., 1966), I, 567, 572.

18. *Ibid.,* 572-573.

19. Lydia Maria Child was a critic of independent political action and refused to join or support the Liberty Party; see Lydia Maria Child to James Miller McKim and Philadelphia Friends, November 24, 1841, in *Collected Correspondence of Lydia Maria Child,* microfiche edition.

20. Joshua Leavitt to James G. Birney, May 19, 1840 in Dumond, *Letters of James G. Birney,* I, 574.

21. *Emancipator,* October 22, 1840.

22. *Memorial of Joshua Leavitt, Praying the adoption of measures to secure an equitable and adequate market for American wheat,* February 27, 1841. U.S. Congress, Senate Document no. 222, 26th Cong., 2nd Sess.; *Memorial of Joshua Leavitt, Praying that in the revision of the tariff laws, the principle of discrimination may be inserted in favor of those countries in which American grain, flour, and salted meat are admitted duty free,* June 23, 1842. U.S. Congress, Senate Document no. 339, 27th Cong., 2nd Sess.

23. "Proceedings and Address of the Liberty National Nominating Convention," New York City, May 12-13, 1841, in *Emancipator Extra,* August 24, 1841.

24. *Free American,* March 18, 1841.

25. *Emancipator,* August 5, 1841.

26. Betty Fladeland, *Abolitionists and Working-Class Problems in the Age of Industrialization* (Baton Rouge, 1984), 64-65; Joseph Sturge, *A Visit to the United States in 1841* (London, 1842), 148-157.

27. John Curtis, *America and the Corn Laws* (Manchester, 1841).

28. *Morning Chronicle,* September 3, 7, 10, 11, October 4, 13, 14, 21, 26, 1841; *National Intelligencer,* October 14,1841; *Emancipator,* August 26, 1841.

29. *National Intelligencer,* October 14, 1841.

30. St. George L. Sioussat, "Duff Green's 'England and the United States' with an Introductory Study of American Opposition to the Quintuple Treaty of 1841," *Proceedings of the American Antiquarian Society,* 40 (1930): 236-265.

31. *Emancipator,* March 31, 1842,

32. *Emancipator,* February 9, 1843; for an account of the reaction of Massachusetts Whigs to the Gilmer letter see Kinley J. Brauer, *Cotton versus Conscience, Massachusetts Whig Politics and Southwestern Expansion, 1843-1848* (Lexington, 1967), 54-57.

33. Hugh H. Davis, "The Reform Career of Joshua Leavitt, 1749-1873," unpublished Ph.D. dissertation, Ohio State University, 1969.

34. *Emancipator,* September 7 and 14, 1843; see also Kirk H. Porter and Donald B. Johnson, *National Party Platforms 1840-1964* (Urbana, 1966).

35. Quoted in Duff Green, *Facts and Suggestions, Biographical, Historical, Financial and Political, Addressed to the People of the United States* (New York, 1866), 151.

36. *Emancipator,* April 15, 1846.

37. Morton Rothstein, "America in the International Rivalry for the British Wheat Market, 1860-1914," *Mississippi Valley Historical Review,* 47 (1960-61): 401.

38. James D. Richardson, *Messages and Papers of the Presidents,* III, (Washington, 1913), 1895.

39. Stanley M. Elkins, "Slavery and Ideology," in *The Debate over Slavery, Stanley Elkins and His Critics,* edited by Ann J. Lane (Urbana, 1971), 377.

"Europe First" and its Consequences for the Far Eastern Policy of the United States

Fred Harvey Harrington

In preparing this essay I have used the writings of William Appleman Williams and his and my students, e.g., Williams's *Tragedy of American Diplomacy; Roots of the Modern American Empire;* "Open Door Interpretation," in Alexander DeConde, ed., *Encyclopedia of American Foreign Policy; America in Vietnam,* which Williams edited with Thomas McCormick, Lloyd Gardner and Walter LaFeber; LaFeber's *New Empire* (Ithaca, 1963) and *America, Russia and the Cold War* (New York, 1967); McCormick's *China Market* (Chicago, 1967); Gardner's *Safe for Democracy* (New York, 1984) and *Economic Aspects of the New Deal* (Madison, 1964); Charles Vevier's *United States and China* (New Brunswick, 1955); David Healy's *US Expansionism* (Madison, 1970); Carl Parrini's *Heir to Empire*

(Pittsburgh, 1969); Wayne Cole's *America First* (Madison, 1953); Richard Thompson's *Yellow Peril* (Salem, 1979). Obviously I have used other publications, including those by authors indifferent or hostile to what has been turned out by the "Wisconsin School of Diplomatic History."

1. Flora Lewis, *New York Times,* May 10, 1985.

2. Manuscript log, New York Public Library.

3. Tyler Dennett, *Americans in Eastern Asia* (New York, 1922), 340.

4. Unpublished paper by Thomas LeDuc.

5. Robert W. Shufeldt, *Relation of the Navy to the Commerce of the United States* (Washington, 1878).

6. Thomas McCormick, *China Market;* Charles Campbell, *Special Business Interests and the Open Door* (New Haven, 1951); Ernest Paolino, *The Foundations of the American Empire* (Ithaca, 1973).

7. Lester Brune, *The Origins of National Security Policy* (Manhattan, Kansas, 1981).

8. Louis Morton, "Germany First," in *Command Decisions* (Washington, 1960).

9. Harry S. Truman, *Memoirs,* vol. 2 (New York, 1956). America First senators, he said, "saw nothing wrong in plunging us headlong into an Asian war, but would not raise a finger for the defense of Europe."

The Evolution of the Monroe Doctrine from Monroe to Reagan

Walter LaFeber

1. William Appleman Williams, *The Tragedy of American Diplomacy* (New York, 1959, 1962), especially Chapter I.

2. Paul Keal, *Unspoken Rules and Superpower Dominance* (New York, 1983), 15. For a more detailed definition, see John P. Vloyantes, *Spheres of Influence: A Framework for Analysis* (Tucson, 1970), 2.

3. Vloyantes, *Spheres of Influence,* 12-14.

4. William Appleman Williams, *The Contours of American History* (Cleveland, 1961), 215.

5. Roosevelt to Hermann Speck von Sternberg, October 11, 1901, in *The Letters of Theodore Roosevelt* edited by Elting E. Morison (Cambridge, 1952), 6 volumes, III, 172.

6. Lynn Etheridge Davis, *The Cold War Begins* (Princeton, 1974), 142-143.

7. Dexter Perkins, *A History of the Monroe Doctrine* (Boston, 1955), 368-393.

8. Transcript of "Newsmaker Saturday" television show, November 17, 1984, 2-3. For one aspect of the resurrection, see William F. Buckley, Jr., "The Monroe Doctrine, I Presume?" *National Review,* XXXIII (April 17, 1981): 446. Also see the useful overview by Gaddis Smith, "The Legacy of the Monroe Doctrine," *The New York Times Magazine* (September 9, 1984): 46; and T. D. Allman, "The Doctrine That Never Was," *Harper's,* CCLXVIII (January, 1984): 14.

9. Richard Van Alstyne, "The Monroe Doctrine," in *Encyclopedia of American Foreign Policy,* edited by Alexander Deconde (New York, 1978), 3 volumes, II, 596.

10. This is a paraphrase of one conclusion in Kenneth M. Coleman, "The Political Mythology of the Monroe Doctrine: Reflections on the Social Psychology of Hegemony," in *Latin America, The United States and the Inter-American System,* edited by John D. Martz and Lars Schoultz (Boulder, 1981), 96-114.

11. This and the following sections of the 1823 statement may be found in James D. Richardson (editor), *A Compilation of the Messages and Papers of the Presidents, 1789-1897* (Washington, 1900), 10 vols., II, 209-220; Edward P. Crapol, "John Quincy Adams and the Monroe Doctrine; Some New Evidence," *Pacific Historical Review,* XLVIII (August, 1979): 414.

12. Charles Francis Adams (editor), *The Memoirs of John Quincy Adams* (Philadelphia, 1874-1877), 12 vols., VI, 193-198.

13. An example of the common interpretation is given in the article reported by Philip Taubman in *The New York Times,* November 9, 1984, 7.

14. Diary of Henry L. Stimson, May 8, 1945, Yale University (microfilm).

15. Transcript of "Newsmaker Saturday," November 17, 1984, 2.

16. For the administration's view, U.S. Department of State, *Resource Book. Sandinista Elections in Nicaragua* (Washington, 1984); and for the opposing view, the "Epilogue," especially, in *Nicaragua, the First Five Years* edited by Thomas W. Walker (New York, 1985).

17. Adams, *Memoirs of John Quincy Adams,* V, 323-326.

18. These remarks from Adams's 1821 July 4th address are reprinted in Walter LaFeber (editor), *John Quincy Adams and American Continental Empire. Letters, Papers, and Speeches* (Chicago, 1965), 42-46.

19. Adams, *Memoirs of John Quincy Adams,* IV, 438-439.

20. *Ibid.,* V, 3-12.

21. Worthington C. Ford, *Writings of John Quincy Adams* (New York, 1913-1917), 7 vols., VII, 371-380.

22. Coleman, "Political Mythology of the Monroe Doctrine," 98-99.

23. *Ibid.,* 104.

24. Van Alstyne, "The Monroe Doctrine," II, 584.

25. Polk's message is in Richardson, *Messages and Papers of the Presidents,* IV, 397; his remark to Benton is analyzed in Perkins, *The Monroe Doctrine,* 77-78.

26. Perkins, *The Monroe Doctrine,* 78.

27. The best discussion is in Frederick Merk and L. B. Merk, *The Monroe Doctrine and American Expansionism, 1843-1849* (New York, 1966).

28. Perkins, *The Monroe Doctrine,* 89.

29. Perkins has useful comments on this point in *Ibid.,* 154-155.

30. G. Pope Atkins, *Latin America in the International Political System* (New York, 1977), 308.

31. Olney to Bayard, July 20, 1895, Great Britain, Instructions, National Archives (Washington, D. C.), Record Group 59.

32. Van Alstyne, "The Monroe Doctrine," II, 593.

33. David H. Burton, *Theodore Roosevelt: Confident Imperialist* (Philadelphia, 1968), 55-56.

34. Roosevelt to Speck von Sternberg, July 12, 1901, in Morison, *Letters of Roosevelt,* III, 116.

35. *Ibid.;* Burton, *Theodore Roosevelt,* 110-112.

36. The quote and a useful analysis is in Dexter Perkins, *The Monroe Doctrine, 1867-1907* (Baltimore, 1937), 408-409.

37. *Ibid.,* 394.

38. James Daniel Richardson (editor), *Messages and Papers of the Presidents* (New York, 1897-1914), XVI, 7375-7376.

39. Burton, *Theodore Roosevelt,* 115-117.

40. Roosevelt to Cecil Arthur Spring Rice, July 24, 1905, in Morison, *Letters of Roosevelt,* IV, 1286.

41. Albert Weinberg, *Manifest Destiny* (Baltimore, 1940), 428-429.

42. Charles E. Hughes, *Pathway of Peace. Representative Addresses Delivered During His Term as Secretary of State (1921-1925)* (New York, 1925), 122-123; also important on this point is Arthur P. Whitaker, *The Western Hemisphere Idea: Its Rise and Decline* (Ithaca, 1954), 86-88.

43. Hughes, *Pathway of Peace,* 123.

44. Hiram Bingham, *The Monroe Doctrine, An Obsolete Shibboleth* (New Haven, 1913), 38-39, 102-103.

45. Bryce Wood, *The Making of the Good Neighbor Policy* (New York, 1961, 1967), 118-121, 355; Atkins, *Latin America in the International Political System,* 327.

46. Gerald K. Haines, "American Myopia and the Japanese Monroe Doctrine, 1931-1941," *Prologue* (Summer, 1981): 101-114; a pioneering overview of this process is in Lloyd Gardner, *Economic Aspects of New Deal Diplomacy* (Madison, 1964).

47. Clayton R. Knoppes, "The Good Neighbor Policy and the Nationalization of Mexican Oil: A Reinterpretation," *Journal of American History,* LXIX (June, 1982): 80-81.

48. Edgar B. Nixon and Donald B. Schewe (editors), *Franklin D. Roosevelt and Foreign Affairs* (New York, 1969), XIII, 207.

49. Haines, "American Myopia," 107-108; another key account on these points is David G. Haglund, *Latin America and the Transformation of US Strategic Thought, 1936-1940* (Albuquerque, 1984), 58-59.

50. Haines, "American Myopia," 104-105.

51. Alan K. Henrikson, "The Map as an 'Idea': The Role of Cartographic Imagery During the Second World War," *American Cartographer,* X (1973): 19-53.

52. Haglund, *Latin America,* 180.

53. George H. Blakeslee, "The Japanese Monroe Doctrine," *Foreign Affairs,* XI (July, 1933): 680.

54. *Ibid.,* 675.

55. *Ibid.,* 676-681 especially.

56. *Ibid.,* 678.

57. Haines, "American Myopia," 114.

58. Perkins, *The Monroe Doctrine,* 364-366; for the US statement of its unilateral rights in 1950, see the discussion in Walter LaFeber, *Inevitable Revolutions; The United States in Central America* (New York, 1983, 1984), 93-94.

59. Radio broadcast by Secretary of State John Foster Dulles, June 30, 1954, in *US Department of State, American Foreign Policy, 1950-1955. Basic Documents* (Washington, 1957), 2 vols., I, 1311-1314.

60. Smith, "The Legacy of the Monroe Doctrine," 127.

61. George Ball, *The Past Has Another Pattern* (New York, 1982), 177, 289, 291; Smith, "The Legacy of the Monroe Doctrine," 128.

62. *Public Papers of the Presidents . . . Lyndon B. Johnson, 1965* (Washington, 1966), 2 vols., I, 469-474.

63. Author's phone call to US Department of State Treaty Division, June 18, 1985; Atkins, *Latin America,* 334-335.

64. Buckley, "The Monroe Doctrine, I Presume?", 446; Allman, "The Doctrine that Never Was," 14.

65. Transcript of "Newsmaker Saturday," November 17, 1984, 2-3.

66. Richard Immerman, *The CIA in Guatemala* (Austin, 1982), has the best discussion and makes the connection.

67. The best overiview of this process is in a forthcoming book by Abraham Lowenthal; the book is as yet untitled, but see expecially Chapter II, "The U.S. and Latin America, 1959-1984."

68. Van Alstyne, "The Monroe Doctrine," II, 589.

69. *Ibid.,* II, 585.

Herbert C. Hoover
and the Dream of Capitalism in One Country

Patrick Hearden

1. For a good description of Hoover's philosophy see Joan Hoff Wilson, *Herbert Hoover: Forgotten Progressive* (Boston, 1975).

2. Melvyn P. Leffler, *The Elusive Quest: America's Pursuit of European Stability and French Security, 1919-1933* (Chapel Hill, 1979), 81.

3. Wilson, *Herbert Hoover,* 104.

4. Michael J. Hogan, *Informal Entente: The Private Structure of Cooperation in Anglo-American Economic Diplomacy, 1918-1928* (Columbia, 1977), 3, 40-41. See also Williams, *The Contours of American History* (New York, 1961), 425-439; and Ellis W. Hawley, "Herbert Hoover, the Commerce Secretariat, and the Vision of an 'Associative State', 1921-1928," *Journal of American History,* Vol. 61 (June 1974): 116-140.

5. Wilson, *Herbert Hoover,* 127.

6. Arthur M. Schlesinger, Jr., *The Crisis of the Old Order, 1919-1933* (Boston, 1957), 155.

7. Herbert Feis, *The Diplomacy of the Dollar, 1919-1932* (New York, 1950).

8. Hogan, *Informal Entente,* 44.

9. *Ibid.,* 96-103.

10. Alexander DeConde, *Herbert Hoover's Latin-American Policy* (New York, 1970), 13-24.

11. *Ibid.,* 25-44.

12. *Ibid.,* 59-89.

13. *Ibid.,* 52-58, 66-78, 125.

14. Joan Hoff Wilson, *American Business and Foreign Policy, 1920-1933* (Boston, 1971).

15. Leffler, *The Elusive Quest,* 229.

16. For an excellent analysis of Hoover's domestic recovery program see Albert U. Romasco, *The Poverty of Abundance* (New York, 1965).

17. *Ibid.,* 184-187.

18. Leffler, *The Elusive Quest,* 270.

19. Wilson, *Herbert Hoover,* 166.

20. Fredrick J. Dobney, *Selected Papers of Will Clayton* (Baltimore, 1971), 21-32.

21. Thomas W. Lamont Memorandum, April 7, 1932; Lamont to J. P. Morgan, Russell C. Leffingwell, and S. Parker Gilbert, April 19, 1932, Box 181, Lamont Papers, Baker Library, Harvard Business School.

22. Thomas W. Lamont Memorandum on Reparations and War Debts, April 5, 1932, Box 209, *Ibid.*

23. Norman H. Davis to Thomas W. Lamont, April 29, 1932; Lamont to J. Ridgely Carter, May 4, 1932, Box 181, *Ibid.*

24. Thomas W. Lamont to Henry L. Stimson, May 23, 1932, Box 209, *Ibid.*

25. Henry L. Stimson Diary, July 11, 1932, Sterling Library, Yale University.

26. *Ibid.,* November 23, 1932.

27. *Ibid.,* December 4, 1932.

28. Edwin O. Reischauer, *The United States and Japan* (New York, 1965), 5-97.

29. Thomas J. McCormick, *China Market: America's Quest for Informal Empire, 1893-1901* (Chicago, 1967).

30. Akira Iriye, *After Imperialism: The Search for a New Order in the Far East, 1921-1931* (New York, 1965), 1-22.

31. *Ibid.,* 278-299.

32. William L. Neumann, *America Encounters Japan: From Perry to MacArthur* (New York, 1965), 193-194.

33. Arnold A. Offner, *The Origins of the Second World War: American Foreign Policy and World Politics, 1917-1941* (New York, 1975), 97-103.

34. Lloyd C. Gardner, *Economic Aspects of New Deal Diplomacy* (Madison, 1964), 21.

35. *Ibid.,* 71.

36. Henry L. Stimson Diary, January 9, 1933.

37. Frank Freidel, *Franklin D. Roosevelt: Launching the New Deal* (Boston, 1973), 104, 120.

38. *Ibid.,* 121-122.

39. Henry L. Stimson Diary, October 8, 1934.

Freda Kirchwey: Cold War Critic

Margaret Morley

The author acknowledges support received from the Northern Arizona University Organized Research Committee.

1. Thomas G. Paterson (editor), *Cold War Critics: Alternatives to American Foreign Policy in the Truman Years* (Chicago, 1971), 7; June Sochen, *Movers and Shakers: American Women Thinkers and Activists, 1900-1970* (New York, 1973), 213-220; Alonzo L. Hamby, *Beyond the New Deal: Harry S. Truman and American Liberalism* (New York, 1973), 94-95; Barton J. Berstein, "America in War and Peace: The Test of Liberalism," in *Towards a New Past: Dissenting Essays in American History,* edited by Barton J. Bernstein (New York, 1967), 311-312; Mary Sperling McAuliffe, *Crisis on the Left: Cold War Politics and American Liberals* (Amherst, 1978), 8-9; Sarah Alpern, "A Woman of 'The Nation': Freda Kirchwey," unpublished Ph.D. dissertation, University of Maryland, 1978.

2. Alpern, "A Woman of 'The Nation,'" 61-62, 71-73, 110.

3. *Ibid.,* 196-198.

4. Freda Kirchwey, "The Nation—1918 to 1955, Outline of a Book," unpublished and undated, 9, Freda Kirchwey Papers; Alpern, "A Woman of 'The Nation,'" 231-234.

5. Kirchwey to Jacob Billikopf, July 3, 1941, Freda Kirchwey Papers.

6. Kirchwey, *The Nation,* Vol. 158, No. 11 (11 March 1944): 302-303.

7. Draft of February 27, 1944 speech, 30, Freda Kirchwey Papers.

8. *Ibid.,* 31-32; Kirchwey, *The Nation,* Vol. 159, No. 12 (16 September 1944): 313.

9. Kirchwey, *The Nation,* Vol. 160, No. 23 (9 June 1945): 633; Vol. 160, No. 26 (30 June 1945): 712; Vol. 158, No. 6 (15 April 1944): 438.

10. Alpern, 203-204.

11. *Ibid.,* 207-209.

12. *Ibid.,* 210-212.

13. Kirchwey, *The Nation,* Vol. 158, No. 11 (11 March 1944): 303.

14. Kirchwey, *The Nation,* Vol. 158, No. 14 (1 April 1944): 381; Vol. 162, No. 1 (5 January, 1946): 6.

15. Kirchwey, *The Nation,* Vol. 158, No. 4 (22 January 1944): 89.

16. Kirchwey, "Outline of a Book," 19.

17. Kirchwey, *The Nation,* Vol. 160, No. 18 (5 May 1945): 501.

18. Kirchwey, *The Nation,* Vol. 160, No. 8 (24 February 1945): 201; Robert Messer, *The End of An Alliance: James F. Byrnes, Roosevelt, Truman, and the Origins of the Cold War* (Chapel Hill, 1982), 52, 173.

19. Kirchwey, *The Nation,* Vol. 160, No. 10 (10 March 1945): 264-265.

20. Kirchwey, *The Nation,* Vol. 160, No. 16 (21 April 1945): 429-430.

21. Kirchwey, *The Nation,* Vol. 160, No. 20 (19 May 1945): 560-561; Vol. 161, No. 4 (28 July 1945): 73.

22. Kirchwey, *The Nation,* Vol. 160, No. 25 (23 June 1945): 684.

23. Kirchwey, *The Nation,* Vol. 160, No. 21 (26 May 1945): 588-589; Vol. 161, No. 1 (7 July 1945): 5.

24. Kirchwey, *The Nation,* Vol. 161, No. 3 (21 July 1945): 52.

25. Kirchwey, *The Nation,* Vol. 161, No. 7 (18 August 1945): 149-150; Vol. 161, No. 20 (17 November 1945): 512; Gregg Herken, *The Winning Weapon: The Atomic Bomb in the Cold War 1945-1950* (New York, 1981), 29-39, 46-49.

26. Kirchwey, *The Nation,* Vol. 161, No. 20 (17 November 1945): 512; Kirchwey, "The Nation 1945-1955," unpublished and undated, 2, Freda Kirchwey Papers.

27. *Ibid.,* 511-512.

28. Kirchwey, *The Nation,* Vol. 160, No. 21 (26 May 1945): 588-589.

29. Kirchwey, *The Nation,* Vol. 161, No. 26 (29 December 1945): 726.

30. Kirchwey, *The Nation,* Vol. 162, No. 1 (5 January 1946): 6.

31. Kirchwey, "Report on the Work of The Nation Associates in Behalf of Republican Spain Before the United Nations," 31 December 1946, Freda Kirchwey Papers; Kirchwey, *The Nation,* Vol. 162, No. 14 (6 April 1946): 389; Vol. 162, No. 16 (20 April 1946): 452-453.

32. I. F. Stone, *The Nation,* Vol. 162, No. 17 (27 April 1946): 499.

33. Kirchwey, *The Nation,* Vol. 163, No. 6 (10 August 1946): 146.

34. Kirchwey, *The Nation,* Vol. 163, No. 17 (26 October 1946): 461.

35. *Ibid.,* 460.

36. *Ibid.,* 461.

37. Kirchwey, *The Nation,* Vol. 163, No. 6 (10 August 1946): 146.

38. Kirchwey, "Draft of February 27 1944 Speech," 32, Freda Kirchwey Papers; William C. Bermen and James Paul Warberg, "An Establishment Maverick Challenges Truman's Policy Toward Germany," in Paterson, *Cold War Critics,* 60-62.

39. Kirchwey, *The Nation,* Vol. 163, No. 11 (14 September 1946): 285-286.

40. Kirchwey, *The Nation,* Vol. 163, No. 13 (28 September 1946): 339.

41. Kirchwey, *The Nation,* Vol. 163, No. 13 (28 September 1946): 337; Vol. 163, No. 14 (5 October 1946): 369.

42. Barton J. Bernstein, "Walter Lippmann and the Early Cold War," in Paterson, *Cold War Critics,* 39; Kirchwey, *The Nation,* Vol. 164, No. 13 (29 March 1947): 349.

43. Kirchwey, *The Nation,* Vol. 164, No. 13 (29 March 1947): 348.

44. Kirchwey, *The Nation,* Vol. 164, No. 12 (22 March 1947): 318.

45. Kirchwey, *The Nation,* Vol. 164, No. 13 (29 March 1947): 348.

46. Kirchwey, *The Nation,* Vol. 164, No. 26 (28 June 1947): 758-759; Vol. 165, No. 21 (22 November 1947): 547.

47. Kirchwey, *The Nation,* Vol. 164, No. 26 (28 June 1947): 758-759; Vol. 165, No. 4 (26 July 1947): 89.

48. Kirchwey, *The Nation,* Vol. 164, No. 13 (29 March 1947): 348-349.

The Atomic Temptation, 1945-1954

Lloyd C. Gardner

1. *Executive Sessions of the Senate Foreign Relations Committee (Historical Series),* vol. 5, 83rd Cong., 1st sess., (Washington, 1977), 114, 127.

2. *Ibid.,* 142-143.

3. *Ibid.,* 142.

4. Harry S. Truman, *Memoirs: Year of Decisions* (New York, 1955), 465-466.

5. Oppenheimer's remarks reprinted in *Robert Oppenheimer, Letters and Recollections,* edited by Alice Kimball Smith and Charles Weiner (Cambridge, 1980), 315-325.

6. *Ibid.*

7. For discussions of the changeover and its implications see Fred Kaplan, *The Wizards of Armageddon* (New York, 1983), and Anatol Rapoport, *Strategy and Conscience* (New York, 1964).

8. Lawrence Freedman, *The Evolution of Nuclear Strategy* (New York, 1983), 1-6; Russell F. Weigley, *The American Way of War: A History of United States Military Strategy and Policy* (New York, 1973), 236-237.

9. John Whiteclay Chambers II, *The North Atlantic Engineers: A History of the North Atlantic Division and its Predecessors in the U.S. Army Corps of Engineers, 1775-1975* (New York, 1980), 8-17; see also, Weigley, *American Way of War,* 59-61, and Russell F. Weigley, *History of the United States Army* (Bloomington, 1984), 144-163.

10. See the discussion in Lloyd C. Gardner, *A Covenant with Power: America and World Order from Wilson to Reagan* (New York, 1984), chapter 1.

11. Speech, March 4, 1919, copy in Woodrow Wilson Papers, Library of Congress, Washington, D.C.

12. Quoted in Weigley, *American Way of War,* 236-237.

13. *Ibid.,* 241.

14. On Roosevelt's hedging his bets, see David Reynolds, *The Creation of the Anglo-American Alliance 1937-41* (Chapel Hill, 1982), 116; and on that question's relation to airpower see also Kent Roberts Greenfield, *American Strategy in World War II: A Reconsideration* (Baltimore, 1963), 54-55.

15. United States Air Force Historical Division, *USAF Historical Studies: No. 89,* "The Development of Air Doctrine in the Army Air Arm, 1917-1941" (Air University, September 1955), 99-101, 103, 110.

16. *Ibid.,* 119-120.

17. For the "negotiations" see United States Department of State, *Foreign Relations of the United States, 1941,* 7 vols. (Washington, 1959), II, 35-72 (Hereafter cited as *FR,* followed by year and vol. number); on FDR's attitude toward Iceland and Greenland see Adolf Berle, diary entry, May 16, 1940, in *Navigating the Rapids, 1918-1971,* edited by Beatrice Bishop Berle and Travis Beal Jacobs (New York, 1973), 312-313. Roosevelt's most "indiscreet" statement about Greenland was made to John Gunther, the journalist. The United States, he told Gunther in April, 1941, "already had full plans to take over the whole Atlantic sphere, including Greenland." For this interview see James McGregor Burns, *Roosevelt: The Soldier of Freedom* (New York, 1970), 59.

18. Chambers, *North Atlantic Engineers,* 87-88.

19. Berle, diary entry, February 13, 1941, in Berle and Jacobs, *Navigating the Rapids,* 356-357.

20. Maxwell D. Taylor, *The Uncertain Trumpet* (New York, 1960), 3.

21. *Ibid.,* 4-5.

22. Some evidence exists that the Germans sought to reach an agreement to limit "strategic" terror attacks, but there was no response in the allied high command. See George H. Quester, *Deterrence before Hiroshima: The Airpower Background of Modern Strategy* (New York, 1966), 147-148.

23. Quester, *Deterrence before Hiroshima,* 167, and Weigley, *American Way of War*, 363-364.

24. Len Giovannitti and Fred Freed, *The Decision to Drop the Bomb* (New York, 1965), 36-37, and Quester, *Deterrence Before Hiroshima,* 168.

25. See Leslie Groves, *Now It Can Be Told* (New York, 1975), 141, 228.

26. For a summary of the arguments raised about strategic bombing and delays in the second front, as well as questions about its impact on combating the German submarine campaign, see William L. Neumann, *After Victory: Churchill, Roosevelt, Stalin, and the Making of the Peace* (New York, 1967), 82-83.

27. The Far Eastern Department in the British Foreign Office thought that an invasion could be made unnecessary by modifying the American demand for unconditional surrender, and by establishing a variety of external sanctions—for example, withholding the treaties Japan would need after the war in order to resume the status of an independent state. See Christopher Thorne, *Allies of a Kind, The United States, Britain and the War Against Japan, 1941-1945* (New York, 1978), 654-656.

28. Giovannitti and Freed, *Decision to Drop the Bomb,* 106-107; and see the letter, Harry S. Truman to James L. Cate, January 12, 1953, The Papers of Harry S. Truman, Truman Library, Independence, Missouri, President's Secretary's File (PSF).

29. Courtland Moon, "Chemical Weapons and Deterrence: The World War II Experience," *International Security,* VIII (Spring, 1984): 1-33.

30. See the discussion in Barton J. Bernstein, "Hiroshima and Nagasaki Reconsidered: The Atomic Bombings of Japan and the Origins of the Cold War, 1941-1945," *University Programs Modular Studies* (Morristown, 1975): 11.

31. "The USSR in the Far East," August 18, 1943, The Papers of Charles Bohlen, National Archives, Washington, D.C.

32. See, for example, diary entries, June 18 and 19, 1945, The Papers of Henry L. Stimson, Yale University, New Haven, Connecticut.

33. Diary Entries, May 13 and 15, 1945, Stimson Papers.

34. Truman, *Memoirs,* I, 34, 104.

35. *Ibid.* For discussion of the decision to delay Potsdam, see Bernstein, "Hiroshima and Nagasaki Reconsidered," 11. For Truman's attitude on issuing a call for Japan to surrender, see diary entry, June 19, 1945, Stimson Papers. Stimson, ironically, was somewhat chagrined by this time that his early "'sell'" job on the bomb had apparently hardened Truman's attitude about rejecting any "concessions" to the Japanese on the matter of retaining the emperor after surrender. The idea that Russia might be asked to join in a pre-Potsdam appeal was suggested by General Marshall. Stimson was impressed: "That would certainly coordinate all the threats possible to Japan." But nothing came of the idea. *Ibid.* Truman always said that he went to Potsdam first and foremost to receive final assurances that Russia would enter the Far Eastern war. There are a variety of interpretations about this matter. For one thing, securing Russian entrance had been Roosevelt's policy, and Truman insisted then and later that carrying out the dead leader's plans was his objective. And then there was a more subtle consideration: after the harsh exchanges with the Soviets over Poland, Truman could "test the ground" with the Russians to see if they planned to continue with Big Three cooperation; Moscow's commitment to enter the war given to Roosevelt at Yalta would be another example of what might be expected, because the Yalta agreement specified the prior conclusion of certain arrangements between Russia and China, including a treaty of friendship with the Chinese Nationalist government, that would, it was hoped, preclude Soviet aid to the Chinese communists. Truman's behavior at Potsdam indicated that he was certainly in no hurry, after word reached him of the successful test of the bomb in New Mexico, either to ask Stalin for a "favor," or to rush the Sino-Russian treaty negotiations to an early conclusion. Saving lives was now one of the tasks assigned to S-1. On this and related points, see Thomas G. Paterson, "Potsdam, the Atomic Bomb, and the Cold War: A Discussion with James F. Byrnes," *Pacific Historical Review,* XLI (May 1972): 225-230. For different emphases on "atomic diplomacy," see Gar Alperovitz, *Atomic Diplomacy* (New York, 1964) and Martin J. Sherwin, *A World Destroyed: The Atomic Bomb and the Grand Alliance* (New York, 1975).

36. Groves, *Now It Can Be Told,* 266-269; Stimson, diary entry, July 24, 1945, *Stimson Papers.*

37. On Truman's reactions at Potsdam, see Lloyd C. Gardner, *Economic Aspects of New Deal Diplomacy* (Madison, 1964), 322-323; Truman's diary entry for July 18, 1945, is reprinted in *Off the Record: The Private Papers of Harry S. Truman,* edited by Robert H. Ferrell (New York, 1980), 53-54.

38. Gardner, *Economic Aspects,* 319-321; Barton J. Bernstein, "The Quest for Security: American Foreign Policy and International Control of Atomic Energy, 1942-1946," *Journal of American History,* LX (March 1974): 1003-1044; Leo Szilard, "Reminiscences," in *Perspectives in American History,* edited by Donald Fleming and Bernard Bailyn (Cambridge, 1968) vol. II, 94-151.

39. Truman to Cate, January 12, 1953, Truman Papers, PSF.

40. Draft, February 13, 1945, "Possible Statement by the President," Manhattan Engineering District Papers, National Archives, Washington, D.C.

41. Stimson to Truman, July 31, 1945, Truman Papers, PSF.

42. Groves, *Now It Can Be Told,* 328-331.

43. Samuel McCrea Cavert, General Secretary, Federal Council of Churches of Christ, to Truman, August 9, 1945; Truman to Cavert, August 11, 1945; Lew Wallace, Democratic Committeeman for Oregon, to Truman, August 7, 1945; Truman to Wallace, August 9, 1945, Truman Papers, OF 692-A; Truman's explanation about the report of his jubilation did not entirely satisfy Mr. Wallace. See Wallace to Truman, August 17, 1945, *ibid.*

44. Truman quoted in Lloyd C. Gardner, *Architects of Illusion: Men and Ideas in American Foreign Policy, 1941-1949* (Chicago, 1970), 83.

45. Truman to Bess Truman, July 20, 1945, reprinted in *Dear Bess: The Letters from Harry to Bess Truman, 1910-1959* edited by Robert H. Ferrell (New York, 1983), 520.

46. Gardner, *Covenant with Power,* 88-89.

47. On this point, see P. M. S. Blackett, *Studies of War* (New York, 1962), 3-16.

48. Stimson to Truman, September 11, 1945, with memorandum, Truman Papers, OF.

49. *Ibid.,* OF.

50. Patterson to Truman, September 26, 1945, *ibid.*

51. Baruch to Byrnes, March 13, 1946, The Papers of Bernard M. Baruch, Princeton University, Princeton, New Jersey.

52. "Memorandum," November 5, 1945, *FR, 1945,* II, 71.

53. Still very useful on the Baruch Plan and the Russian response is P. M. S. Blackett, *Fear, War and the Bomb* (New York, 1949), chapter 12; on Soviet theory see Herbert Dinnerstein, *War and the Soviet Union* (New York, 1962); the quotation from Stalin is taken from a Russian source reproduced in David Holloway, *The Soviet Union and the Arms Race* (New Haven, 1983), 20.

54. See *FR, 1945,* II, 12-47.

55. Searls to Secretary of State Byrnes, October 24, 1946, *FR, 1946,* I, 963-966.

56. Going back to Truman's discussion with Charles de Gaulle in August, 1945 (see footnote 46), American policy makers were determined to break down the prewar European pattern of exclusive defense alliances that had led to war. Truman's admonition to the French leader to concentrate instead on economic recovery was finally made into a general policy with the Marshall Plan in 1947. America's atomic shield was to provide external defense, and a powerful stimulus for a generalized alliance. NATO was the result. See Gardner, *Covenant with Power,* chapter 4.

57. Though he would later oppose the militarization of the Western alliance, George F. Kennan offered some thoughts to members of Baruch's team along these lines, suggesting that failure of the Russians to agree with the American plan could

be predicted, unless the United States took steps, such as military staff conversations with the Canadians and the British, that demonstrated we were serious about pursuing a military alternative to international control. "Memorandum of Conversation," November 12, 1946, *FR, 1946,* I, 1011.

58. Diary, July 24, 1946, in David E. Lilienthal, *The Journals of David Lilienthal: The Atomic Energy Years* (New York, 1964), 69.

59. David Alan Rosenberg, "U.S. Nuclear Stockpile, 1945 to 1950," *Bulletin of the Atomic Scientists* (May 1982): 25-29.

60. *Ibid.*

61. The best discussion is Harry R. Borowski, *A Hollow Threat: Strategic Air Power and Containment Before Korea* (Westport, 1982).

62. "Personal Interview of Dean Acheson," March 26, 1970, typescript in author's possession.

63. David Alan Rosenberg, "The Origins of Overkill, Nuclear Weapons and American Strategy, 1945-1960," *International Security,* VII (Spring 1983): 3-71; and David Alan Rosenberg, "American Atomic Strategy and the Hydrogen Bomb Decision," *The Journal of American History,* LXVI (June 1979): 62-87.

64. Herbert York. *The Advisors: Oppenheimer, Teller and the Superbomb* (San Francisco, 1976), 34.

65. July 14, 1949, *FR, 1949,* I, 482-484.

66. "Minutes of a Meeting of the Policy Planning Staff," November 3, 1949, *FR, 1949,* I, 573-576.

67. Diary entry, January 31, 1950, Lilienthal, *Journals,* 629-630.

68. Dennison to Truman, November 9, 1949, Truman Papers, PSF.

69. "NSC-68: A Reappraisal," *Naval War College Review,* XXXIII (November-December 1980): 4-14.

70. Nitze to Acheson, July 27, 1950, with enclosures, Papers of the Policy Planning Staff, National Archives, Washington, D.C.

71. Press Release, November 30, 1950, copy in Truman Papers, OF 692-A.

72. "Memorandum for the Record." December 7, 1950, *FR, 1950,* VII, 1462.

73. Draft, "Soviet Intentions in the Current Situation," December 2, 1950, The Papers of Dean Acheson, Truman Library, Independence, Missouri.

74. Untitled Memorandum, December 4, 1950, Acheson Papers.

75. Truman to Lodge, December 22, 1950, Truman Papers, OF.

76. Eisenhower to John Foster Dulles, September 8, 1953, The Papers of John Foster Dulles, Princeton, New Jersey.

"Every System Needs a Center Sometimes"
An Essay on Hegemony and Modern American Foreign Policy
Thomas McCormick

1. Fernand Braudel, *Afterthoughts on Material Civilization and Capitalism* (Baltimore, 1977), 86.

2. William Appleman Williams, *Contours of American History* (Cleveland, 1961), 285.

3. Immanuel Wallerstein, *The Modern World-System* (New York, 1974), 239.

4. Braudel, *Afterthoughts,* 81.

5. *Ibid.,* 91-92; Wallerstein, *The Capitalist World-Economy* (New York, 1979), 18.

6. Wallerstein, *Politics of the World-Economy* (New York, 1984), 17.

7. Nigel Harris, *Of Bread and Guns: The World Economy in Crisis* (Bungay, Suffolk, 1983), 231-232.

8. This opening conceptual section owes its major intellectual debts to William Appleman Williams, Immanuel Wallerstein, and Fernand Braudel. Williams's work first introduced me to the concept of hegemony, though he preferred other phrases like Brooks Adams's American Economic Supremacy or Henry Luce's American Century. Moreover, he always used a comparative framework that moved easily back and forth between the Pax Britannica of the nineteenth century and the Pax Americana of the twentieth. Wallerstein's work in the last decade is that most often identified with world systems analysis. The very language and the typologies of this essay, as well as significant insights, derive from Wallerstein's writings. And finally, Braudel's monumental work on early capitalism provided ample evidence that world systems analysis was not simply a set of sociological abstractions, but could be plausibly and persuasively grounded in empirical evidence.

9. That insightful witticism about the open door policy belongs to my good friend and colleague, Harvey Goldberg.

10. Williams, *The Tragedy of American Diplomacy* (Cleveland, 1959), 91.

11. My thanks to Beth McKillin, a dissertation student at Northwestern, for educating me to the deep divisions in organized labor's approach to foreign policy, and especially the persistence in the 1920s of democratic, anti-imperialist elements centered in city labor councils.

12. My treatment of the 1930s owes much to Patrick Hearden's manuscript, "Hitler versus Roosevelt: The Nightmare of a Closed World," due to be published late in 1986 by Northern Illinois University Press.

13. Gore Vidal, *Washington, D.C.* (Boston, 1967), 242-243.

14. Thomas McCormick, "International Conflict: The U.S. Role," in *Perspectives on War and Peace: A Newsletter* (May 1985), vol. 3, no. 2.

15. Fred L. Block, *The Origins of International Economic Disorder* (Berkeley, 1977), 33-82. For another excellent discussion of the postwar world economy, see William Borden, *The Pacific Alliance* (Madison, 1984), especially the opening chapter on "multilateralism."

16. For a fine discussion of the American developmental model and its underlying assumptions, see Nathan Godfried, "American Development Policy for the Third World," unpublished Ph.D. dissertation (University of Wisconsin-Madison, 1980).

17. The best coverage of Japanese economic recovery is Borden's *Pacific Alliance.* My account of European recovery derives largely from Michael Hogan's manuscript, "The Making of the Marshall Plan," in preparation for publication by Cambridge University Press.

18. Fred Block, *Origins* and William Borden, *Pacific Alliance* are outstanding in their understanding of the restraints imposed by national capital and a nationalist

Congress in internationalist options; and in pushing them to the political expediency of what they call "military Keynesianism."

19. See especially Joyce and Gabriel Kolko, *The Limits of Power* (New York, 1972); an even more interesting book on rereading.

20. Harris, *Of Bread and Guns,* 31. Harris is a radical British economist to whom I owe much for his analysis of the Long Boom and the Long Slump. His statistical data are especially good.

21. Wallerstein, *World Inequality* (Montreal, 1975), 36-37.

22. Williams et. al., *America in Vietnam* (Garden City, 1985), 48.

23. Harris, *Of Bread and Guns,* 38.

24. Block, *Origins,* 96-109.

25. *Ibid.,* 152-155.

26. Harris, *Bread and Guns,* 51-52.

27. Block, *Origins,* 144-149.

28. See Gunnar Myrdal, *Rich Lands and Poor* (New York, 1957).

29. This section on Vietnam is based on Borden, *Pacific Alliance* and my essay in Williams, *America in Vietnam,* 45-60.

30. Harris, *Bread and Guns,* 73-99.

31. *Ibid.,* 120 and 145.

32. COMECON stands for Council on Mutual Economic Assistance and includes the USSR, Eastern Europe, Cuba, and Vietnam.

33. Harris, *Bread and Guns,* 180-186.

34. *Ibid.,* 80-82.

35. *Ibid.,* 188-194.

Index

Acheson, Dean, 117, 185, 189, 191, 193, 194

Adams, John Quincy: slavery views of, 86, 87, 89, 91, 99; on Monroe Doctrine, 124-129 passim, 139

Alpern, Sarah, 157, 158, 159

American Historical Review, 9, 21

Asia First, 106, 117, 118, 119

Atomic bomb: American, 162, 163, 170-172, 177, 181, 182, 184, 188, 189; Russian, 189-190, 210

Atomic diplomacy, 169-194 passim, 210, 211

Attlee, Clement, 193

Autarky, 199, 201, 202, 206, 207, 220

Balance of Power policy, 50, 51

Baruch, Bernard, 186, 187

Baruch Plan, 186, 187, 188

Beale, Howard K., 6, 13

Beard, Charles A., 6, 21, 45-52 passim, 58, 59

Beard, Mary, 45-49 passim

Becker, William H., 25, 26, 28

Bender, Thomas, 45, 46

Berle, Adolf, 176, 177

Bingham, Hiram, 133, 134

Birney, James G., 92, 93, 94, 95, 99, 102

Bradley, Omar, 169, 170, 192

Braudel, Fernand, 196, 197

Bretton Woods international monetary system, 83, 216

Brown, A.J., 7

Bush, Vannevar, 186

Byrnes, James F., 163, 164, 165, 181

Calhoun, John, 128, 129

Capitalism: 48-62 passim, 201-202, 204, 206; and imperialism, 65-83 passim; in one country, 143-155 passim; international nature of, 196; golden ages of, 198; and single power hegemony, 198-199; crisis of, 200, 210, 211

Central Intelligence Agency (CIA), 137, 138, 139

Child, Lydia Maria, 86, 87, 88, 91, 99

Chile, 140, 147

China, 73, 74, 75, 79, 108, 112-119 passim, 152-155

Chinese Consortium, 110-114 passim, 201

Cold War: 51-58 passim, 106, 157-168 passim, 187, 190, 205, 209, 213, 215, 219; and Eastern Europe, 160, 161, 164, 167; Williams's views on, 29-33 passim

Coleman, Kenneth, 123

COMECON, 217

Commission on International Exchange, United States (CIE), 73

Conant, Charles A., 66-74, 81, 83

Containment policy, 166, 167, 187, 188, 208

Corn Laws, 92-99 passim

Crapol, Edward P., 24, 25

Cuba, 23, 54, 55, 131, 138, 140

Curti, Merle, 6

Curtis, John, 96, 97

Detente, 215-217

Dewey, John, 58

Dodge Plan, 207, 210

Dollar Gap, 205, 206, 210, 212